STROKE REBEL

Linda Rådestad

BRAIN REHAB DISTRIBUTION Ltd.

A division of Brain.rehab Ltd.

Although the author and publisher have made every effort to ensure that the information in this book was correct at press time, the author and publisher do not assume and hereby disclaim any liability to any party for any loss, damage, or disruption caused by errors or omissions, whether such errors or omissions result from negligence, accident, or any other cause. The author has tried to recreate events, locales and conversations from her memories of them. In order to maintain anonymity, in some instances, she has changed the names of individuals and places in addition to some identifying information and details such as physical characteristics, occupations, and places of residence.

Please note that this book is not intended as a substitute for the medical advice of physicians. The reader should regularly consult a physician in matters relating to his/her health and particularly with respect to any symptoms that may require diagnosis or medical attention.

ISBN 978-9925-7633-0-6

Cover design by Debraj Dey

Cover photograph by Andreas Sjödin

Special thanks to:

My husband Remco and my children Maarten, Elle, and Madeleine, for believing in me when I hit rock bottom.

All my friends and family for their continuous support and proofreading.

The therapists and doctors at Klimmendaal and Rehab Station.

Professor Frank-Erik de Leeuw, MD, PhD, because you are still searching for an answer to why I suffered a TIA followed by two strokes at a young age.

Norman Doidge and Michael Moskowitz, for writing books that changed my life.

My editors: Jan Eise Kuipers (you were only 16 when I asked you to become my editor), Remco de Vries, Deborah Harmes, and Sarah Bercot.

Arjan Kuipers, my best friend and peer.

And my special thanks to Claire Wineland. Even though I never had a chance to meet you in person, I know that we could have become the dearest of friends.

To every stroke survivor and brain-injured person out there,

I know how it is.

I wrote this book for you because I care about you, and I want you to discover that, even if you think you tried everything in your pursuit of recovery, so much more is possible.

Why I wrote this book

The two strokes that I experienced changed everything. The believes I had of myself and the world were thrown upside down.

For the better, I can say now!

After hitting rock bottom, I went on a self-examination tour. I took a good look at myself. I did not like what I saw. Besides the visible aftermath of my strokes, I saw a sleepless workaholic that put too much value on extrinsic values.

Following this realization, I decided that things had to change. I started reading and listening to hundreds of books and research papers. I compiled what I learned from reading into a "trial and error" toolbox. This toolbox, created mostly of new habits, allowed me to put theory into practice and helped to recover this far (doctors consider me a medical miracle) and, what I am most proud of, I became a better person through the process.

Most importantly, I want other stroke survivors to be part of this and help them through what I learned. This has been my biggest drive why I wrote this book.

Oh and a word of warning before you read on, The contents of this book reflect my thoughts, I am known to be direct and I am afraid I may use some strong words, please do not take offense. If so I apologize in advance.

Table of Contents

STROKE REBEL

Linda Rådestad

Introduction

We all have our own story. You are about to hear mine. What I am doing is very uncomfortable for me since I'm an introvert. I am accustomed to only ever sharing superficial bits of my story such as where I'm from, what I do, what my hobbies are, and the like. However, now you are getting the whole story from me—authentic, bare, and completely vulnerable.

Science supports everything I have written in this book (see endnotes), but it is not meant to be a research paper. It is more of a complete expression of my own struggle as well as a bit of an operating manual about how I survived my two strokes and ultimately got my life back.

I hope you will find helpful wisdom and practical advice with naked authenticity, along with some guidance concerning the emotional and physical stamina that helped me through my recovery. What I offer you, in addition to my story, is a sort of CliffsNotes version of all the books and research papers I've read in the past three years, plus my personal observations. My goal is to provide you with a plan for recovery from the bad cards you've been dealt, along with my suggestions on how to become a happier and more joyful individual again.

Using my observations, I guide you through the stages of my stroke story, from my life as a businesswoman that "had it all" to waking up in my version of hell, paralyzed on half of my body, unable to make a sound, and wearing a diaper. I was diagnosed with a severe stroke, and doctors doubted that I would ever walk or utter a word again. They also repeatedly told me that hardly any recovery would take place after the first six months.

In this book, you'll read how I alleviated chronic pain and became able to walk normally, move my fingers, and even run again. And although it is not perfect at present, I also recovered my ability to speak. All of these things were accomplished AFTER the initial six months. How was I able to recover as well as I have so far, despite all the naysayers?

Once I got my overwhelming neuropathic pain under control, I made the conscious decision to ditch my victim mentality forever. Overcoming my pain not only freed up my energy but also taught me the essential lesson that it is possible to rewire my own brain.

I took control of my own biology and improved my body and mind. I became a biohacker.

Anyone who views herself as an experimenter doesn't get upset when things don't go the way she wants. She merely collects more data, makes a note of it, and tries to apply that data differently next time. This is how I see myself now—as a somewhat obsessed experimenter-biohacker. I will continue to try everything available, whether proven or experimental, to fully recover. My body and brain are now a running experiment on neuroplasticity.

Before my stroke, I was always searching for something. I don't know what it was (perhaps wealth and status). But I'm not searching anymore. I have found my "Ikigai," a Japanese word meaning my reason for being. You will hear about it in chapter 28.

It is my sincere wish that you gain wisdom, practical advice, and most importantly, an abundance of hope from the pages of this book. If not, I think you'll still find it inspiring and even entertaining!

I am determined to not screw up my second chance in life. I wouldn't change any of the things that I have learned in the past three years, not a single thing.

As a result of the events I am about to describe, I have become more aware, centered, happier, more appreciative of what life has to offer, and more authentic in my approach to life.

Anything wise that you read within these pages should be attributed to the authors of books and research papers on neuroscience; the experts on neuroplasticity, willpower, habits, health, and sleep; and to the writings of stoic philosophers I have read. Any unwise assumptions can be taken as my error.

If you are a stroke survivor, I urge you to not give up. There is a path to recovery. Take your steps in the right order. Be patient, do not doubt, and become your new, better self.

Stroke Rebel is my first book, but it will not be my last one. I'm going to keep you updated on my recovery!

Chapter 1

Autobahn

It was near the end of summer 2016. I didn't care what day it was. I hardly slept for three consecutive days, and the pain was overwhelming. The doctor diagnosed me with neuropathic pain,[»1 »2] adding that he could do little to nothing about it. It was up to the medication I was taking to deal with the pain, medication that did not offer any relief. By that time, I didn't care about much of anything anymore.

It was as if my life had ground to a halt with very little meaning left to it. My sense of worth plummeted, and I felt terrible about myself and my situation. Those impressions lingered for quite a long time. I didn't see a single ray of light in the following days, months, or years, for that matter.

At some point later in time, I found myself walking on a paved road through the woods, if you could even call it walking. I was holding a cane with three legs as I dragged myself toward my turn-around spot in a very painful slow motion. That day, though, was my endpoint. I was convinced of that.

Since my left arm was paralyzed and I didn't have any real feeling in my left leg anymore, I had the cane in my right hand. It was like an extra limb to help me keep balance, but I could only move it 10 cm at a time. Any progress that I made movement-wise was excruciatingly slow and breathtakingly painful.

It was a 450-meter walk to the viaduct, yet it felt like forever. Ironically, I couldn't keep myself from calculating how long it would take me to go 450 m using a cane that took 30 seconds to move, 10 cm at a time. I stopped and thought about this for a little while, my brain struggling to calculate, divide, and multiply. In my normal state, this would've taken me five seconds, but now...all the numbers came streaming in as a strange, sluggish mix of German and Spanish.

I can't do it, I thought. *I can't do anything. And I'm a loser.*

It was getting dark by that time, and the wind blew so hard that my sweater fell off. I bowed down to fetch it but fell to the ground. I tried to scream, but all that came out of my mouth was an unrecognizable mess of sound. I sat there for a while, trying to move my numb left arm. It wouldn't move at all.

"Damn it!" I mumbled and closed my eyes. *Please take me out of this dream, out of this terrible nightmare.*

I didn't believe in God, but I was extremely angry with him. Then, just in case he did exist, I added, *What have I ever done to you? I'm a good person. Why didn't you just leave me in a wheelchair? I would've gotten the hint, if that was supposed to be my wake-up call. I could've become a wheelchair tennis Olympic champion, like Esther Vergeer*[3]*, or even the next champion wheelchair ballroom dancer. I could've made something of my life by helping others. So, why did you have to give me this unbearable pain? Why did you make me mute and lame, too?* Then I thought to myself, *It doesn't matter anymore now. I'm going to die anyway.*

I decided to try and get up by switching my legs and forcing my right leg under my body, pressing the cane back, holding it firmly, and moving my right leg into the correct position. It took ages. But finally, I got up. I ignored the sweater I left behind and started dragging my body toward the road again.

While slowly stumbling forward, everything felt like a horror movie playing on a screen inside my head. How could I go from having it all to absolutely nothing in just a few months? I was a burden to my husband and kids. I couldn't even talk to them. I couldn't give them a word of advice or comfort. None of it was getting any better.

Maybe this was the lesson that God (or whoever) wanted to teach me—learning to be dependent on others? I don't think so, God. I didn't come this far in life to let that happen. I somehow managed to put on a sarcastic smile, but since my mouth drooped on the left side after my stroke, it must have looked like a very crooked smile.

I heard the sound of something heading in my direction. Was that the "old man" coming to stop me and tell me it was all just a dream? Whoever he was, he was walking fast, and I couldn't see his face at first. As he passed by, I saw that it was just a neighbor.

He didn't even try to say hello. I didn't really blame him. I hid my face, leaning against a tree, trying to catch my breath. At this point, I was also quite close to the viaduct. As I let my thoughts run loose in my mind, I was conflicted about whether or not I would throw myself onto the highway, without looking. The fall itself would undoubtedly kill me, but I didn't want to hit someone else's car and kill them too. I decided to watch for a clearing in the traffic below and wait until the right moment.

Then I heard something else, like a voice that couldn't have been there. *I'm probably hallucinating*, I thought.

This time, I heard it out loud quite distinctly and turned around. There was a shadow approaching me, but I couldn't see who it was. I could just hear someone coming forward. As he came into view, I realized it was Maarten, my son. The thought of seeing him immediately lifted my spirits. But I was confused by his sudden arrival. Nothing made any sense. I had left him and the rest of the family in the car some hours ago and watched them drive away. They must have turned around for some reason.

"Mom, I'm hurt," Maarten said. "Look." He was bleeding all over his outstretched hand. I was even more confused by what I was seeing, and my reactions were incredibly slow. I sat there looking at him for a long time before I could summon the energy needed to put my arm around him.

In the distance, the car was approaching, and we walked towards it together. We didn't say another word. I figured there would be time for me to make my move. The viaduct would always be there, patiently and unemotionally waiting for my return.

Chapter 2

Stroke

This will work, I thought while I rolled over in bed and squeezed my husband's nostrils very firmly. Shutting my eyes tightly against any light, I waited.

Remco's eyes flew open, fluttered. He looked at me with a shocked expression. Then, as if nothing had happened, he shook his head, turned around slightly, and fell soundly asleep again. It was 2 a.m.

I hated him when he snored. Lying there, my jaw clenched in frustration, I wondered why he couldn't just agree to get some help about it. I have a hard time falling asleep again when I'm jolted awake. My restless "monkey mind" took over whenever I woke up in the middle of the night (which I usually did).

I began to plan my day and make mental lists of everything I had to accomplish in the next 18 hours. There was always so much to do.

I usually began by taking Maarten and Elle to the train since they headed to school at 6:50 in the morning.

"Are you sure?" they would ask, rolling their eyes dramatically. They were both typical teens now—healthy, self-assured, and completely convinced they could handle an 11-km bike ride to the train. I knew they could do the distance and get there on time. But it was the other commuters that worried me, especially on the one-kilometer dyke section of the ride. That part of the journey could be quite unsafe if a cyclist was not very visible to other drivers in the dark.

"Besides, we're going with Femke," Maarten continued.

"Then I'll take her with us too," I replied. Femke was our next-door neighbor.

Their usual comeback: "Why are you such an uber-protective mother?" or "You need to relax." I had a quick response to those remarks too. Oliver, Maarten's best friend, had been hit by a car while riding his bike to school and missed an entire year of school afterward. Elle couldn't seem to help herself. "Everything turned out alright with him, though, right?"

She got me thinking. *Were they right? Was I a control freak?* They were probably right, and I needed to let go a bit. They were 16 and 17 at the time.

There was evidently no returning to sleep, so I thought about making their lunch. If I got up early, I would have enough time to make a quinoa salad with coriander and avocado. Elle would like that. Maybe I could take some to my office as well.

I had four people working for me. The tough economic times were coming to an end (I hoped, since the financial crisis had taken a heavy toll on my company). The global financial downturn had started back in 2008 while I was pregnant with Madeleine (our third child). It still broke my heart to think about how I took her to the office a week after she was born so I could go back to work and breastfeed her at the same time. That felt so long ago and foreign to me now. I was possibly a bit insane to do it!

At that time, I was the owner of about 10 websites that specialized in electrical components. During the financial crisis, it was necessary to downsize from 12 to four employees and then find additional ways to save money. I bought a new 200-m^2 office and rebuilt it to save on rent. I had also just launched an American website (the dollar was strong at the time), and I thought I would make use of that overseas turnover as well. Electrical components were high in profit margin since our customers were usually companies buying them in large quantities.

That day, I needed to work on a specification file explaining to our programmers in Ukraine that I needed to downgrade Magento, the software I was using.

As my to-do list grew in my head, I must have fallen asleep again. Then I heard snoring, snoring, snoring, and I found myself waking up once more. As I came out of a deep sleep, I noticed it was difficult to open my eyes completely, but I did.

I rolled over, shook Remco, and then tried squeezing his nostrils again. He finally stopped. I felt myself trembling with agitation. Why couldn't he just go and sleep in another room? We had talked about it several times before, but he refused to deal with it. He ended up saying, "I don't snore," and that *I* could always sleep in another room. That was true. But I never made the move despite the fragmented sleep.

Instead, not sleeping well became an ongoing habit. I also knew I had a lot of other bad habits to work on, like drinking five to six glasses of wine a week, not working out enough (at least for my standards), and an addiction to light cola and coffee. But most of all, I needed to improve my sleeping schedule. I planned to tell Remco after dinner the next day that he was going to be sleeping in another room until he solved his snoring problem.

Snoring, snoring, snoring...

What? I was barely back into REM sleep when he woke me again.[»1 »2]

I bolted upright and sneered at him. "Do you realize you've been waking me up about three times every night? I am fed up with it! I'm going to the office since I can't sleep here anyway." The next thing I knew, I was putting on my clothes.

"I am sorry," he said. "Come and lie down. I'll cuddle you to sleep."

I responded angrily, "No! I won't. Every time I'm about to fall deeply asleep, your snoring wakes me up! I'm better off if I go and get some work done. But when I come home, we're sleeping in separate bedrooms."

I was furious! I intentionally made extra-loud noises while brushing my teeth to piss him off. Then I looked at my watch and saw that it was 3:30. I went downstairs and grabbed a light cola from the fridge, and off I went. I was smart enough to avoid looking at myself in the large mirror downstairs. I must have looked horrible with those dark shadows under my eyes.

There was no one on the street in Elten, the German town where we lived. It was a 10-minute drive to my Dutch office across the border in 's-Heerenberg, and I loved taking the highway at that time of day. There were a few cars but no *Nur Links* drivers, as my husband calls them. These were Dutch people (the NL on their license plate indicated that they were indeed from the Netherlands) who didn't seem to understand that the Autobahn had no speed limit. The *Nur Links* drivers would drive in the left lane at 130 kph, and Germans came roaring up behind them at 220. It was not a good match.

I was pleased to see that there were no "left drivers" on this particular morning, so I hit the gas and sped to 140, then 190 kph. But I was so tired, I didn't get the kick out of it that I usually did.

When I reached my office building, I noticed that I must've forgotten to turn the lights off the previous day. When I tried to turn the key, the door was already open. I glanced over at the parking lot and saw Marianna's car. Was she here at 4 a.m.?

When I walked upstairs, I saw her and smiled. She was sitting behind her desk, working on a Word file and translating emails into English. I had given her that assignment because her mother came from the US, and Marianna spoke excellent English.

"I couldn't sleep," she said smiling.

I smiled back. "Do you have a snoring husband as well?"

"No," she replied, "but I couldn't sleep, and I had to finish these documents anyway. The continual ringing of the phone during the day disrupts my flow."

I nodded. She had initially come in temporarily to cover for a former employee that I had to let go. I liked Marianna. She was 47 years old but looked a decade younger. Her husband was an entrepreneur, and I could tell she was used to hard work. That's why she was diligently sitting there at 4 o'clock in the morning!

I sat down behind my desk and picked back up on the Word file I intended to send to the programmers in Ukraine. We each worked in silence until 8 o'clock, when Sonja came in. She was the manager when I wasn't there, which didn't happen often, and she was the quiet type as well—no-nonsense and never talked behind other people's backs. She was a hard worker, too, like me. My respect for her was well-earned during the 10 years she had been working for me.

We all continued to work, three quiet women, each on their own tasks. After a while, I decided to head downstairs for a bathroom break and to get another light cola from the fridge. When I came back upstairs and put the Coke on my desk, I noticed I felt a bit strange. My leg felt tingly like it was half asleep. *That's weird,* I thought.

I took a moment to try and stretch my leg out by leaning on the table. But just as I began to extend my leg, I fell slumped down into my chair.

Within seconds, I realized something was seriously wrong with me. My left arm was now unable to move. My leg hung limply to the side. When I tried to say something to Sonja and Marianna, I opened my mouth and nothing came out. I sat there, unable to call out for help or move. They were a mere few meters away, Sonja with her back to me and Marianna sitting three meters to my side.

I was stuck in place, unable to make a sound, and my entire left side was in a contorted position. I was forced to sit and wait for them to turn around and see me in such a state of distress. It felt like hours, although it probably took only a few minutes. It was obviously before 9 a.m. because the phone hadn't begun to ring in the office yet. I waited and waited until Sonja's gaze shifted, and she saw me first.

"Are you alright?" When I didn't answer, Marianna looked up and gave Sonja a worried glance. They both walked over to me, gently laid a hand on top of my leg, and continued talking. But I was unable to answer.

As calmly as possible, Marianna said, "Let's call Remco." His office was quite close to mine, and he was there within minutes.

"It looks like a stroke," he said, remaining calm. "Let's call an ambulance."

Marianna made the call for assistance. While she had them on the phone, she shouted at me to move my right arm, apparently getting instructions from the person on the other end of the phone. I was able to move my right arm.

"Move your left arm!"

Nothing.

She tried again. "Move your left arm!"

Nothing.

"The ambulance is coming," she said after she hung up. They were there in 20 minutes. I remember them carrying me down the stairs and putting me into the ambulance. Then I blacked out.

Chapter 3

The Neurologist

My eyes had been closed for most of the past hour, but I nevertheless noticed the movement of the ambulance as we traveled to the hospital. I also felt my body being transferred onto a stretcher and wheeled down to the examination area.

Soon after my arrival at the Slingeland Hospital emergency room, I was examined by a neurologist. She was a young brunette woman, probably in her late twenties or early thirties. The staff informed the doctor that they had already done a CT scan. They also told both my husband and the doctor that there was no evidence of bleeding or blood clotting.

My body may have looked slumped and loose, but inside I felt rigid with anxiety. It seemed to me that this neurologist was my only hope just then. I knew I had to convince her that something was seriously wrong. Trying to draw her attention over by staring at her quite intensely, she finally noticed what I was doing and came over to examine my limp arm and leg further. Using a calm tone of voice, she continued to talk to me throughout the examination, but I was unable to answer.

My husband told me later that the neurologist concluded that I had suffered a TIA (transient ischemic attack).[1,2,3,4] She probably had little to no experience with such a young woman having a stroke.[5,6,7,8] As a result, the neurologist only did a further five minutes of examination and discussion before she left the room.

I had an unexpectedly strong reaction when I saw her leaving and became frightened and panicked. I wanted to cry out, "Wait! Ms. Neurologist! There is something seriously wrong with me!" But no matter how hard I tried, nothing came out of my mouth.

Instead of doing any further assessment, they moved me down the hall to a sort of common room. I was lying there in shock, silent, waiting...but for what?

My two oldest children were there along with my sister-in-law who had brought them to the hospital. My husband had also called my brother Thomas, an internist in Sweden. Again and again, I tried to get up but couldn't move. I tried to talk, but I couldn't. After waiting for who knows how long, I blacked out again.

"Why are you keeping us waiting?!" my husband yelled to a nurse in the hallway. "Get the doctors now!" I was briefly conscious again after hearing his angry voice. I attempted to talk to him, with no luck.

"Do another scan now!" My husband was frantically shouting orders to someone in the hallway. "She's having a stroke!" I blacked out a third time.

The next time I woke up, a nurse was sticking a needle in my arm. I heard my husband say, "They finally got the blood thinners." By that time, it was past noon, and I had been in that state of limbo for several hours. Those thoughts had just passed through my head when I blacked out again.

Awakening to the sound of angry voices, my now red-faced husband was yelling at someone in the hall. "I am going to take her to a hospital in Germany if you don't do another scan right now!" His enraged words must have stirred them to action because I was taken away for an MRI scan soon after that.

It had been five and a half hours since I first came into the hospital.

What they saw on the brain scan was shocking. A full third of my right brain hemisphere was dying due to a lack of oxygen.

An older, more senior doctor came to speak to Remco. "They are going to transfer her to another hospital and remove the blood clot. If we hurry, there may be a chance that no further damage is done."

The next thing I remember is being in an ambulance again, this time with a kind-faced paramedic sitting next to me. As he held my hand and spoke to me in a gentle voice, I cried for the first time in a long time.

Chapter 4

Coffee Lady

When I arrived at the Rijnstate hospital, the medical staff was waiting for me. A woman whisked me away to the hall where I would have the surgery to remove the clot, a thrombectomy. My husband later explained that they made a small incision and went directly into a vein with a tiny camera-instrument combination. Traveling up to my brain, those devices then sucked out the clot. The procedure was supposed to take half an hour.

Entering the operating theater, I could see that my surgery would be performed by a young doctor who couldn't have been more than 30 years old. He had pleasant features and brown hair. There was another doctor present to assist him and a nurse on hand too. All I could think about at that moment was how badly I needed to pee, but that would have to wait.

The surgeon moved closer to my face and looked me straight in the eyes. "We're going to remove that clot now."

I just stared at him, silently. I wanted to say, "Be careful, especially at the brain part." The nurse swabbed my thigh with disinfectant and, scalpel in hand, the doctor made an incision to create an entrance into a vein in my hip.

A large overhead monitor displayed the interior view of my vein. Everything was clearly visible to the doctors and, somewhat surprisingly, to me as well. As they worked and talked among themselves, I tried to be as still as possible because I understood any movement could cause more damage to my brain or my vein.

More than an hour passed instead of the 20 or 30 minutes I was told to expect. They only managed to remove a part of the clot. My thinking processes were still intact and questions were racing through my mind. Were they having problems because the doctor was so young or inexperienced? Had he ever been in charge of a procedure like mine?

The following day, Remco held a clear glass tube up to the light so I could see it. In the tube was the clot that the surgeon had removed. It was huge.

Right after the surgery, the doctor asked me a question. I was silent, unable to answer him. Next, he commanded, "Raise your left hand." Nothing happened. He was more insistent the next time as he stated firmly, "Raise your left hand." Again, nothing happened. I could clearly understand him, but my body and voice simply would not respond.

Shouldn't the removal of most of the clot have solved my issues, allowing me to move and talk right away? That seemed to be what the medical staff was expecting, and I felt like I was letting everyone down.

A devastating thought raced across my mind. *They must have already been too late.* Quietly contemplating that was overwhelming.

The next morning, I slowly opened my eyes, expecting to be suffering from the effects of a hangover. At least, that's what it felt like as I woke up. Wondering if I needed to sit up, I tried to shake off the frightening nightmare I must've had. I expected to see my familiar room, my bed, and my husband lying next to me.

Bright, shimmering light entered through the windows and bounced off unfamiliar white sheets and a blue curtain that surrounded my bed. With a dull thud in my heart, I knew I was not at home. I had not been dreaming. The events of the previous day had indeed happened. This was a living nightmare, not a sleeping one.

Trying to sit up in the bed, I discovered that I couldn't move or lift myself. The entire left side of my body was as heavy as a brick wall and just as unmovable. Slowly reaching out, I noticed that everywhere I touched felt numb under my fingers. There was a tiny bit of movement in my left leg, but I couldn't make it move up and down or flex my foot.

A nurse came into my room while I was poking at my useless limbs. I wanted to ask her how long it usually takes for a stroke patient to be able to walk again. Looking straight at her face, I opened my mouth to speak, but nothing came out. Again and again, I tried to talk with no success. Beginning to feel quite worried, I decided to try to stay calm and ask the doctors when they returned.

"I am going to change your diaper now!" the nurse shouted. She talked to me like I was hard of hearing.

A diaper? Is she talking to me or the old man lying in the bed next to mine? Oh God, she's talking to me! What was happening, and why couldn't I wake up from this nightmare? I shuddered and allowed her to change my diaper. She never spoke another word to me after that first announcement.

Another woman came into the room shortly afterward. She spoke much more sweetly. "Hello, Linda. I'm here to give you your breakfast." What a very different attitude and energy she had compared to the diaper-changing woman!

She told me her name, but I couldn't seem to remember it. She was a small brunette woman in her forties with a springy walk and happy face. She smiled practically non-stop as she brought our meals, poured coffee, and cleared the trays. She also talked to herself a bit as she tidied up the room. Finally, and most importantly, she took the time to make direct eye contact and speak individually to *me*.

Without the ability to respond, I merely watched and observed, living up to my reputation among family and friends as an analytical person. Her pleasant face and happy demeanor spread good energy all around the room. She served our meals, cleaned up any mess, and then spent valuable time encouraging me, bringing light into the room.

Since I couldn't talk or laugh with them, it seemed even more important to analyze the people around me and the events that were unfolding. I was already formulating a strategy. Perhaps this ability to observe and assess might help me recover. As I continued to observe the kind and encouraging Coffee Lady with the happy face, I knew in my heart that she honestly wanted the best for me. I could feel it without her needing to say it. I could see it in her eyes and in the way she put her hand on my arm.

One year later, I read a book written by Jill Bolte Taylor called *My Stroke of Insight* that struck me with its authenticity.[1,2] She is a neuroscientist who suffered a stroke herself and describes the process of recovery. The author explains that those in contact with people who are ill, traumatized, or in recovery should be "responsible for the energy they bring" to patients.

It was only the second day after my stroke, but I made an important decision right there in the hospital. I would surround myself with kind people who were generous enough to bring me a flow of positive energy, people without any agenda, people who only wanted the best for me so that I could recover.

Since I was constrained by my lack of speech, I would need to embrace the art of human observation. I also wanted to be able to learn from others without having to ask questions. Soon, I should be able to determine who are the authentic ones, the ones that I could safely allow in. I would learn to tell who those special people were by the relaxed expressions on their faces, their smiles, the way they touched me, the way they treated me, and from the sparkle in their eyes. I had already noticed that the positive kind of people all seemed to have that sparkle in their eyes—consistently and without reservation.

Chapter 5

The Doctors

A hospital's atmosphere is chaotic almost every day. In my case, the following 12 days were filled with intense activity and emotions. People arrived and departed in waves.

My family kept their brave faces firmly in place as they walked into my room. They all encouraged me to sit up, and they spoke to me in a normal way. My husband even made jokes. We all knew that it was vital for me to regain strength and never lose hope.

Elle brushed my hair. Madeleine made beautiful drawings to hang over my bed. But Maarten, my oldest, looked worried most of the time. He withdrew and became quiet. He was there but, at the same time, not entirely there. This hurt the most—not because he withdrew into himself, but because I was unable to speak any words of comfort to him. I still couldn't make a sound. These were the crucial weeks leading up to his final gymnasium exams, which is a sort of

Dutch equivalent to prep school. But Maarten never had any problems with studying in the past and assured me that he had it all under control.

The hospital put me through a lot of tests to assess the damage to my body and brain. At physical therapy, they tested my arm and leg for responsiveness and to learn how much control I still had. Since I couldn't move my left arm, they put it in a blue triangular bandage around my neck. This fabric sling made sure my arm didn't just hang uncontrollably.

A speech therapist worked with me too. My goal was to make any type of sound at all. But nothing came out. I was completely mute.

She put a mirror in front of me one day. "Say aaah," she tried. "Say oooh." I thought she had run out of ideas and options after over a week, but she surprised me. Walking over to a drawer, she asked, "Do you like music?" Then she pulled something out of the drawer—a speaker.

She watched my face to see if it would change. I didn't react to any of the songs she played. Then she tried "For Bitter or Worse" by Anouk. When she saw my expression change, she asked, "You like Anouk? Let's listen, then." I nodded. She was hoping that I could finally make a sound, listening to this song.

Looking into the mirror, I could barely recognize myself. The entire left side of my face drooped noticeably, my unwashed hair was greasy, and deep, dark shadows had formed under my eyes. They filled with tears as I listened to the song.

Who was ever going to want me again? Who would want to be with me when my face was sagging and misshapen, I couldn't walk or talk, and last but not least, I was wearing a diaper. As the emotions rolled over me, I knew I was crying out of self-pity, not stress from the stroke. I am ashamed to say this, but I was crying over my lost looks.

The following week in the hospital was even more exhausting for me. More tests were necessary, and lots of people came to visit. I remember the visits from Isabelle and Karin the most.

Isabelle is my sister, and she has been a lawyer in Brussels for many years. She came prepared, as always. She brought dice with letters on them, one of those magic drawing boards and, of course, some nice shampoo, conditioner, and skin cream. I wanted to thank her for *not* bringing flowers since there were already enough of those in my room. Instead, she thoughtfully brought things I could actually put to use. I looked at her and smiled. She smiled back. No words were needed at that moment. I knew she was going to support me in my recovery.

When she left and I was alone for a while, I tried playing with the dice. I knew they were letters but couldn't figure out how they worked. Whenever I was alone for five minutes, I would secretly practice with them. But I would get exhausted within a few minutes, forcing me to stop.

Karin came to hug me and, as she took my hand, said the sweetest words. She had been married to Remco's uncle, but they were divorced now. She'd gone through a period of burnout from the stress of being a big-shot lawyer and partner at Baker McKenzie. So, she knew firsthand how it felt to be in a difficult situation. We bonded, and I don't know how long we just sat there while she whispered kind words to me. When she left, she looked at me once more and smiled. It was only then I noticed she had that sparkle in her eyes.

My time in the hospital was coming to an end, and we were waiting for the doctors to give us a report. They were going to tell us how I was doing just then, after which they would tell us what we could expect for my future. As we sat in the doctor's waiting room, I could see that Remco was nervous.

I was nervous too. As the door opened, I thought to myself, *Please give me some good news.*

The doctor who walked in was quite young, in her late twenties at most, and had long, nearly black hair. Her appearance made me wonder if she was Persian; as she spoke, I could hear that her Dutch was impeccable. Although we had never interacted before, she was familiar to me since I had seen her around the hospital.

She sat behind her desk and began to speak, mentioning that I had suffered a very severe stroke. Nobody had told me, yet. "A major stroke," she had said. Those words echoed through my head while she continued talking.

Referring to the thrombectomy procedure performed to get the clot out,[1,2,3] she said, "We did everything we could." She continued, saying that the stroke killed a lot of nerve cells in my brain's right hemisphere.[4,5] Then she paused for a moment.

"It is only fair to tell you that you will most likely never get out of that wheelchair and talk again."

What? She couldn't be referring to me! I continued to breathe slowly, hoping she wasn't talking to me. It felt like I was inside a movie scene, but I was merely observing the action in the room. I didn't cry at that moment. I was cold, chilled, and silent.

My husband began to ask a lot of questions. His face looked desperate. I didn't want to stay in that room. *That woman has no idea what she's talking about,* I thought. *In fact, she has no clue.* I started rolling my wheelchair toward the door—not an easy task with only one working hand.

"Are you leaving?" the doctor asked.

I nodded. I thought to myself, *Yes, I have work to do.* I was thinking about the magic drawing board my sister had brought me, the one I had secretly been working on.

The day after that first confrontation with reality, our family knew we had received a wake-up call. It was time to make plans. My husband and children talked to a rehabilitation center called Klimmendaal. The center informed them that they had made arrangements for my stay, a stay lasting at least six months. I would receive rehab during the week, safely surrounded by nurses, therapists, and physicians. That staff would take care of me, put me to bed, help me shower, and feed me. The goal of those months of therapy was to let me return to a life I could manage.

When my husband told me I would be going to Klimmendaal the next day, I was happy to get out of the hospital. I had been there long enough. The typical sounds that echo throughout any hospital had kept me awake during the night. I was ready for the next step.

While sitting in my hospital room the last day, my children began to gather my things to take with us. Among them was my magic drawing board. Elle saw it first and asked, "Did you write my name on here?" She couldn't hide her excitement. I nodded, and she put her arms around me saying "Yeaaah!"

Maarten and Madeleine rushed over to me as Elle explained, "Mama can write my name!" Instantly the children were all hanging on to me. I smiled and they laughed. Then they stopped, looking stunned.

"You made your first sound!" Maarten said.

Really? I thought about it. Then I tried, and succeeded, to make an "aaahh" sound. I could barely believe it. I was no longer silent!

They were all laughing and filming at the same time. I cried and they cried. That was one of the first truly happy moments imprinted in my brain, or what was left of it after the stroke.

That felt good. *More* than good.

The words of the young doctor echoed through my memory again. "Most likely, you may never make a sound again..."

One point for me. Nine hundred and ninety-nine to go.

Chapter 6

The Husband's Story

It was Friday, April 8, 2016, and I had just dropped off our youngest daughter at school. I had walked into the office and was sipping my first coffee when I received a phone call from one of my wife's colleagues at 8:20.

"Something is wrong with Linda. Hurry up and come to her office." I jumped up, ran to my car, and arrived at my wife's office four minutes later.

I walked over to her desk. Linda was leaning to one side, motionless, and her eyes were glazed-over, looking at nothing. My immediate instinct was that this was a stroke. I told Marianna to call an ambulance.

While we waited, I went online and did a web search to see if there were any immediate actions we could take. Giving her aspirin to thin the blood was not advised due to the possibility of bleeding in the brain.[1,2,3]

The horror that unfolded from that point is something I still don't feel like writing about. This book is designed to be about hope and strength, so I'll keep it short.

It took the hospital five and a half hours to decide that this was not a TIA but a stroke. Valuable hours were lost to incompetence and indecisiveness. Irreversible harm had been done to my wife's brain. She was eventually transported to another hospital so they could perform a thrombectomy, but if this had happened just a few hours earlier, a lot less harm would have been done.

The next morning I was sitting by her hospital bed. My wife was awake. She could see me. She couldn't say a word, couldn't even make a noise. She was lying in a hospital gown, and I could see she was wearing a diaper. It was Saturday, so our children had come with me.

What was there to say? Only words of support came to mind. I considered it important that we were going to fight this together and focus on the good things. At the time, I truly believed that it might take her half a year to recover at most. How misinformed I was, looking back now.

Half of her mouth was numb and drooping. She could not get up, and her left side was completely paralyzed. Nurses were speaking loudly, clearly, and slowly to her, as if she were near-deaf and 95 years old.

"MRS. DE VRIES, CAN I GET YOU SOMETHING TO DRINK?"

There was my wife, the prettiest woman I had ever seen, a natural Swedish blonde, still in the prime of her life. At only 43 years old, she was raising three children, running her own company, and had graduated cum laude with a degree in law from the University of London. She always cared about honesty and values. She lived a healthier life than most. I thought, *She is the last person on Earth to deserve this!*

She had been a model in her twenties and used the income from modeling to get through those expensive years of college. The youngest child of a single-mother family of 10, she ended up a thousand miles away from her hometown of Stockholm. Now she lived with me in a German town not far from the border of my own home country, the Netherlands.

In the days after the stroke, we tried speaking with some of the doctors about what was going on. What prognosis could they give her after the stroke?

Basically, this is what we were told: "She has had a severe stroke. It is too early to tell what permanent damage has been done. She will recover for three to six months, and realistically, it is safe to say that she will come out of this with permanent damage. We doubt that she is going to be able to get out of a wheelchair. Because she can't make any sound at the moment, she might not be able to speak again."

Together with Linda, I went to see one of the assistant doctors. She told us more or less the same thing. Maybe I was not ready to hear this yet, and Linda was not going to accept what she was being told about her future. Tears filled her eyes. I knew what she was thinking. She would beat this. She was the exception to the rule. Although she was crying, she could not yet produce a sound.

Chapter 7

Klimmendaal

The day I was released from the hospital, Remco arrived in the morning to pick me up. As he rolled me out of the room, my favorite nurse came up and kneeled alongside my wheelchair. She asked, "Are you leaving now?" I nodded a nonverbal yes and smiled my crooked smile.

After helping us with the luggage, we stepped into the elevator. Remco mumbled, "And off we go," as he pushed the button for the ground floor.

Waiting in the wheelchair at the hospital entrance while Remco retrieved the car, I looked at the other people in the main hall. Each of those patients had their own story, their own suffering.

Finally, I can leave this place. Within a few minutes, Remco's car appeared. He helped me get out of the wheelchair and safely tucked into the car seat. Even though I still needed help getting into the car, I felt relieved to be leaving the hospital.

Sitting behind the steering wheel, Remco looked at me and grinned. "Now, let's take you out for a ride first. There's no rush to get to the clinic right away." He turned up the volume of the car stereo, and to my surprise, Talk Talk's song "Happiness Is Easy" was playing. This 1986 song was one of our all-time favorites. When we first became a couple, back in the early 90s, this was one of the songs that Remco taped onto a cassette for me.

There it was, right at that moment—happiness. All the struggles of the past two weeks had so badly worn us out, we both burst into tears. We drove to the north of Arnhem, towards De Hoge Veluwe National Park,[1] and Remco encouraged me to sing along to the loud music. He sang out loud, although he had never been much of a singer. The volume was high enough that it didn't matter. "No one is going to hear you," he shouted.

Those 30-year-old songs made me nostalgic, and then they really made me want to sing! I used my mouth to make noises. Still only able to produce sounds with the right side of my mouth, I moved it into different positions to generate a bit of sound.

We drove around for a while, then parked the car facing the lush natural landscape right in front of us. It was wonderful to be there in that beautiful place. It was also a drastically different sensation from those two weeks in the hospital surrounded by medical noises and people. We turned down the music and sat silently as the sun began to break through the rain showers. I could hear birds singing and knew they were preparing for the mating season. I wondered if birds ever got strokes. It was an odd thought, but I later read that birds can indeed get strokes, just like humans.

After an hour of silence, we drove on for another 15 minutes until we arrived at a giant contemporary building.[2] It rose above the trees in front of us. I was pretty nervous, but

Remco was excited. "This is going to be your new home, for the next six months at least."

We still hadn't become accustomed to the process of getting me out of the car and into the wheelchair. It took a few tries before we managed it. As Remco pushed my wheelchair up to the entrance of the clinic, we noticed the four-meter-high statue in front of the entrance. The sculpture of a tall man was missing an arm and leg. *Wasting no opportunity to rub it in,* I thought wryly.

The building was attractive and looked somewhat new. A long hallway with glass on the outer wall showcased the numerous trees outside.

We were welcomed by a smiling older man who said, "Good morning. You must be Linda." His thinning gray hair was combed away from his forehead and toward the back. He was not very tall. "Let me show you to your room."

Remco continued to push my wheelchair as he followed the man into the elevator. On the second floor, we walked along a straight hallway with doors on both sides until we arrived at what would be mine. "This is your room," the man said. Glancing around as I entered, I discovered that it was a private room with a pleasantly large window overlooking the grounds. There was also a small hospital bed, a chair in front of a table with a computer, and a closet. "The bathroom and shower are in the hall, and the assistant doctor will be with you soon," the man explained.

Remco began unpacking my clothes before helping me go to the bathroom. When we returned to my assigned room, the assistant physician was sitting there with a smile. "Hi, I'm Erwin." Erwin was an attractive-looking man in his forties with brown hair that was beginning to turn gray.

Erwin and Remco discussed my background, running my own business for the past 15 years, our three children, and my determination to get better. Erwin told Remco that I would get a daily schedule with customized training sessions. Then, looking at me, Erwin told me what I could expect from the rehab.

After the assistant physician left, Remco turned to me. "I have to go to the office now, but I'll visit you every day after work, and I'll bring the kids with me. You'll be able to fully focus on your recovery here."

As he held me, I cried. I had so many things I wanted to say to him just then. I was sorry for making our life such hell at the moment. I was sorry for getting mad at him the night before my stroke. I wanted to apologize for everything. But of course, I couldn't speak.

After he left, I was alone in my room. I realized I had to relearn how letters worked, but I could concentrate for only five minutes at most before I became fatigued. I still couldn't write, except for my daughter's name. *Elle.*

Weeks had passed since the stroke, and there were still so many words that I couldn't remember, even simple, everyday things like "door" or "window." When my sisters Anne and Isabelle came to visit me at Klimmendaal, Anne came up with an idea to put Post-it notes around my room. That way, I could begin to remember that a table was called a "table" and a curtain, a "curtain," by looking at the Post-it on the surface of the object. Still, I was unable to say it.

I was eager to meet my physical and speech therapists, but I dreaded meeting the psychologist. *Why would I need a psychologist?* I thought. *There's nothing wrong with my mind. With my brain, yes, but not my mind.*

My brain might have been working incredibly slowly, and it frustrated me that I still couldn't talk, write, or count. But I was capable of analyzing things and above all, people.

"Hi. I'm Daphne, and I am going to be your speech therapist for the next six months." I was sitting in my room, eating a sandwich as she began. "I will start by observing how you eat normal food, not the mashed food that was served to you in the hospital."

At the hospital, I had been eating soft, mashed foods and thick fluids, and I didn't know why I had difficulty swallowing at the time. Much later, I looked it up and discovered that difficulty swallowing (or dysphagia) is a common problem after a stroke because the fine control over the muscles of the throat diminishes.[3,4,5] As a result of this condition, food and drinks can end up in your airpipe, entering the lungs.

I observed Daphne. She was blond, had small lips, and she was tall—the description of a typical young Dutch woman. I soon passed the test for eating normal food, just like I had passed my own test for not wearing diapers anymore. I had worked very hard on that, training my body by pressing my pelvic muscles together every time I felt like peeing. It took me about 15 days before my hard work paid off.

I still had not decided whether or not I liked the speech therapist. The following day I met the occupational therapists, Joy and Jenny. Occupational therapy is meant to help clients with physical, mental, or developmental conditions to recover or maintain their daily skills and activities. Joy, a brunette in her thirties, was always friendly to me. She took me into a room with a lot of toys, games, and plastic balls.

As she put my numb hand on a table, she asked, "Can you stretch your fingers for me?"

I tried hard, wanting to be a good student, but I couldn't. She talked to me quite a bit about the importance of stretching, since the primary goal of that therapy was to enable me to stretch out my fingers again. "Without being able to stretch your fingers or grasp objects, a hand is more or less useless," she explained.

There were so many things I wanted to ask her but couldn't. I wanted to know how long it would take me to regain the ability to stretch my fingers, but of course, she couldn't answer my unspoken questions.

My two daily sessions were meant to be 25 minutes each. But the therapist arrived late 80% of the time. That tardiness reduced my session times to between 15 and 20 minutes total.

The other occupational therapist was Jenny—about 30 years of age, not too tall, and with short blonde hair. Although she had a friendly face, there was something about her that nagged at me a bit, something I just couldn't put my finger on. I would need more time to analyze her before I decided how I felt.

Jenny's approach to making my hand move again was significantly different. She put my arm and hand in an ice-cold bath. I could vaguely feel the cold, but she told me that it was actually intended to help reactivate the blood flow in my hand and arm.

I had several other physiotherapists during my time at Klimmendaal. I won't describe them all, but Herma deserves to be mentioned. She was a bit boyish and looked about 45 years old. She was a good therapist, and I liked and respected her. She was intelligent, and she spoke to me as if I was smart as well. That mattered to me, especially at a time when I felt so vulnerable. As she examined my individual problems, she made detailed notes.

"I am going to tape your shoulder," she said and then explained why she needed to do that. Of all my therapists, I liked Herma the most. She seemed to understand that I was silently screaming for specific information on how to recover from a stroke.

"We are going to tape you to prevent shoulder subluxation," she said.[»6 »7] "Your muscles are too weak right now."

More specifically, the connection between my brain and muscles did not work correctly anymore. "The tape will be able to keep your shoulder in place."

Herma told me that my muscles were fine at the moment, but I had no control over them. "In a few weeks," she said, "I will teach you how to walk again."

She smiled as I reacted positively. I was sitting upright with my ear pointed towards her like I didn't want to miss a single word of what she said. I thought to myself, *Really? She was going to teach me how to walk again!* I wanted to hug her in that moment for saying those words, but I just smiled.

At my next session, I saw Daphne the speech therapist.[8,9] She tested me to see what sounds I could make, and it didn't go well. She gave me a piece of paper with eight sounds written on it. I could practice those—not actual words—just eight sounds. I took the paper and nodded. Determined to practice those sounds until I could make each one, I promised myself that I would practice every single one of the exercises during my breaks when I was back in my room. My discipline was undoubtedly still intact. In fact, it was better than ever.

That night I slept well, a lot better than I had in quite a long time. The words of Herma echoed through my head: "In a few weeks, I will teach you how to walk."

I hung on to those words like a lifeboat, bobbing up and down in the rough water.

Chapter 8

New Friends

"This is Linda. She is recovering from a stroke and will be here for some time."

My favorite nurse was the one who introduced me as I wheeled myself over to one of the dining tables. The new wheelchair I got had been modified so I could use it with just my right hand.

As I glanced around the dining hall, there were about nine other patients staring back at me. Two of them were in wheelchairs, and the rest were walking with or without a cane. There were two other people at the table I chose, and a smiling woman sat across from me. Smiling back gave me a chance to take a closer look at her.

She was a small woman, about 55 years old, and she introduced herself as Maria. Maria had suffered a TIA, and she was only going to be in Klimmendaal for six weeks. She later told me that she was originally from the Philippines and had moved to the Netherlands for work. Her husband passed away a few years earlier, and she had two teenagers. She spoke Dutch with a notable accent.

When she talked about her children, she got a certain glow on her face. I could tell that she was very proud of them and that she loved children in general. When my six-year-old daughter Madeleine visited me, Maria always seemed to walk by coincidentally. Then, on Madeleine's birthday, she gave her a colorful card and some pocket money.

At the table that day, I tried to say my first word to my new friend Maria. But all that came out was an annoying "shhh" sound. It seemed as if the entire room went silent and all the other patients were looking at me. They obviously didn't get new patients in their dining hall every day.

I even overheard one man at the next table saying to his dining buddy, "She can't talk!" Unexpectedly, there was genuine excitement in his voice as he continued, "I'm glad I can talk again after my stroke. Can you believe it? She can't talk to her kids if she has them. That must be horrible for her!"

He said every word loudly and clearly. I managed not to flinch, but I did get tears in my eyes and anger welled up inside. Why do people forget that even if you can't talk, you can still understand what they're saying? *You can talk, alright, but you don't know when to shut up,* I thought.

"I'm Jeroen," the guy opposite me said, as if trying to save me from the less thoughtful man with the big, uncensored mouth. "I had a severe brain injury," he continued.[»1 »2 »3] He told me this was his last stop in a three-year rehab period. Next, he was going to live on his own for a while in a place with on-call paramedics in case of an emergency. After that, he hoped to return to his wife and children.

Later, he told me the rest of his story. He was a computer programmer, 35 at the time, and had just taken his daughter to school on their bikes. After he dropped her off safely, a passing car took the wrong turn, missed seeing him completely, and crashed into him. Jeroen flew off the bike and hit his head on the concrete, shattering his skull (he was not wearing a helmet).

Three years had passed since the accident, but on the front of the top of his head, it was clear that some of his skull had been replaced. Jeroen considered himself a lucky man, though, because he could walk and talk now. He explained that he'd had many epileptic seizures, and those seizures frightened his wife. He was quite sad about that because it meant, for the time being, they could not live together. When he told me his story, I got tears in my eyes. I tried to smile at him, and he smiled in response. "Looking back doesn't help," he said. I nodded.

After dinner, Maria said in a motherly tone, "Let me roll you to your room." She must have looked at me the way she looked at her own daughter. She didn't seem to care whether I could talk or not since she talked enough for two people, and I liked her. She was a kind woman who laughed a lot. I needed a little laughter in that new environment. We were in the hallway when I suddenly pulled the brake on my wheelchair. Not too far from my room, there it was, sitting in the hallway—an exercise bike. I stopped and stared at it.

"Do you want to go on that bike?" Maria asked. "You can't go on it without the supervision of a physical therapist," she warned me. I had no intention of waiting around for permission. I just rolled my wheelchair over to the bike and tried to stand up. "What the heck," Maria said as she helped me get on the bicycle.

It took at least 10 attempts to get in the saddle. Then, it took us at least 10 minutes to get my left foot into the pedal straps. Finally, I managed to get on and was sitting on the bicycle.

"Go on then," Maria encouraged me now. On the sixth try, I managed to get the wheels to go around. My left leg was turned inward and she had to hold it steady for me as I smiled at her.

We started laughing. For the five minutes it lasted, it was a remarkable feeling. At that very moment, I decided that I would work harder than ever to recover. I couldn't just wait to have supervisors present to get my training time in, since they didn't have enough time allotted to me each day. Maria was my partner in crime from then on. Each time the rebel (me) knocked on her door, she immediately knew what to do, looking to the left and right to see if a nurse was coming. Then, when the coast was clear, she helped me get on the bike as quickly as possible.

Jeroen was there during some of these episodes. I tried to talk to him while I continued to struggle on the bicycle. But most of the time, he couldn't understand the unrecognizable jumble of sound that came from my mouth. Later, when I learned how to make some sounds that resembled words, Jeroen helped me learn how to pronounce those words. There was a computer in my room with software for that purpose, and Jeroen would loudly pronounce the word that appeared on the computer screen. I sat, studying the position and shape of his tongue and teeth. Then I would try to repeat the word as best I could, trying to use my tongue and teeth just like he did. We went on like this for quite a few afternoons, and I had a feeling that he enjoyed being of use to me.

A few weeks into my stay at Klimmendaal, my mom and my oldest brother came to visit me. My mom was 84 at the time, and since she lived a thousand miles away in Stockholm, Sweden,[4] I had not seen her since the stroke. We hugged for a long time. She brought me a CD player and some audiobooks on CD. "Then you can relax and listen to a book," Mom explained. She was in her eighties and not acquainted with current technology, so she probably had no clue that I could download books on my phone nowadays. I just hugged her. It was sweet of her to think of a gift like that.

My oldest brother Arne is a doctor (gynecologist) in Stockholm, and he asked the nurses a range of questions about my care. When he was visiting on another occasion, he gave me his phone. "Listen to this," he said. It was a radio interview with a stroke survivor. Just like me, she had aphasia. I listened to it for an hour but then fell asleep. When I woke up, I immediately looked for Arne's phone. I needed to know if the woman was ever able to talk again.

As I finished listening to the interview, I found out that she eventually (mostly) recovered and even went back to her job! That happy ending made me feel responsible good.

Chapter 9

Brain Fog

He kept staring at my breasts as the water dripped into my face. I turned my face away from him, not wanting him to know how humiliated and vulnerable I felt. Naked and sitting on a chair in the shower, I was unable to tell him to stop looking at me—or leave.

It was odd and unnerving to have a male intern who couldn't have been more than 19 years old as the person assigned to help me shower.

Please, someone get me out of here! This thought echoed through my mind at least a dozen times as I sat there in silence. Ten minutes passed, with him staring at me, before he finally handed me a towel that allowed me to cover my breasts.

"Get out of your wheelchair, then," Herma commanded in a friendly voice. It was later that day, and I was sitting in my wheelchair with two long bars on each side of me. I called them my ballet barres because they reminded me of the wooden rails attached to the wall in a ballet studio. I stood up, wiggling from one side to another. "Put your right arm on the bar and walk toward me," Herma continued. There was a large mirror in front of me. As I watched myself in that mirror, I slowly began to walk forward.

I was immediately dismayed by what I saw reflected back at me. My hips didn't move in an even line, my left shoulder hung down, my left leg made a spastic movement, and my foot wouldn't flex. I looked terrible, and it shocked me.

Herma could see the expression on my face and was quick to comfort me. "Not bad for the first time," she said. "Look," she continued, "the first walk is always the worst, and it will only get better from here." I gave her a tired smile and grabbed onto her arm. I wanted her to know that I appreciated the positivity she offered.

Realizing how important it was to train, I made every effort to excel in my sessions with Herma. I also practiced on my own whenever I was alone in my room. What I had heard was correct: You get tired more easily and swiftly after a stroke. But I was stubborn, and I just ignored the advice to rest that people gave most of the time. In my mind, the precious recovery time was ticking away too quickly. I needed to grab every available minute.

Herma had given me a walking cane with three legs at the bottom. Having that cane inspired me to do more of my own practice sessions when I was alone in my room. I "walked" from my bed toward the wardrobe, two meters. But one night, a nurse caught me doing that and took the cane out of my hand. Speaking to me like I was a small child, she said, "You broke the rules. You can only practice with this cane under a staff member's supervision."

Undeterred, I managed to get the cane back the next day. I was determined to continue my solo practice sessions every moment that I had the energy to do so.

Daphne stood in my doorway one morning and said, "We are going to do some tests today." Then she rolled me to the room where she did her speech therapy sessions. "Look at the computer screen and tell me which animal you see. Try to say either the entire word or just the first letter." During the past weeks, I had somehow improved my speech enough to make a limited number of sounds and some syllables.[1] In spite of that progress, I still sounded like a baby learning its first words, and my vocabulary consisted of sounds like "bah," "duh," and "maa" instead of full words.

The first image on the screen showed a dolphin, and I recognized it as a creature that I had seen swimming in the sea several times. Competitive as I am, I wanted to do well on this test. I was thinking hard about it, but I just couldn't figure out that the animal in the picture was called a dolphin.

The next picture showed a giraffe. Again, I thought hard about it and names like "long-neck," "small-head," and "leaf-eater" crossed my mind. I kept staring at the enormous neck and small head, but I couldn't figure out the name of that animal either. Daphne showed me eight more pictures including a monkey, lion, and cow, but I was unable to guess a single one of them. When the test was over, I was both exhausted and disappointed. For the first time in my life, I felt completely stupid.

Over the next two weeks, Daphne gave me more tests. I failed all of them. Then came the clinic's family day when partners and children could come for a visit and join the therapy sessions. One particular day, my husband and two oldest children joined my session with Daphne. She showed my husband and children the test.

"She is suffering from aphasia, apraxia, and dysarthria," she said. Then she explained to us what those terms meant. "Aphasia is the inability to comprehend and formulate languages. Apraxia is a lack of control over planning your speech. This can be caused by either a problem with the memory of words or the ability to put tasks in the right order."

Daphne continued. "Dysarthria is a motor speech disorder. Problems occur with the muscular movement and the muscles that help produce speech. This can often make it very difficult to pronounce words. As we know, Linda is left-handed, and she is one of the few people who have their speech center in the right brain hemisphere. I will be working with her to improve her speech over the next three to six months" she said.

Remco looked surprised and asked, "Three to six months? Why is the program limited to just six months?"

"There is hardly ever any improvement after that," Daphne answered.

"What about the multiple languages she spoke before her stroke?" Remco asked. "She spoke five languages. Does that affect her rehabilitation?"

Thinking aloud, he went on, "Are those languages stored in different areas of the brain? She seems to remember Swedish children's songs a lot better than everything in Dutch she learned 20 years later."

"That could make the recovery go even slower," Daphne answered.

Those conversations with the therapists had made it clear to me. The pressure was on, and I could feel the weight of that knowledge. I would need to work harder than ever before those six months were over. I tried to calculate how many weeks were still left, but the numbers came out in German and Spanish, and I couldn't make sense of them anyway.

Six months, I thought to myself. That fixed time-period had now been mentioned by the occupational therapist, speech therapist, and physical therapist. *That's how long I will stay here.*

I should develop my own plan on how to fully recover in six months. The time bomb started ticking.

I was not aware of how wrong I was at the time. The tests Daphne gave me shouldn't have been part of my recovery program at such an early stage. Much later, I read that ischemic stroke patients have neuroinflammation around the affected area, and inflammation is strongest for the first six to eight weeks after the stroke.[2,3,4,5,6] Doing those tests within that period gave the worst possible results. Looking back, I can confirm that during the first two months after the stroke, I had an overwhelming amount of brain fog, which only slowly started to disappear after three to four months.[7,8,9]

Luckily, one of my best friends came to see me soon afterward. Ann-Britt was a warm and friendly Norwegian woman living in Vansbro, Sweden. The first time we met was in Milan in 1992. We were both working as models there at the time, and I met her on a job. About a year later, I arrived at the Ford Modeling Agency in Tokyo and, much to my surprise, the first person I ran into was Ann-Britt. In a time before the convenience of mobile phones and social media to stay in touch, we were lucky to connect and spend three wonderful months together in Japan.

Now Ann-Britt had arrived to visit. She looked at me and smiled, but I turned the left side of my face away from her, not wanting her to see my crooked lips and asymmetrical face. "You are beautiful," she said. I laughed and thought, *Liar!* We cried and hugged for a long time.

"I'll give you a massage. Remco told me that you are suffering from some annoying back pains." This was true. I had begun to notice an irritating pain in half of my back that turned up now and then. Ann-Britt massaged my arm and back until I fell asleep. I knew that despite being unable to see each other very often, she was a true friend for life.

The following week, I woke up with a strange feeling one morning. I was having problems with my eyesight, as if there was a half-opened grey curtain directly in front of my right eye. I was frightened and immediately called for the nurse from my bed. The nurse quickly called the doctor who then examined me. By that point, my right eye had gone from seeing a little bit to seeing nothing at all. "We have to take you to a hospital. This might indicate a new stroke," the doctor said. "I'll call your husband."

There was a taxi waiting downstairs, and my favorite nurse accompanied me. I was scared. "Go as fast as you can," she told the taxi driver. And off he went at full speed.

Chapter 10

Glass

It was unsettling to find myself back at Rijnstate, the same hospital I was taken to immediately after my stroke and where I had my thrombectomy. The delays didn't help my uneasiness. A seemingly endless amount of paperwork needed to be completed before they moved me to a room. I wondered if I might have been examined more promptly if I had arrived in an ambulance instead of a taxi.

The nurse who had accompanied me from Klimmendaal held my hand as I waited. I cried as I tried to say "husband" to her. She squeezed my hand tightly and nodded to let me know she understood. "He will be here soon," she said in a soft voice.

During that wait, my right eye regained its sight for five minutes, but then the gray curtain returned. Remco blanched when he finally arrived with our son Maarten soon afterward. He was experiencing a frightening replay as he saw me lying there helplessly without a neurologist in sight.

Another 30 minutes passed before the emergency room neurologist came to see me. This young woman immediately reminded me of the doctor that had kept me waiting for five and a half hours while a clot caused havoc in my brain and killed an endless number of neurons. Remco stood nearby, telling her the essential information about my previous stroke and thrombectomy. His voice was agitated since he could see that the same situation was unfolding again. He had driven 40 kilometers to meet me at the hospital and had beaten the doctor to my bedside by 15 minutes, when she was only down the hall.

Remco knew from experience what could happen with that sort of long delay. "You should scan her immediately," he demanded. The doctor's body language indicated that she was annoyed at him for being insistent or offering an opinion.

As she finished examining me, it was almost as if she slowed down while writing out her instructions for an echo and visit to the hospital eye doctor, saying, "Someone will take you there." She didn't seem to be in any hurry whatsoever.

Minutes ticked away, at least another quarter of an hour, as Remco regularly returned to the nurses' station to ask why it was taking so long. When the doctor returned, she made it clear that there was no one available to take me to the scan. She suggested that she walk us out of the emergency room and Remco could bring me back into the main hospital himself for the scan. As Remco turned my wheelchair around a tight corner, he accidentally hit the doctor's ankle with the chair. To her, "Ouch!" he replied, "We're in the emergency room, so don't worry, you can get treated right away." She gave him an icy, deadly look.

As all of the unpleasantness with the doctor unfolded, my right eye continued to open and close that shadowy curtain, sometimes with crystal clear vision, then totally blind, then back to partial vision. Hours passed like that as we waited to be seen for the echo. My face and throat were scanned. I was told that there was no visible blood clot, so we were instructed to proceed to the eye clinic next.

We entered the waiting room in the eye clinic and could see that it was filled with patients, most of them over 70 years old. I was exhausted and beginning to grow impatient with how long everything was taking and how many departments we were sent to. Remco and Maarten seemed worried as well. When Remco tried to convince the receptionist that I was an urgent case, she rather brusquely said, "Sit down, Mr. de Vries. The doctor made no notes about anything urgent regarding your appointment."

We waited another hour and a half as more old people came and went to their appointments. When we were finally called in by the eye doctor's assistant, she asked a range of questions before the doctor arrived. He was a middle-aged man, and we were told that Remco would need to answer for me if it wasn't a simple yes or no response. As the doctor began a more thorough look at my eye, he turned to Remco and asked, "Why didn't you get an MRI?"

"I don't know," my husband replied, looking somewhat startled.

Suddenly, the doctor was in a hurry, signing papers and handing them to my husband with the brisk instruction: "Go to the stroke unit right away!" Remco hastily rolled my wheelchair to the stroke unit where they took a scan and injected blood thinners immediately. But by that time, my right eye had lost all vision. They assigned me to a hospital bed in the stroke unit, and I waited. My sight never returned.[1,2,3]

Later that day, Remco was asked to talk to the supervisor of the ER doctor that "helped" me that morning. The supervisor told him that the young doctor felt threatened by his remarks, and Remco said that he understood. But he also explained his side of the story. The bottom line was that he couldn't really have cared less about what she thought or felt when he had been right all along. The outcome was precisely what he had feared.

Remco and I were in complete agreement. We were both fed up with Rijnstate, just as we had been fed up with Slingeland Hospital months prior. When I had a chance to see my medical record at a later date, there was more written up about my husband's perceived threat to the neurologist that day than the serious implications of my medical condition.

Lying in the hospital bed gave me time to think and ask myself some questions. *What's wrong with me? Why have I had two strokes within a couple of months? I already had blood thinners after my first stroke. What's next, a third stroke?*

I felt hopelessness seeping into me. I really wanted to leave, to get out of there. In all honesty, I did not feel safe in that (or any other) hospital just then. Remco and our two oldest children were there, and I could hear them out in the hall, talking to a nurse.

That was my chance. I could make my move. It took me at least five minutes to get the railing of my bed down so I could put my feet on the ground. Next, I managed to get my slippers on. Then I unhooked myself from the IV. Taking my three-legged cane, I made sure to use the sides, the walls of anything that appeared for support. I wiggled away slowly. The most important thing was to keep my drop foot in place. I did that by turning the foot outward. *I'm getting out of here,* I thought.

The annoying old man sitting in the bed next to me sneered, "You can't do that!"

I just looked at him and thought, *Yes I can!*

It took me three minutes to walk the three meters to the door. I was pretty happy that I managed to calculate that. *I'm on the run now.* I was slowly heading for the end of the hallway, at one meter per minute.

I bumped into the right wall several times because I was not accustomed to being blind on the right side, but I also needed the wall for support. Where was I going? It didn't matter. I just felt like leaving. I went without stopping. The left side of my back hurt enormously. Doctors and nurses walked by. When someone looked at me, I immediately looked away and toward the wall. I felt liberated walking on my own. No one knew where I was.

One eye. That's not too bad. My inner voice was chatting away as I tried to build my confidence.

I was about two meters from the elevator when I heard a voice behind me, "Here she is!"

Shoot, they found me. My first escape attempt had lasted for a staggering 20 meters.

"Mom. Mom?" It was Maarten calling me. "The nurses are looking for you." I mumbled a response, something intended to sound like "home."

Remco had a concerned face as he caught up with us. "I will do my best to get you back to Klimmendaal as soon as possible," he promised. "You don't want to be here right now. I understand. Sit down in the wheelchair, please, and let's go for a meal in the cafeteria."

Our trip to the cafeteria did not help, and the day continued to be anxiety-inducing. Losing sight in one of my eyes forever and the fear that this kind of thing could happen again at any given moment were both depressing thoughts.

When I returned to the hospital room, Remco had somehow convinced one of the doctors to come down to talk to us. The doctor listened carefully as he explained that I did not want to stay in the hospital. She understood. She countered that it was risky to let me go with so many blood thinners in my body. She asked me, "Do you still want to leave?"

I gave her a sharp look and sarcastically replied, "*Toedeloe*" (slang for "goodbye" in Dutch). Maarten and Elle couldn't keep themselves from laughing a little.

But I did not end up leaving that night because Remco and the children convinced me to stay. It turned out to be a long night. I couldn't unwind and rest. I asked the nurse for a sleeping pill, something I wouldn't usually request. Unfortunately, the medication never took effect, and I remained awake for most of the night as my back hurt more than ever. That type of pain is what they call "neuropathic pain,"[4,5] and doing something to get rid of it entirely—sooner rather than later—seemed unavoidable.

A few days later, Mr. and Mrs. Professor came to see me. This is how we refer to my sister Ingela and her husband Gunnar, one of our family's inside jokes. They are, in fact, professors. My sister is a Professor in Caring Science at Sophiahemmet Högskola in Stockholm. Her husband is an MD and a Professor Chair in Clinical Cancer Epidemiology at Gothenburg University.

Remco was exhausted and glad to have them present because he knew he could use some help and additional insight. He knew that the doctors had kept me waiting too long the first two times, unnecessary delays that had devastating results. Remco also believed that I would not survive a third stroke.

"Look," Gunnar said in a calm voice, "we will have to get Linda's medical file first. Then I will find out through my contacts at Sahlgrenska Academy hospital who the best neurologist in the Netherlands is. We will take Linda to him. Period." Immediately, I could see the relief on Remco's face. It was as if Gunnar had taken a massive weight off his shoulders.

Gunnar received a response from his colleague in Sweden the next morning. His name is Frank-Erik de Leeuw, and he is a neurologist and professor at Radboud University's Nijmegen medical center. "How far away is that?" Gunnar asked.

He was unaware that 90% of the Netherlands could be reached within an hour from where we were sitting. "It's just 20-30 minutes away," Remco replied.

Gunnar continued, "I'll write him an email first. If we get no response, we'll go and visit him. We should, however, make sure we have Linda's file from Rijnstate before we go."

My sister Ingela took care of me that day and accompanied me on several appointments with Herma, Joy, and Marlijn. Marlijn was the psychologist I had grown to like and trust. I felt that she was on my side when she made arrangements to help me cope with the pain. One of the methods she used was EMDR (eye movement desensitization and reprocessing), an integrative psychotherapy most commonly employed in the treatment of traumas.[6]

If my therapists measured my pain on a scale of 1 to 10, a level of 3 was uncomfortable but bearable, and a continuous pain at 7 or above was too intense to cope with. My pain level was usually around 7 at that time and using EMDR brought it down to 4 or 5. However, at night, the pain always came back. When I was eventually able to say some words, I tried to convince her that I needed some additional changes made with my occupational and physical therapists.

Basically, I wanted to change Daphne, my speech therapist, and have the opportunity to see more of my favorite therapists.

Herma, Lisette, and Jeroen were my favorites. I only saw Lisette a few times, but I immediately noticed that she was very competent and had a lot of experience. I met Jeroen, my physiotherapist, a few times during hand electrical stimulation. During those sessions, he observed how little my pinky finger moved. Electrical stimulation pads were taped onto my arm, and a small device sent electrical waves through my nerves in the hope of activating the connections between my brain and my arm again.[7][8][9][10]

Much later, after I had left Klimmendaal as an intern, I wrote a note to Jeroen—something along the lines of "Do you want to be my therapist at home when I leave Klimmendaal?" Unfortunately, he replied, "I can't do that. Klimmendaal doesn't allow me to see patients outside of the clinic."

That disappointed me. Of the dozens of therapists I had seen, I would have preferred to only work with Herma, Lisette, Jeroen, Marlijn, and Femke, a brilliant speech therapist I connected with later in my recovery period. My reasons for choosing that specific group of people were related to the Coffee Lady I observed in the hospital right after my stroke. No matter the therapist, I always took the time to observe them carefully. My favorite therapists were all smart, no-nonsense people. They treated me like an intelligent human being that fully understood what they said. Last but not least, they were all kind.

In my mind, a kind person is someone who lives in a more awakened state of mind, making the right ethical choices from within his or her heart. A kind person carries consciousness within and has a continuous concern for fellow human beings.

In a book I read some 10 years earlier, *The Art of Being Kind* by Stefan Einhorn, the author proposes that only 20% of the population possesses the type of kindness I just described.[11] The remaining 80% do not. Looking at the world around us, that made sense.

My sister Ingela took care of me. She wondered out loud one day, "Why are you wearing jogging pants all the time?"

Soon after, she returned with some lightweight pants, a t-shirt, and a pair of easy-to-put-on Velcro sandals since she often took me outdoors. One day, she also brought a ball I could put my left hand on and around. That was rather difficult for me since my spasticity seemed to be getting worse every day. The spasms made it difficult to keep my fingers open, and my left hand was cramping almost continuously. I couldn't set my fingers down on the ball without first prying them open with my right hand. Trying to force my left hand open with my right hand also took several minutes due to all the ongoing spasms.

It was time to get more language back. "Focus on the Swedish words," Ingela said, so I did. We took opportunities throughout the day to work in time to practice. Once, we were having lunch with the whole family. The Ronald McDonald House above the clinic provided a perfect family-like environment and got us away from the hospital atmosphere. We had just ordered sushi when Gunnar held up a glass and asked me, "What is this?" I sat there, thinking hard, trying to come up with an answer to his simple question. I concentrated more and more, but I still couldn't come up with the right word.

I had failed once again. I hated feeling stupid. A strong sense of determination took hold of me in that moment. I needed to remember that a glass was called "glass."

Two days later, I was checked out of Klimmendaal for a weekend at home with family. We went to a restaurant for dinner, and Remco's sister Carmen also came along. I made sure to catch Gunnar's eye, pointed at my glass, and casually said, "Glass." He smiled back at me, and I felt enormously proud.

Gunnar didn't know that I had been practicing for hours and hours on the word "glass" for the previous two and a half days.

Chapter 11

C9H17NO2

I looked to my left and right, making sure no one would see me. After entering the railway station, I found a suitable place right at the start of the platform. From this position, the train would still have enough speed. I rolled my wheelchair closer to the edge of the platform until I found the perfect spot. Now I would be able to make it onto the track.

The blue and yellow train approached the station. I needed to be patient because my timing had to be perfect. As I started counting down in silence, it seemed like an eternity before the train reached the platform.

Ten...nine...eight...seven... The train passed the last railroad switch routing it to the platform I was on. *Six...five...four...* I continued counting as I thought, *This is it.*

Three...two...one... I stopped thinking and just pushed my wheelchair forward.

Immediately, a massive flash of pain went through my back. I opened my eyes. The unbearable pain had woken me. *Damn, it was only a dream.* I silently wished I hadn't been dreaming. *I wish I was dead.*

Lying beside me, Remco rubbed his eyes. The shock that had gone through my body as it was waking me up had woken him up too.

"I wan die," I said, or thought I said. He just looked at me.

"What did you say?" he asked.

"Pain," I said. "I wah die."

I was crying in agony when I told him that. My pride had never before allowed me to have these types of thoughts. Now I did.

Remco just held me. Poor Remco. My stroke had turned our lives upside down, and now he had to deal with a wife with suicidal thoughts as well. "Yu proms me. Helb... me do... end ma... pain," I asked him. I needed his help in case my life became unbearable. Remco responded vaguely, with some words that sounded reassuring. I felt so sorry for him.

Klimmendaal had sent me home on Friday. From that point on, I was expected to be at the clinic on Monday, Tuesday, Thursday, and Friday to receive therapy. Of course, my whole family was happy to have me home. But I felt guilty since I was now an extra burden on them.

From the beginning, Remco helped me get dressed in the morning because, if he didn't, it took an hour to accomplish. Then he prepared breakfast. Madeleine and Elle massaged my aching body at night, and Maarten drove me the 30 kilometers to Klimmendaal, four days a week, and waited around until I was finished with my therapy. I felt like a burden to them.

About a month after the stroke, I began to notice the neuropathic pains. In the beginning, they were annoying, ranging from pain levels 3 to 5. Living with that amount of pain was manageable and wouldn't prevent me from doing rehab.

Millions of people live with some form of pain every day, so I didn't complain initially for that reason.

However, the pain continued to escalate and reached a level where it began to interfere with my rehabilitation. A terrible burning sensation in my back, with pain levels of 7 and up to 9 at night, completely wore me out. It was impossible to fall asleep when my back felt like it was being barbequed, and sleepless nights were the consequence.

The pain wore me out to the point where I was no longer able to take in new material in my therapy sessions. A person's body needs sleep to remember and "save" newly acquired skills.[1,2] My sleeplessness was preventing me from doing this. Given the recovery time frame that had been set, three to six months, I began to worry even more about all the time I was wasting.

Dealing with unbearable pain was probably the most challenging part of my whole recovery process. We tried warming cushions, cold baths, warm baths, wet towels, tapping on the painful spots, and squeezing my neck. But none of those things eased the pain, and sleeping pills did not help me fall asleep. Those pills could not extinguish the barbeque-like sensation in my back and left me feeling foggy the next morning.

A few weeks before, while still at the clinic, Remco and I had discussed the severity of the pain. I hesitantly asked the doctor to prescribe me something to deal with it. As naive as I was at the time, I thought there would be some Advil-type medication (non-steroidal anti-inflammatory) I could take to make the pain disappear. The doctor told me there was no Advil to take for neuropathic pain. There were two options, but neither of them would work immediately. The doctor decided to give me gabapentin (C9H17NO2).[3,4,5]

Gabapentin is a medicine that was initially developed to treat epilepsy. It affects the brain by preventing brain cells from firing too rapidly, thus preventing an epileptic seizure. Often triggered by stress or sleep deprivation, an epileptic seizure is a state where brain cells fire too quickly and the body loses control and/or consciousness. Neuropathic pain is also a process in which brain cells that deliver pain signals spin out of control by firing rapidly. The doctor explained that it could take up to a month for the gabapentin to have any effect, so until then, I was not to expect any pain relief.

The following two months were a blur—filled with confusion, tormenting pain, and a general lack of sleep. The medication did very little to lessen the pain. My days weren't so bad if and when I somehow managed to get a reasonable amount of sleep. However, at around 3 or 4 in the afternoon, my pain level would often increase and the struggle would begin again. My life seemed to be nothing but chaos, an uncontrollable mess that I was not accustomed to.

Pain and sleeplessness can make you go crazy. Once, I barely slept at all for three nights in a row. On the fourth day, I tried to make my way over to the viaduct. This is the day I describe in the first chapter. Of course, I am not proud of those moments, but for this book to be authentic, it must include the moments that I would rather forget as well. Later in this book, I will explain how I finally managed to overcome my pain without medication.

Before the story continues, though, I would like to quickly address the "love-hate relationship" I have with my stroke. I do hate what happened to me because it almost made me end it all. But, I can accept and maybe even "love" the stroke because of all the new doors that hitting rock bottom opened for me.

When gabapentin did not work at all for pain reduction, I switched to amitriptyline. Amitriptyline is an antidepressant also used to help people with insomnia and neuropathic pain.[6,7,8] It took another month for the pain to go down from a level 8 to 5. Eventually, I took three 20-mg pills of amitriptyline a day and slept during the night, but I always started the day with a hazy feeling.

I didn't like the idea of taking medication for an indefinite period of time, but level 5 pain wasn't something to settle for either. In the interim, taking that medication enabled me to regain a somewhat decent sleep schedule. The reduction in pain also meant that I could think straight again when my morning haze cleared.

After switching from gabapentin to amitriptyline, I also stopped having suicidal thoughts. This was a direct result of being off the gabapentin. It all started to make sense after I read a leaflet on gabapentin. It states: "Can increase the potential for suicidal thoughts."

According to Wikipedia's page on gabapentin, "In 2009 the U.S. Food and Drug Administration (FDA) issued a warning of an increased risk of suicidal thoughts and behaviors in patients taking some anticonvulsant drugs, including gabapentin, modifying the packaging inserts to reflect this. A 2010 meta-analysis supported the increased risk of suicide associated with gabapentin use."

I am sharing this information so you know that, if you have experienced a stroke and develop neuropathic pain for which you need medication, you need to be aware of the possible effects of gabapentin. It almost certainly increased my suicidal thoughts because I started to see killing myself as a very plausible way to end my pain.

Now that I had some of my sleep and a little energy back, I knew it was time for me to educate myself. No more destructive medication. I wanted to take charge of my life again.

Chapter 12

Hero

As he handed me the small box of business cards, I smiled at him. "Just in case you get questions from someone you don't know," Remco said. "If you can't think of the right words to say, just give them one of these."

I looked at the card on top. Its headline read: "My name is Linda, I have aphasia." Beneath that, in smaller font: "I understand everything in English, Swedish, Dutch, and German, but finding the right words can be slower right now. This speech problem started in 2016 after a stroke. I am recovering."

I was startled for a while, seeing that on a card that belonged to *me* left me speechless (how ironic). Sometimes, I still believed that I was in the middle of a bad dream.

Remco gave the cards to me when we were in Stockholm, six and a half months after my stroke. I was just out of my wheelchair. My Swedish family had arranged for me to go to Rehab Station Stockholm (Spinalis) [1] for two weeks to receive intensive training there.

While I was at the center, Remco and our children were going to travel around Canada. They deserved a break from all the stress and extra work I had given them recently. Remco accompanied me to Stockholm and would fly back the next day.

I had begun to read some of the books Remco gave me a few months earlier, including *The Brain that Changes Itself* and *The Brain's Way of Healing*, both written by Norman Doidge.[2,3,4,5] Back then, I couldn't make consistent progress in those books since my left eye only allowed me to read for five minutes before it fixated on the center of the page I was reading. The same center focus occurred when I was writing. Instead of starting in the upper left corner of a piece of paper, I would start writing in the middle of the paper. It took me two to three months to get over that. Only after that was my left eye able to start at the left side of the paper.

Those two books really grabbed my attention, and I couldn't get enough of them. After reading them through once, I purchased the audiobooks. That allowed me to listen to them every day, since I didn't want to miss a single bit of what they contained. It was breathtaking information. It's hard to give an all-inclusive survey of Norman Doidge's books, but I'll try to summarize what I found most important.

Neuroplasticity

The word perfectly captures the amazing capabilities of our brain. ***Neuroplasticity*** is the brain's capacity to adapt, recover, and grow.[6,7,8,9,10] Brain cells can (and will!) take on a new function when required. The remaining part of the brain can also remodel its structure. This allows a new function to replace the old one. Lost functions can, therefore, reestablish themselves elsewhere in the brain. In short, this is why you can regain lost function and why it is nonsense that this recovery process is limited to a certain amount of time.

If this is true, why did they tell me my recovery would last no longer than six months? I researched this subject on Google, YouTube, in audiobooks, printed books, and published articles on the topic of neuroplasticity.

Here is a small part of what I discovered:

We have understood neuroplasticity for about 50 years, but professionals have only begun to make full use of its potential in the last 10-20 years. It has only been possible to scan the brain at different moments in time since MRI scanners became more widely available in the past two decades. Doing research with the MRI confirmed what had already been stated by the pioneers on neuroplasticity for many years beforehand. Scientists like Edward Taub,[11] Michael Merzenich,[12] and Paul Bach-y-Rita[13] showed that the concept of neuroplasticity is beneficial when dealing with a stroke or brain injury, regardless of its extent. They did so decades before the (functional) MRI found its full way into research.

Although information on the brain's capacity to change is becoming more widely accepted by the majority of professionals working in stroke rehab, there's still not enough being done to maximize this information. Outdated rehabilitation routines and financial restrictions often steer rehab efforts toward completion within a relatively short time period. Even if you don't undergo any treatment at all following a stroke or brain injury, you would still see some recovery. After the initial phase of physical recovery, we become dependent on the plasticity of the brain. It is up to the patient to reprogram his or her own brain.

Examining this in more detail, the nerve cells (neurons) produce more protein when stimulated or given commands. This extra protein makes the cells more stable and can also be used to build nerve tracts. A nerve tract is the growing of sprouts out of the nerve cell, connecting the cell to its surrounding cells.

After a stroke or other serious brain injury, when the brain is left with a damaged area, the surviving neurons and healthy cells at the border of the affected areas can start to take over the role of their deceased neighbors. This can be achieved by stimulating the brain to perform the lost task(s). As you might know, all cells in our body carry our entire DNA. Each of your cells holds the complete blueprint of your body. Our nerve cells are no exception, and they are therefore programmable to perform any function. Both its location and the influence of neighboring cells end up deciding a cell's function. If the need to take on a different function arises, the cell can do so because the required DNA is already present in its center (the cell nucleus).[14,15]

Specificity is the key.

The capacity of the brain to heal itself does come with a catch, though. To regain a function, the brain parts that need to be repaired or reorganized have to be stimulated very precisely and with the right intensity.[16,17] What this means for you is that you will have to use what is not functioning, even if that seems impossible (at first). Moreover, it will take a lot of work before you start seeing small improvements. Significant improvement won't be achieved in either days or a few months, but can take several years. Lots of patience and a large amount of determination are critical to your recovery.

I thought about this for a while. *Determination and patience.* Determination, that I had for sure. Patience...not so much. But while researching patience, I came to the conclusion that I had to concentrate on small wins. A combination of these incremental victories leads to larger and greater accomplishments.[18]

I was now hooked on the subject of neuroplasticity (hence the subtitle of this book). As I realized it was my "get out of post-stroke jail free" card, I decided to spend every afternoon looking up more information. *Neuroplasticity.* I was going to cling onto those two words—"neuro" (nervous system) and "plasticity" (the quality of being easily shaped or molded)—like it was a matter of life or death.

In fact, my life did depend on it. I had begun to feel like the brain's unlimited ability to improve was providing me with much-needed motivation to fight for my recovery. I knew it was not going to be easy and lots of hard work lay ahead. I knew all of that, but I still started to see myself as a guinea pig in my own study on neuroplasticity. Even though I had no idea how to proceed, I was going to give it my best shot. All I knew at that point was one simple fact: I was going to do my best to succeed.

The Brain's Way of Healing also had an interesting section on chronic pain. A doctor named Michael Moskowitz had reprogrammed his brain to no longer feel the chronic pain that he had been suffering from for 13 years.[19] I needed to look into that. I realized pain might become the biggest enemy of my recovery.

Remco flew home to take his trip to Canada with our three children. I was not going to see them for over two weeks, which was entirely new to me. I was going to stay in Kungsholmen, a pleasant area in Stockholm, with my brother Urban and his lovely wife, Monica. Urban is a Swedish Royal

Navy commander and a dentist. I felt safe and welcome in their large apartment.

Monica gave me massages when I was in pain, and all of my brothers and sisters took shifts taking me to and from Rehab Station, just outside of Stockholm.

I met a lot of friendly and encouraging people at Rehab Station. Many of the physical therapists who worked there had experienced accidents themselves and were in wheelchairs. That aspect created a special bond between therapists and their patients. One example was Danny, the gym instructor. He was able to stand up and walk for a bit, but he could not walk steadily yet. He shared his story with me one day. He had fallen from scaffolding at a construction site, and the fall left him with a spine injury.

One evening, Monica asked me, "Do you want to see a documentary about the founder of Spinalis?"

"Yes," I replied. The documentary on Claes Hultling was more than inspiring. He had done the extraordinary.

Claes Hultling was an anesthesiologist at Karolinska Hospital in Stockholm.[20] In 1984, three weeks before his wedding, he was on an island in the archipelago of Stockholm when he dove into shallow water and broke his neck. He became paralyzed from his chest down.

After an initial mental breakdown, he convinced himself that the show must go on, so to speak. He refused to see himself as a victim. He also made it his mission to aid and support people with spinal cord injuries.

A few weeks after his accident, he did indeed get married—in the hospital, with a hundred guests. He also convinced the hospital's emergency helicopter pilots to fly him out to his summer house in Landsort for the weekend to celebrate his honeymoon. From the outset, he was a rebel who saw opportunities instead of obstacles.

Along with his friend Richard Levi, a neurologist and colleague, Claes went to the US and Australia. They wanted to learn how to work with and take care of people with spinal cord injuries.

When they returned to Sweden, they possessed more than enough motivation and information to start their own spinal cord injury unit. They managed to get funding from the private sector with the assistance of Hans Norbert, an ice hockey player who had broken his neck. With the ice hockey World Cup, a fundraiser was launched. Corporate Sweden followed up with donations.

In the following decades, Spinalis became the Swedish authority on research and treatment of spinal cord injury victims. In 2010, Spinalis helped set up a similar spinal cord facility in Botswana.

After watching the video, I couldn't put the documentary out of my mind for several weeks. Claes Hultling had set the example for me. He was my new hero.

Chapter 13

Pain Unlearned

"Come on, you can do it," Sandra said. I was lying on my stomach on a therapeutic table. My legs were stretched out, and I was being told to raise my lower left leg up to a 90° knee bend. "You can do it," she kept encouraging me. But as much as I tried, I just couldn't get my leg up. Not even a centimeter.

"We will have to do quite a bit of work on you," Sandra said. Originally from the north of Sweden, Sandra was a small young woman and a good therapist who knew what she was doing. She methodically went through each of my muscles to see how much control I still had over them. Since my stroke, I had lost a lot of muscle mass in my left arm, shoulder, and leg.

Although I had learned to walk again, I could still only walk with a brace and cane, and my walking didn't look anywhere near perfect. Most of the therapists at Klimmendaal seemed to concentrate their efforts on speed, not proper movement.

They regularly timed my walk with a stopwatch, and with their mantra of "the faster, the better," I soon noticed there was almost no focus on *how* I walked. Treatment in clinics seemed to be primarily gauged by measurable improvements. I also considered it strange that the patient's age appeared to carry no weight whatsoever on how the treatment plan was structured.

The Klimmendaal file said, "Linda walks the block in seven minutes and 21 seconds." To them, this indicated an improvement of more than one minute compared to three weeks earlier. They interpreted those numbers as evidence that I was making "progress" with my therapy, as if it didn't matter how I walked.

In contrast, at Rehab Station, more focus was put on my muscle control. Training the muscles would improve control over them, so Sandra taught me to exercise my weakened muscles as much as possible.

I continued to practice the exercises with Sandra every morning, working out hamstrings, the back of my left buttock, my front lower leg, my left foot, and many other muscles that I didn't have sufficient control over. I had not used those enough over the past few months, so they had shrunk considerably.

The movement of my knee exacerbated the shrunken muscle issues, since my left knee would overbend. I was also dealing with a left foot that would not extend (lift up), also called a drop foot. At Klimmendaal, they continued to assert that they weren't sure if I would ever be able to get rid of the brace that kept my foot somewhat extended at all times.

I chose to ignore that negativity and be a little more optimistic. I had regained some control over my left large toe and thought to myself, *That's a start, at least.* Reading about neuroplasticity had convinced me that if I exercised every day, my brain would slowly increase its control over the damaged area again. I was similarly optimistic about my arm and shoulder. My arm had remained in an awkward position since my stroke, bent over my stomach with my hand rigid and cramped.

The levels of pain I mentioned before had become my main problem and began to obstruct my recovery. Every day at around 4 p.m., the pain became unbearable. At Rehab Station, they made an appointment for me with their pain doctor too. He suggested spreading out the times when I took pain medication instead of taking it all at night. I was hesitant since I was already dealing with the drug's side effects and spreading out the hours of intake might cause me to have that unfocused and hazy feeling more often throughout the day.

There has to be another way, was my only thought. There was.

I had been reading about a man named Moskowitz[1] in *The Brain's Way of Healing*. Doidge begins by explaining a bit about Moskowitz's background. Michael Moskowitz, MD, is a psychiatrist who turned himself into a pain specialist and set up a pain clinic in partnership with a friend. Bay Area Medical Associates (BAMA) in California was set up as a place where people with chronic pain could be treated.[2] The people who seek out this clinic typically have tried all available painkillers and drugs including nerve blockers, general injections, acupuncture, and other potential options for easing their pain.

When those patients arrive at BAMA, all mainstream and alternative treatments have usually failed them. As Moskowitz states in Doidge's book, "Everything that can be done for you, has been done for you. They come here to die with their pain."

In Doidge's book, I read all about chronic pain.

It is important to realize how pain works. The central nervous system consists of the brain and spinal cord. When the body encounters an injury, the nervous system transmits a signal through the spinal cord to the brain. The pain center in our brain receives this signal and fires up the cells in the pain mapping areas. Our brain receives the signal as an acute pain that says, "This is where you are hurt. Attend to it."

The external zones of our body are represented in our brain in specific processing areas called brain maps. Each body part is connected to its own brain map. If the neurons in our brain maps get damaged or reprogrammed after an acute pain, they will continue sending signals. This false alarm makes us believe that the pain is located in our body while it is, in fact, located in our brain!

In the case of neuropathic pain, we are dealing with the negative effect of neuroplasticity.

Sure, my pain mapping cells had been damaged as a result of my stroke, but why did my pain extend and get worse? It was as if my brain was reprogramming itself to extend the pain maps.

These pain signals are still being sent long after the body has healed, so acute pain develops an afterlife: chronic pain.

You may have heard of phantom pains occurring in amputated limbs. The pain receptors of that limb are still marked on the brain map.[3] As long as these receptors keep sending pain signals, the brain projects the pain onto missing limb areas, as if it were there.

One of the core laws of neuroplasticity is, neurons that fire together, wire together.[4] This can be described as follows:

When a child learns the alphabet, the visual shape of the letter A is connected to the sound "ay." Each time the child looks at the letter and repeats the sound, the neurons involved (audio-visual combination) fire and wire together.[5,6] If the child repeats this again and again, it makes a word recognizable without having to spell out each individual letter.

A good example of how neurons are trained in reading language is an experiment where you are to say the color in which a word is written. It's an easy task, unless you compile a list of words like "green" in red ink and "blue" in green ink. Now there is a mismatch between the color and word, and the task becomes more difficult.

Synaptic connections get stronger and circuits get better at performing their tasks through training. However, the opposite is also true. When a person stops performing an activity for an extended time period, the involved connections are weakened and in most cases, lost over time. The expression "use it or lose it" rings true. *Hmm*, I thought. *The more my left arm keeps hanging there, the more functionality I will lose. If I don't use it, I'll lose it.*

It all makes so much sense if you think about it. That's how humanity managed to evolve to the technology-loving, creative, and resilient *Homo sapiens* of our day and age—by constantly evolving higher order skills (and losing body parts we no longer have a use for, like a tail).

Why did it take so long for science to come up with this? I thought. To defeat my pain, I now had to manipulate the "use it or lose it" principle to rewire the unwanted brain connections causing my chronic pain. Not an easy task!

My pain had increased by then, and I was taking one more amitriptyline pill (I now took four or five each day), which didn't help. My brain was becoming accustomed to the drug, and it was losing its effect.

If I sat down to take a rest, the pain would immediately become worse. The moment I sat down, my pain began to increase dramatically. It seemed as if sitting or lying down triggered my brain's pain maps. I tried to avoid sitting or lying down during the day, but I was eventually forced to sit when exhausted.

It seemed like my brain recognized sitting down as a trigger for my pain. The pain slowly spread to neighboring areas and now had started to descend to my hips. It was a neuroplastic brain trap! I was desperate. If there was a PhD in pain, I would certainly have a shot at it. I realized I had to either be a zombie for the rest of my life or take a chance on this new "Moskowitz endeavor." I took the chance.

Moskowitz defines chronic pain as "learned pain"—when the brain's pain maps are stuck in ON mode because the pain receiver has failed to remedy the cause of acute pain, therefore damaging the central nervous system.

How did Moskowitz get rid of his pain?

According to Doidge's book, Moskowitz started by reading around 15,000 pages on neuroscience, basically everything he could find on the subject of neuroplasticity. He learned that we can strengthen circuits between brain areas by getting the involved neurons to fire all together through learning a new skill.[7] Even more interesting to him was that he discovered we can also weaken connections since neurons that fire apart, wire apart. Could he use this concept to weaken the links that had shaped his painmaps?

He had learned that, according to the "use it or lose it" principle,[8,9] the workings of the brain could be described as a constant struggle for cortical "real estate." This creates a situation where the brain's most regularly performed activities take up more and more space by essentially stealing that space from other, less regular activities.

Moskowitz made a picture of the brain in a state of acute pain by drawing 16 circles in red. He then created a picture of the brain in a state of chronic pain by drawing 16 large expanding circles in red. He continued by drawing a picture of a brain that did not register any form of pain. Next, he analyzed the 16 areas that fire during episodes of chronic pain. He observed that many of those areas, when they are not processing pain, are used to process sensations, thoughts, images, movement, emotion, visual information, and beliefs. In a chronic pain state, all those areas are hijacked to process pain.

Thinking there may be a way to use competitive plasticity in his favor, Moskowitz wondered if he could redirect those pain processing areas when he was in pain. He proposed the idea of forcing himself to come up with counter stimulation, thus stealing the cells back. This was all based on the ongoing competition for cortical real estate. Since he knew that a considerable part of the brain is dedicated to visual processing, he surmised that visual activity would make for the best possible counter stimulation. He had been living with constant pain in his neck for over 13 years and was highly motivated to find a solution.

Moskowitz consciously imprinted the brain drawings that he had made in his mind so he could remind himself that the brain is capable of changing. Each time he was in pain, he began by looking at the drawing of chronic pain with the expanding red circles. Then he made himself believe that the pain area was shrinking so that it would eventually look like the drawing of the brain without any pain.

"I had to be relentless," he explains. "Even more relentless than the pain signal itself."

In the first three weeks, he did feel a small reduction of pain when visualizing the shrinking pain area. After a month, he got the hang of it and applied the visualization each time he felt a pain spike coming on. His method worked!

Six weeks later, the pain between his shoulders and back disappeared entirely, never to return. After four months, he began to experience completely pain-free periods, and within a year, this increased to being quite consistently free of pain.

Maarten ordered another book for me: Moskowitz's *Neuroplastic Transformation Workbook.*[10] I read it within a week and then began to implement an adapted form of it.

I usually began by looking at the image in the book that contained the large red circles. I'd imagine the pain on my whole left back and neck shrinking a little around the edges. Then I imagined the pain maps in my brain getting slightly smaller too. Next, I continued by looking at the image of the brain without pain. I even took a picture on my phone of the no-pain brain and set it as my phone's screensaver.

Each day from 4 to 7 p.m., when my pain was at its worst, I practiced visualizing my pain area getting smaller and smaller for two hours straight. I sometimes used a vibrating massage unit on my neck to make my body send additional feedback (a counterattack) to my brain. But nothing happened during the first eight weeks, and the pain remained the same.

When those eight weeks had passed, however, I began to feel the pain area shrinking slightly.

I got the hang of the process too. It was like I entered a "flow state" during the visualization. I sat there for two, sometimes three hours, but it felt like 20 minutes!

I still didn't fully believe it, but the pain area had been slowly receding upward from my hip, and a little bit inward and to the left from my spine. During that period, I reduced the amitriptyline from 60 to 50 mg. Within a week, though, I felt the pain level rising again. I continued my focus on decreasing the pain area. After three months, the pain area was reduced by 60%, and I had also reduced my pain medication to just 20 mg of amitriptyline each day.

Shortly after that, I decided it was time to stop taking pain medication altogether. I continued to do the visualization every day since I had far better results with that method than I did with the medication. In total, it took me three and a half months to go from a state of constant pain to being completely pain-free.

I was thrilled—no medication, yet free of pain! I continued to keep my pain medication within reach, just in case. But in the end, I never used it again.

I am proud to be one of those people that could be helped by Moskowitz's method.

Of course, I understand that many people might be a bit skeptical of all this. But I know from my own experience that your brain *can* be reprogrammed to change! You may also think that this visualization is just some sort of "spiritual stuff." To put it in perspective, before my stroke, I was a down-to-earth businesswoman who was not into any kind of spiritual stuff. And while it's a relatively unknown topic now, more and more research is regularly published on mental imagery and pain.[11,12,13,14,15,16,17,18,19]

We still know so little about the human brain. If you don't believe it, google this question: How much do scientists know about the brain? Some are of the opinion: as little as 1%. Neuroplasticity wasn't even recognized by most doctors and scientists until 25 years ago, and it wasn't part of most theories regarding brain science until the functional MRI became more widely available. That's rather strange when you realize that the "use it or lose it" principle has been well known in science for quite a while.

Moskowitz had figured out a way to unlearn pain. And I still have the brain map screensaver on my phone, just to remind me of how lucky I am.

Chapter 14

Finding Realistic Hope

Quietly sitting there on the couch, I felt vulnerable as the woman approached me. I wasn't sure exactly why I felt so sensitive just then. Perhaps it was due to my less than positive memories of my speech therapist at Klimmendaal.

"Hello, Linda," she said. "I'm Emma." She sat down next to me on the couch in the waiting room and gently touched my shoulder. Looking directly at her, I immediately noticed the sparkle in her eyes.

Emma continued to talk as she got up to walk toward her treatment room. "We are going to do some speech therapy." I gave her a shy nod as I picked up my cane, trying to look nonchalant while following her down the hall. The way I walked must've looked dreadful since my hip was drooping on the left side and my hand was curled up in a tight, awkward position.

Once inside the treatment room, she said, "I'm going to do some tests with you today, and at the end of these next two weeks, we'll retake them. That way we can see if you've made improvements."

Shoot, not another test, I thought. As I sat there, remembering all the failed speech tests at Klimmendaal, I shrugged and responded, "Uhh, okay."

She put a tape recorder in front of me and said, "Name as many fruits as you can within one minute."

"Apple," I said after 10 seconds. Then I tried to figure out the name of the round orange fruit I was picturing in my mind. It took me at least 20 seconds, although it felt more like 20 minutes. "Orange," I said. Then I thought about a banana, but I remembered that there was a debate over whether a banana was a fruit or a berry. Bananas met the botanical requirements to be a true berry, but in the culinary world, it was still considered a fruit.[1]

"Time's up!" Emma said.

Shoot. I was disappointed in myself, believing that my perfectionism had stood in the way of scoring the best result. Why was I thinking about a banana being a berry instead of just shouting out, "banana"? I felt like I didn't pass.

After Emma had given me a few more tests, she said, "Look, there is a lot of improvement that you can make. You're at how many months post-stroke now, seven or eight?" I nodded in response. "You still have the rest of your life to improve your speech, and if you practice every day, you will hardly notice that you once had a speaking problem in something like five to ten years."

I almost fell out of my chair.

I had recently found out about neuroplasticity, but I wasn't sure if it could apply to my speech too. This was the first time I heard a therapist say that, and I got tears in my eyes.

Emma was putting the tape recorder back in her bag, so she didn't see my tears. I quickly slapped myself on both cheeks. It was a habit I began as a child to stop myself from complaining or crying. It worked immediately. My tears stopped, and I dried my eyes. I was smiling when she looked at me again.

I got along well with Emma. I could've listened for hours to her talking about her travels to Cuba, Kenya, Gambia, Vietnam, and many other places. Although I had done some traveling to a variety of countries in my modeling days, I had not been anywhere she mentioned. I felt inspired to make a bucket list of new places to visit in the future.

During our sessions, I made some small improvements in my Swedish. Each word still took a significant amount of time and effort, even though I could envision those words perfectly in my head.

People who didn't know me might have thought I was "stupid" if they just casually observed me. I was having a difficult time speaking, so who could blame them?

The truth is, my thoughts were still processing relatively quickly, I understood everything people told me, and I almost always had a reply sorted out in my head. However, it took additional time to process the words and then say them out loud. I no longer had a rapid, semiautomatic way of pronouncing words. I also knew there were quite a lot of words I hadn't been able to remember yet.

So, let's say I wanted to process a self-issued command six months after my stroke, for example, "I will significantly recover my speech in five years." My brain would then follow these steps:

1. Which language did I want to speak? English? Check.
2. Were all the necessary words available? No. First I had to figure out the English for *språk*. After a while, I was able to find the right word: "speech."

3. Did I know how to pronounce all the words? No, something like "significantly" was still too difficult. Since I couldn't pronounce it, I would replace it with "a lot."
4. I needed to solve the issue of a Spanish word like *cinco* coming to mind instead of the English translation I wanted. So, how do I translate *cinco*? Ah! It's "five."
5. I was finally able to pronounce the sentence: "I... will... reco...ver... my... speets... a lot... more... in... five... years."

No wonder talking went so slowly! Numbers came to me in German or Spanish just after my stroke. Later in the book, there will be further details on the topic of aphasia and why I was having these kinds of issues.

It had been a long journey so far, from not speaking at all to being able to make some sounds that were understood by others. For the first two months after my stroke, I couldn't speak at all. After six months, the left part of my tongue was still partially paralyzed.

I was usually exhausted after my sessions with Emma. But she gave me the one thing that I needed most at that time—a realistic sense of hope.

I thought about hope for a while. *What is hope anyway?*

I looked it up on Google: "Hope is the belief that the future will be better than the present."

I figured that I should formulate my goals based on hope, so I made it my goal to be able to speak normally again.

Next, I deconstructed the words Emma had said, because I realized those words were utterly important to me. Emma said that if I "practiced every day," this would give me a sort of agency (the power) to achieve my goal.[2,3] Her words, "five to ten years," was a realistic timeframe. And that I would "hardly notice" my previous speech problems told me that some people would notice and some wouldn't.

Thanks, Emma! You gave me realistic hope.

My mind wandered off to the conversation I had with a young doctor in the hospital after my stroke. I left in the middle of her explanation. She gave me a rundown on my status in a way that had probably been taught to her in med school. I can only wonder at how they instruct students to give the "bad news lecture" to a patient. Imagine the checklist in the textbook:

- Do not forget to specify the medical condition to the patient.
- Never provide the patient with false hope.
- Give the patient a realistic assessment of your findings.
- Don't speculate on the future.

That type of training was probably what made her say, "I doubt Linda will be able to walk and talk again." Unfortunately, that was a typical anti-hope message.

Hopelessness is a state of mind in which the future is expected to be worse than the present. Her message was good for exactly one thing: causing hopelessness.

Since a patient with a brain injury starts at the bottom of the ladder, at least some recovery is to be expected. She should have instead said something like: "You have severe brain trauma. I cannot make any promises about your recovery, but I can tell you that the brain will recover at least a bit over the next few months. After that, it is all about neuroplasticity. Your brain can relearn more than you think. Relearning is all about training and repetition, for which an enormous amount of willpower is going to help. To maximize results, ensure that you train consistently, get sufficient sleep, eat healthy food, and avoid stress. Then you can surprise all of us with your recovery."

We now know that all of those factors play an essential role in how well a patient recovers. So, think about it. (I'm speaking to you, doctors.) Realistic hope is important!

When Daphne (my Klimmendaal speech therapist) told me, "Your recovery will last for three to six months. After this period, hardly any recovery will take place," it put an enormous amount of pressure on me. I am convinced that she was not at all aware of two critical factors: my perfectionism and my tendency to be a workaholic. She did not realize that she switched on a ticking bomb by putting a time limit on my recovery.

I believe that she probably didn't have any intention of causing that level of anxiety in me, so I can forgive her. But the truth is, any therapist can easily learn to give realistic hope to a patient. They could have told me, for example, "Linda, you now have a speaking disability caused by the damage in your brain. I cannot promise you anything, but if you work hard enough, you will make improvements for years to come. However, exactly how much you are going to recover is still difficult to determine."

I wondered how many other patients had seen and been impacted by the young doctor with her bad news lecture and way of dispensing information? How many patients had fully trusted so-called professionals like Daphne, causing them to accept unnecessary limitations? No statistics are kept on these issues. Certainly, adding an extra chapter to medical school textbooks about instilling hope in patients and urging them to move forward with optimism would increase the motivation of many who find themselves in a situation similar to mine.

The positive conversation with Emma sparked my motivation to succeed. I knew that I had to reformulate my goals straight away. I also needed to make a realistic plan for how to achieve those goals, which were:

- regain normal speech[4][5][6]
- regain the ability to walk normally
- regain full control over my hand

At that moment, I wasn't sure how I would do it, but I knew I was going to figure it out.

Sitting in the airplane on my way home to Germany, I felt motivated. I knew that my future was going to be *a lot* better than my current situation.

Chapter 15

Madeleine

I watched her comb her hair as she stood in front of the big mirror in our living room. It was 7:35 a.m. I smiled at her, but she didn't seem to notice. She was busy doing her own thing, thinking her own thoughts, when she suddenly raced up the stairs as if hunted by a wild animal.

"Papa, wake up!" She exclaimed. "We need to leave in 15 minutes."

Running back down the stairs with her bathing suit and towel in her left hand, Madeleine put them into the backpack she used for her swimwear. Thursday was swim day at school, and she moved quickly, wasting no time. I recognized myself in this behavior. It reminded me of how, before my stroke, I would routinely multitask.

Rushing to the fridge, Madeleine took ham and four slices of bread and moved to the kitchen counter to make two sandwiches. She began eating one sandwich while putting the other in her red lunch box.

When Remco came downstairs, I noticed that his face looked tired. He came closer and kissed me briefly and gently on the cheek. Suddenly Madeleine commanded, "We have to go in one minute." She kissed me goodbye, and off they went.

I was speechless. Why hadn't I noticed when she started doing for herself all the things I used to do for her? She may have only been seven years old, but she had grown up so much in the past months! Tears were rolling down my cheeks as I blamed myself for not spending enough time with her. I was so busy with my recovery that I hadn't been available for enough time with my child.

Let's change that, I thought. *We can spend more time together and play games like Memory. I can put her to bed every night, rubbing her back until she falls asleep.* I knew she needed some quality time with her mother after the events of the past few months.

When I developed severe pains about three months after my stroke, Madeleine would massage my back. I could see that she felt good about being able to help. She had always been a "giver," not a "taker." She was also good at sports and excelled academically. I grew more proud of her each day.

Madeleine had been born right in the middle of the 2008 global financial crisis. My company was severely impacted as the crisis spun out of control nine months before she was born. After I had to lay off six people while I was pregnant, I felt I couldn't afford to stay home when I could no longer delegate all the tasks needing to be done. On the day I gave birth to Madeleine, I was still working in the office.

She only weighed 2,510 grams, or 88.5 ounces, or 5 pounds and 8 ounces (depending on how you measure such things)—just enough to keep her out of an incubator. In spite of the strain I was under during the pregnancy, she was a healthy baby who gained weight in no time. While searching online about fetal stress, I found an article in *The Guardian* that gave the results of a study on the children of mothers who experienced unusually high amounts of stress during pregnancy. In most cases, the IQ of those children was 10 points below average.

Luckily, our daughter was turning out to be a smart cookie. Her teachers even told us several times, "If you wanted her to, she could skip a year." We declined since we thought it was better for her to stay with the friends she had already made in her class. Age-appropriate social development is necessary too.

There was one thing about Madeleine that worried me a bit, though. She was a perfectionist and showed signs of OCD-like behavior.[1] But hey, so did I. She went through a phase of hating any seams in her clothes, and I remember the challenge of looking for seamless clothing all over the web. Happily, her OCD[2,3] signs have reduced significantly over the years. She now plays the piano, plays soccer three times a week, participates in street dance classes, and plays golf once a week.

Two months after my stroke, she turned seven. I remember that we celebrated her birthday on the top floor of the clinic at the Ronald McDonald House. She was so happy about it being her birthday. Jeroen, my friend and fellow patient with a brain injury, helped me carry her present to the Ronald Mcdonald House. Her gift was a child-sized version of a Segway on which she could stand and roll around.

There was plenty of space at the Ronald McDonald House, including a dedicated game room with a typical Dutch *sjoelbak*. The game (*sjoelen*) dates back to the 1500s when English gentlemen played it. Madeleine always got quite upset when she lost any game, and to be frank, at that point, she always beat me at Memory.

I used to tell her, "You can only win or learn." But since Remco and I never liked losing when we were children either, I guess she came by her temperament naturally.

The Ronald McDonald House also had a kitchen and dining table available for us to use. Remco's mother had prepared a meal for us, and we were glad to accept her help. Remco picked up the food after work that day, and we warmed it in the microwave. By eating our dinner together at the table, we tried to establish a bit of family time that evening.

I still occasionally needed Remco, Maarten, or Elle to help me shower and fall asleep, so there was not always someone to put Madeleine to bed each evening. She never complained, though. It wasn't in her nature. She didn't even complain when it was suddenly necessary, at only four years old, to have an hour-long scan in a scary machine that made loud, strange noises (an MRI). The events leading up to that MRI are noteworthy because they probably triggered my first set of physical problems.

Madeleine had a soft hump of fluid under the skin on top of her head. It had been there since she was a small child. The hump appeared after a fall, and we went to the hospital the day it happened. Although they sent us home the following day, the amount of swelling of the hump changed daily.

At four years old, Madeleine never seemed to notice it, but we always brought it up at the yearly visit to the children's doctor in Germany. Whenever he looked at it, he usually concluded, "The closing of the fontanel can take time, and it is not unheard of that the fontanel only starts to close at the age of..."

During a rare visit to my Dutch GP, I asked her to take a look at Madeleine's hump as well. Since Madeleine was almost five at the time, the GP suggested that we go to Slingeland Hospital for a scan. An appointment was made, and Madeleine had a CT scan of her head a few weeks later. We were told that it would take some time to process the image and that our doctor would contact us later with the findings.

Two weeks later on a Friday afternoon, I received a call from the doctor at Slingeland Hospital. She explicitly asked if we could come to the hospital that same day. She mentioned that it was no problem if we couldn't make it until 5. The doctor also said nothing that took away our concerns when she declined to tell us anything about the results over the phone. The sound of urgency in her voice made us nervous, and we drove to the hospital in absolute silence.

A blonde-haired woman came into the waiting room, introduced herself as Madeleine's doctor, and asked us to follow her to her office. After getting us settled into chairs in front of her desk, she sat down behind it and began. "As we know, Madeleine had a small skull fracture from a fall when she was five months old. There is only ever a 1 in 1500 chance for an infant who suffered a linear skull fracture to develop a growing skull fracture.[4,5] A growing skull fracture is caused when the fast-growing skull grows apart at that linear fracture because the meninges, membranes that envelop the brain and spinal cord, prevent the two sides from growing back together."

As I listened, my mother instinct to keep calm took over, and I did not initially allow myself to cry. But as the doctor turned her monitor in our direction to show us the picture of Madeleine's skull, I burst into tears when I saw the photographic rendering of the CT scan. It indicated what was quite clearly the top of Madeleine's skull. We saw it plain as day, the enormous gaping hole in her head, as round and large as an extra eye socket.

The doctor gave us a compassionate look, saying, "Madeleine will have to be examined further. Since we have no specialized child neurologists here, we'll send her to the Radboud University Medical Center in Nijmegen where they do have specialized doctors. A growing skull fracture is a very rare condition, and I have personally never come across one in my career. I had to do some research, but there is no reason to assume that Madeleine's situation requires immediate attention since she has been doing fine with this fracture for years. An operation may be necessary."

My emotions finally got the best of me. My youngest child had a gaping hole in her skull, and I felt frantic. "What's going to happen next?" I asked.

"It's hard to say since I'm no expert. And of course, it's going to depend on further research. An operation to close the hole will be needed sooner rather than later. The operation in question is, of course, not without risks since the brain is right there in the same area. There will always be a risk of brain damage."

That was how we started our weekend. When we got home, I began an internet search on growing skull fractures that lasted all night long. As the doctor had told us, the condition was pretty rare. But being the control freak that I am, I wanted answers, and waiting was not an option. I could feel the stress starting to build up inside me. Somehow, Remco always stayed quite a bit calmer than I ever could, sometimes to the point that it almost seemed as if he didn't care. Of course, I knew that he did care, genuinely. But how could he stay so calm?

Over the next few days, I contacted several doctors. One doctor in Düsseldorf even told us she could perform surgery on Madeleine the following day.

Then I called my brothers in Sweden. They showed Madeleine's brain image to a fellow doctor, a brain surgeon. He told us not to operate just yet.

We decided to listen to the Swedish doctor and waited 12 long days until our appointment in Nijmegen for Madeleine to get her MRI scan in order to see if immediate surgery was necessary. That Wednesday, our poor little four-year-old child had to be in the MRI scanner for nearly an hour. In the scanner, you have to lie completely still in a tunnel-like machine while thumping, pulsing, and vibrating noise is all around you. For a child, that must have been frightening.

Madeleine said she understood the procedure completely when it was described to her, and she did what had to be done. A week later, we met Dr. Van Lindert, a very friendly and understanding child neurologist at Radboud. He explained his findings from the MRI, telling us that Madeleine was the only documented case he could find where the skull fracture seemed to have almost completely closed again on its own.

He couldn't believe his eyes as he went through the different layers that the MRI scanner had mapped. Only a small hole was left, allowing the cerebrospinal fluid to create the swelling outside the skull. He had good hopes that the gap would close by itself in the coming years, and his suggestion was not to perform any surgery at all. He explained that there were more risks involved in the operation itself than in doing nothing. Then he suggested that we make another appointment in two or three years.

There was one warning though. The doctor told us that we should be extra aware of an increased risk of meningitis if Madeleine were to ever injure her head.

We emailed the MRI scan to another doctor in Berlin and asked him for a second opinion on Dr. Van Lindert's findings. That doctor must have been a very kind and warm-hearted person because he replied that same Sunday. He wrote that he completely agreed with the findings of Dr. Van Lindert and wished us a pleasant weekend.

I could finally escape my stress, that sensation of being in survival mode. Now that my mind was at least somewhat put at ease, I could relax again. We went out for dinner to celebrate the fact that Madeleine did not have to undergo surgery. The tension had begun to leave my body, but I also noticed that I was starting to feel a bit weird.

The following day, I went out for a 20-km run. When I came home, I had to sit down because I started feeling sensations like needles in my legs and ants crawling on my arms. I figured it would disappear overnight, but it didn't. I kept working as usual, but I could feel my body protesting.

A month passed. Instead of disappearing, my symptoms became more worrisome. I decided to go for a medical check-up, but the doctor couldn't find anything concrete to explain what was happening to me. When my symptoms gradually worsened, I returned to my doctor who decided to refer me to a neurologist.

The neurologist told me in a very straightforward manner, "It looks like you're experiencing the symptoms of burnout."

"Burnout," I said. "I don't believe it!" I walked out of the room.

And so, I went straight back to work. Back then, I thought burnout was for losers. In hindsight, that was the wrong way of thinking about what the doctor had tried to tell me. But instead of listening to the advice, I turned to the internet and started googling my list of symptoms. I could hardly sleep at that point.

Lyme disease made more sense to me, and a lot of the symptoms matched.[»6, »7, »8] I had taken some antibiotics for a tick bite two years earlier when a red ring appeared on the back of my knee. The internet's stories on chronic Lyme disease were pretty scary, and I read that two weeks of antibiotics could allow the Lyme to survive and cause neurological damage when the body was weakened. *That's it!* I thought.

As I went to revisit the doctor, I realized that I had seen more doctors in those three months of searching for answers than I had in the 40 years prior. Based on the information I gathered on borreliosis, which causes Lyme and can stay undetected in your body, I advised the doctor to prescribe me more antibiotics. She didn't give them to me, though. Instead, she prescribed oxazepam so I could fall asleep again.[9,10]

The symptoms had gotten so bad that I was admitted to the hospital twice during our vacation in Sweden, once in Gothenburg and once in Stockholm. The cause of my symptoms remained frustratingly unknown. My sleeplessness peaked as well since I was trying to get off the oxazepam, a drug that can cause side effects like sleeplessness and anxiety when you stop taking it.

I ended up going to a specialized Lyme doctor in Germany. She started treating me based on all the symptoms I had and gave me a three and a half months' supply of antibiotics. I was also instructed to take two months off from work. After carefully following the prescribed routine, my neurological symptoms disappeared. At the time, I was unsure of what had initially caused those issues, but I was relieved and happy that they were finally resolved.

Looking back now, I believe I did have burnout due to stress. Since so much time has passed, no one can ever be sure. The many effects of stress on your central nervous system and how you can get rid of stress will be explained in a later chapter.

Through it all, Madeleine helps me remember to put things into perspective with her child-like spirit of acceptance, her supply of jokes, and lots and lots of love.

Chapter 16

Silent Breakdown

When my sister walked into the room, I was on YouTube watching Lara Boyd's TEDx talk on neuroplasticity (for the fifth time) called "After watching this, your brain will not be the same."[1]

"Are you still watching that brain stuff?" Isabelle asked me. "Let's go swimming."

I gave her a one-word answer: "Okay."

Isabelle had invited me to a two-week training course in Marbella, on the sunny south coast of Spain. Given by a Swedish company called Enriched Life, the course wasn't restricted to stroke patients. There was also an MS[2,3,4] and Parkinson's[5,6,7] group in attendance. At the time, I could walk slowly with a cane and brace, and say approximately 30 short words but no compete sentences.

Isabelle stayed with me for the first week and then, when she needed to go back to work, Maarten flew down to take her place.

Maarten had finished gymnasium (high school) while I was at Klimmendaal, my rehab clinic. He was accepted into Harvard University[8] on December 10, 2015, after only a single application. I made a video of him opening the email from Harvard and have watched that video at least a hundred times. It still gives me goosebumps!

He was so incredibly happy to be accepted. But then Maarten decided that Harvard could wait. He took a gap year to take care of me as I recovered. He drove me to Klimmendaal each day, waited for hours, and then drove me home. I'm forever thankful to him for that.

The Marbella hotel was a luxury resort. Enriched Life's business model is to rent an entire hotel during the off season, then assign an on-site Swedish staff consisting of a nurse, doctor, psychologist, speech therapist, and several physical therapists. It seemed like no expense was spared, with one notable exception. The swimming pool was far too cold for patients whose nerves functioned better in warmer temperatures. Spasticity had a tendency to increase in cold water.

I was enjoying the time spent with my wonderful sister. She sat with me while I had my physical and speech therapy. I tried to tell her several times, "Don't bother with this boring stuff. Just go sit in the sun and read something, or walk down the beach and relax." But she stayed firmly by my side. It was as if she felt responsible for me like she did when we were children. I was three years younger, and like all sisters, we'd had some quarrels when we were young. Later, however, Isabelle developed into one of the warmest and kindest human beings I've ever met. She didn't seem inconvenienced by being with me, and she helped me with the hand movement exercises I got from Ulla.

Ulla was a talented physical therapist, and she was also the most educated I had met to date since she had a PhD.

She was in her late fifties and typically Swedish, a kind woman with blonde hair and blue eyes. She had also worked in California for a couple of years. I looked up the topic of her PhD thesis. She had specialized in spasticity and the use of Botox in arm and hand therapy. Before we met, I had already read some articles about Botox treatment for arm and hand spasticity.

Botulinum toxin (Botox) is a "nerve block" that stops the release of chemicals in your muscle cells.[9,10] These chemicals normally signal your muscles to tighten up. As a result, it disrupts the tighten-and-relax system for the muscles. This allows Botox to address the symptoms of spasticity by targeting the muscle. The cause is not actually addressed through the use of Botox, though, since the spasticity is created by impaired brain-muscle communication.

When a stroke damages the motor cortex, it affects the brain's ability to send signals to move your muscles. When muscles don't get any messages from the brain, they cramp and shorten as a way of protecting themselves. From an evolutionary perspective, this kind of protection was useful not too long ago. A lion would have a harder time getting hold of your cavewoman arm while it's curled up against your chest.

After Botox is injected into a muscle, it's necessary to do additional rehab exercises to strengthen the muscles that are not subject to the Botox. Botox wears off in about three months. After that, a new injection is required.

Ulla was pro-Botox and so was my sister. For some reason, I was skeptical and felt I needed to do more research before I made a decision. I did make an appointment with a doctor in Stockholm who Ulla recommended, a specialist in Botox injections, but I decided to cancel the appointment. It just didn't feel right for me.

I will leave out a discussion of the pros and cons since I believe that everyone should decide for themselves whether or not to use it. I made my decision not to use Botox based on this reasoning: I figured that if I used Botox, it would shut down the brain-muscle communication between my arm and my brain. Of course, without Botox, I also had no control over my arm. According to the studies on neuroplasticity, I should've been able to learn to relax my arm and regain brain muscle control by slowly training it to do the right movement during repetitive practice.

At dinner one evening, I overheard some of the specialists from Enriched Life discussing a study being done in California about stem cell treatment and the potential for promising results in treating brain injury.[11,12,13] I had read about this study before I arrived and even contacted the scientists conducting the trial.

Without thinking, I tried to join the conversation. I wanted to say, "I know about this study. It's being conducted at Stanford University, and I've already contacted them to volunteer for their research since the initial results seem very promising."

What came out of my mouth was an unrecognizable mess. Looking around the table, I noticed that no one was able to understand what I was trying to say. Instead, they all gave me a compassionate look.

I wasn't sure which I hated more, the fact that people felt sorry for me or that I couldn't even take part in a decent conversation!

I didn't cry in that moment. I knew there was no use in getting angry about the situation. I just decided to work so hard on my speech that one day, I couldn't be ignored anymore.

Later that night while I was in bed and my sister was asleep, I did shed a few tears. No, a lot of tears. I sobbed like a baby for hours, weeping my way through a whole box of Kleenex tissues.

Right this minute, as I write this chapter, what comes to mind is: *Why did I promise to make this book as authentic and truthful as possible? I hate feeling stupid, and I hate feeling uneducated.* My self-pity had struck again, and I hated that, too—even more when I noticed other people's pity for me.

Still feeling sorry for myself, I snuck out to the toilet so I wouldn't wake up Isabelle. There, I had a silent breakdown. I'm not proud of this now, but at first, I felt like blaming the doctor who kept me waiting for five and a half hours in the hospital. After that, I blamed every hospital, every doctor, and every therapist I'd seen since the stroke. At that particular moment, everyone was to blame except me. I even blamed the hotel staff for not delivering an extra box of tissues to my room that day.

The next morning, I went to breakfast as if nothing had happened. The calm facade that I presented to the world seemed to be me in a nutshell.

Much later, I received an answer from Stanford University about their stem cell treatment trials. The treatment consisted of inserting modified stem cells from the bone marrow into a chronic stroke patient's brain.

Since they denied my application, I guess I'll never find out if it could have worked for me.

Chapter 17

Maarten

"Do you know this book?" Maarten asked. "You're going to like it."

It was 7 o'clock in the morning. We were getting ready for our 40-minute drive to Klimmendaal. I could smell the fresh and earthy scent of rain in the air that morning.

Maarten showed me the audiobook he was talking about on his iPhone, *The Daily Stoic* by Ryan Holiday and Stephen Hanselman.[1,2] He must've noticed that I was somewhat disappointed by the subtitle: "366 Meditations on Wisdom, Perseverance, and the Art of Living."

"You need a break from the brain," he said.

Maybe he was reading my mind. I thought, *I don't need these kinds of books. I have brain damage, remember? I need to recover, so I have to read about the brain.* Instead of telling him that though, I answered with a simple "alright."

"Do you know anything about stoicism?" he asked.

"Um, a little bit." I learned a few things in high school, but I didn't remember what could make it so special that I now had to listen to an entire book on the subject. "Tell me about it," I continued.

"Stoicism is an ancient philosophy containing a lot of great wisdom," Maarten explained. "I think it can help you accept and make the best out of your stroke. It's not going to make you give up your dream to fully recover, though. In fact, those who practice stoicism are known for their steep yet attainable goals.[3][4][5][6] They'll do almost anything within their reach to achieve them."

My curiosity was piqued at this point. I liked this!

I thought about my own goals to talk fluently, walk, run, and be able to tie my shoelaces using my hand again. "I'm listening," I said.

Maarten gave me a short rundown: "Stoicism was the most influential philosophy in ancient Rome. Its foundations were laid in the third century BC, in Athens, by Zeno of Citium. 'Stoic' comes from the Greek word 'stōïkos' meaning 'porch,' and it refers to the place where Zeno taught his philosophy. Zeno[7] was succeeded by other famous philosophers like Seneca, Epictetus, and Marcus Aurelius."

Now, those names started to ring a bell. I remembered Aurelius. He was that "good guy" Roman emperor. Maarten continued his lecture. "The authors of the *The Daily Stoic* think that Stoic wisdom is still very relevant today. Let's listen to it," he said. It had become a habit, listening to audiobooks during our morning trip to the rehab clinic.

I clearly remember the first thing that drew my attention to Stoicism. It was a question by Epictetus, a former slave. After he was freed, he became one of the most prominent Stoic philosophers and a teacher to Marcus Aurelius. Once, during one of his lectures, he asked something like, "What kind of boxer are you?" He then continued, "If you are in the ring and you get hit in the face, would you just walk out of the ring? Of course you are going to get hit. That's inevitable when competing in boxing. Now, if you get hit in life, which also is inevitable, will you step out of life and give up? What is the whole point of training, then? Whether you are a boxer, wrestler, or any other human being, you'll have to train yourself to be able to deal with a very strong opponent. That's life. You are going to get hit sometimes."

I hit the pause button and thought about this for some time. Then I listened to it again. I was ashamed of myself. Thinking back, the stroke was the challenger, my "very strong opponent." At first, I could handle my new challenger. But when the challenge got tougher due to neuropathic pain, I felt like my opponent was too strong. I had then tried to leave the ring. Basically, I was at the point of giving up.

Where had my fighting spirit been? I always wanted to win at games when I was a kid, continually aiming to be the best at school.

It seems that the Moskowitz method to fight my pain came at the very last moment. It had slowly awakened my inner warrior. I grew in my role as a fighter after I began to become a master over my pain.

My stroke had knocked me off my feet, literally and figuratively. Now I had to stand up, face my opponent, and punch it straight in the face. I would not stop until the referee declared me the winner. I had never felt so sure about anything in my life.

How wise Maarten was. He was only 17 at the time. *Did he really come out of my belly?* I thought with a grin.

I still remember the first time Remco and I were confronted with his exceptional intelligence and memory. He was two years old when the supervisor of his kindergarten called us in for a private conversation. We thought he had done something terrible.

As is often the case with young children, there had been some biting or fighting incidents at kindergarten. We assumed Maarten might have done something along those lines. It turned out that they wanted to address something else altogether. They asked us if we realized that he displayed some rather "unusual" behavior. Writing his name was not so astonishing, but they wondered how it was possible that Maarten knew all the different cars on the street.

Maarten had liked cars for about a year by then. It began when Remco asked him, "Do you know what car we drive?" Remco explained to him that it was a Mercedes and you could tell by the star logo on the car.

Soon, Maarten wanted to know about every new logo he noticed on cars. A Mercedes was easy for him after that, and he continued by learning BMW, Volkswagen, Citroën, Chrysler, and so on. The list got longer and longer. Within weeks, he knew that Opel had the Corsa and Astra, and Volkswagen had the Polo, Golf, and Passat. Mercedes had the C Class, E Class, and S Class. He would point and say, for example, "Peugeot 205." Then he pointed again, "Ford Mondeo." If he didn't know a car, he just hadn't been told about it yet. To us, it seemed pretty reasonable. You taught your kid the name of a car, and then he remembered it. He was our first child, so what did we know?

I remember one time, when he was seven, Maarten had to give a speech on the subject of his choice. After he prepared it on paper, he read it aloud to me. When he finished speaking, he told me, "Now I'll adjust my presentation to speak with simpler words, so the kids in my class can understand me."

When I heard him say that, it not only blew my mind but also made me realize he had recognized that he was different.

Since he disliked being too different, he adapted to fit in with the rest of the kids. He had, by that point, developed an early form of social awareness.

Maarten had planted a seed. I became hooked on the principles of stoicism and still am today. Since then, I have read a few books on stoicism among which are *Meditations* by Marcus Aurelius,[8] Epictetus' *Discourses*,[9] and Seneca's *Letters from a Stoic*,[10] and I have listened to Brian Johnson's marvelous app, Optimize.

There is an abundance of wisdom to be found within stoicism, so I picked out a few things to share that helped me deal with my stroke:

1. Clarity

> *"Some things are within our control, while others are not. We control our opinions, choice, desire, aversion."*
>
> *"The chief task in life is simply this: to identify and separate matters. I say clearly to myself which are externals not under my control, and which have to do with the choices I actually control."*
>
> - EPICTETUS, *DISCOURSES*, 2.5.4-5.

To summarize Ryan Holiday's take on these words, Epictetus basically says the following: All other things (besides "our opinions, choice, desire, aversion") are beyond our control. Holiday gives the example of a flight that is delayed because of a storm. No amount of yelling at the airline representative will end that storm. The same goes for our health. You can refrain from smoking and maintain a healthy diet but, in the end, we do not "control" our health in a strict sense.

I had a stroke due to a blood clot in my right brain hemisphere. I ate a healthy diet, there was nothing wrong with my weight, and I did a lot of sports. Unfortunately, *shit happens*, whether you like it or not. According to stoicism, I do not control the external event that took place. In my case, this external event was my stroke. You can decide for yourself if it's fair or unfair, but you have no control over things like this. However, you can control what you think about it.

2. Amor fati

In this case, it would be easy to say, "I think it sucks that I had a stroke." But stoicism helped me take a different point of view. "The art of acquiescence" is to accept, rather than fight, everything that comes our way in life.

Many centuries later, Nietzsche put it a bit differently when he named it *amor fati* (a love of fate).

American author Byron Katie[11] wrote that we need to practice "loving what is." She tells us to "quit arguing with reality—but only because we lose every time we do so anyway." It's a simple approach, which I still think is hilarious!

Could I learn to love my fate? Could I accept the things I could not change? Could I courageously change the things I was able to? I couldn't change the stroke, but I could change my attitude toward the whole stroke situation. *That is doable,* I thought.

Another book by Ryan Holiday comes to mind, *The Obstacle Is the Way.*[12] Should I see the stroke as an obstacle? Should I rise up and show what I'm made of?

Marcus Aurelius said, "The impediment to action advances the action. What stands in the way becomes the way."[13] When we convert this into understandable English, we get "the obstacle is the way."

I get goosebumps whenever I read this. I hope that, by describing it in this book, I can inspire a few stroke survivors to apply the same knowledge to aid them in their recovery. I could easily fill this entire book with my admiration for stoicism, but I'll leave that to the books and authors I mentioned before since they are specialized in this. I'll add a few more insights, first.

Something that struck me funny in the lectures of Epictetus is a question he would ask: "What would have become of Hercules, do you think, if there had been no lion, no hydra, no stag, and no boar? Obviously, he would have rolled over and gone back to sleep." This tells us that Hercules became who he was by overcoming his obstacles.

"Oh my God! Why did this thing (my stroke) have to happen to *me*?" That was what I would have said previously. But that changed to, "Hm, ok, awesome challenge." Stoicism teaches us that it's all a matter of acceptance and making the best out of things, and I would use my obstacle to become who I could be.

We need to discipline ourselves to care only about the things that are within our control. The trick is to get good at separating what is within our control from what isn't. It is also essential to practice making wise choices about what we control rather than spend time worrying about things we cannot influence.

In fact, it's like playing a game of cards. When you're dealt a bad hand, there is no use in getting upset about it. The only thing you can do is play your cards as wisely as possible. In my case, this means doing lots of rehab, reading about the brain and learning to understand it better, eating healthy, maintaining a good sleep schedule, and most importantly, being a warrior. Being upset is not going to bring you (or me!) anything.

Thinking about my stroke this way gives me a clear and tranquil feeling. It allows me to enjoy life much more. However, don't believe that stoics have no emotions. This is not about being emotionless but instead about having the right emotions. Try not to let irrational feelings take over.

3. It takes time.

Another valuable lesson I learned from the Stoics is one I learned from Epictetus: "Nothing important comes into being overnight, even grapes and figs need time to ripen. If you say that you want a fig now, I will tell you to be patient."[14]

It is going to take time to recover. As an impatient perfectionist, I found this small lesson to be exceptionally helpful.

4. Choose your friends wisely.

To lead a quality life, it is vital that you choose your friends carefully. I took this advice and began to select more carefully who I spent my time with.

Seneca wrote, "Associate with people who are likely to improve you. Welcome those whom you are capable of improving. The process is a mutual one. People learn as they teach."[15]

I started to replace the negative thinkers, those that drained energy every time we met, with warmer people. How to recognize those warmer people? After spending time with someone, you should be able to see whether the person was like a leak, causing air to flow from your personal balloon of energy, or filled you with additional energy.

Move away from people that offer you fake kindness. Allow kindness only when it is sincerely given. Otherwise, the hypocrisy will drag you down. "There is no companionship with the immature," as the Buddha said.

5. Reach for your highest potential.

Epictetus said: "Step forward and make use of what you have learned." He continued, "What we need now are people applying their learning and bearing witness to their learning in their actions."

I guess I am writing this book because I took this quote literally. I have but a single goal with this book. If I can make one or two stroke survivors' lives more acceptable and more joyful again, I will have accomplished my goal.

The Stoics taught me to be determined and see my stroke as a challenge of post-traumatic growth, not simple adversity. I can either break down and give up, or grow from the stroke. I was determined to grow.

Chapter 18

Kicked Out and Happy

She had tears in her eyes when she welcomed me. We hugged for a long time. I somehow managed to say, "I'm still smart."

She just looked at me and said with a smile, "I do not doubt that."

I was seeing Sonja for the first time in my office, and my return was warm and welcoming. She was the manager now and doing very well. Sonja had hired a new employee for the shipping department to get the packages out via UPS, and she was also in the process of hiring someone to replace Marianna. We were all grateful that Marianna had stayed on for almost a year to help out, but now she needed to leave and work in her husband's business.

My decision to start a website directed at the US market had been a sound one. We sold only electrical equipment from premium brands such as ABB, Schneider, and others. That segment of the business was growing and profitable.

The only questions we ever got from clients were queries about whether the equipment was genuine or what they called "Chinese garbage." We were proud of the products we supplied, so when we could confidently assure them it was the "real thing," clients returned again and again for additional orders.

Sitting down at my desk created some strange sensations. *Here is where it all happened,* I thought. A few memories flashed through my head—the ambulance workers carrying me on a stretcher down the small stairs, and people watching.

It had not been the first time I was taken away by ambulance from my office. The year before my stroke, I had gone into a portion of the building that was being reconstructed, and I was helping put up the prefab ceiling. Trying to talk on the phone and climb a ladder at the same time was not a good idea, and I fell, bringing a portion of the wall down on me, breaking my knee and leg. That episode resulted in a plate and 13 screws inserted into my right leg.

From the time I turned 40, I saw more hospitals and doctors than I had my whole life prior. It seemed to be one thing after another, including experiencing burnout/Lyme disease, breaking my leg, and then a severe stroke. The Universe was apparently trying to send me a message, but I was ignoring the hints. I'd had a TIA two years before my stroke and couldn't see out of one of my eyes for a few hours. But when my vision returned, I went back to work and never bothered seeing a doctor about it.

Finally, there was the stroke. I knew I should've been listening to the hints I was getting from who knows what or where, but I didn't—even after the stroke. I returned to the office thinking I could work four hours a day. I believed it would all work out if Maarten could drive me straight from the rehab center to my office each day.

When I made contact with the programmers in Ukraine, they were happy to hear from me again. We communicated through Skype, and it was hard at first to type in English. Since I had lost my ability to spell, I used spellcheck, quickly learning that a number of words are not spelled as you pronounce them.

After being back at work for two weeks, exercising my hand during breaks and falling back into multitasking once again, I realized that my eye couldn't manage that. It had begun to get blurry after one hour of work, and I had headaches and pain. I decided to listen to my body, probably for the first time ever.

I wasn't going to go to the office anymore. I would work from home for half an hour at the most each day, skyping with the programmers. My priority would be to get well first, then work. Period.

At Klimmendaal, my only individual sessions were with Femke, a new speech therapist who was referred to me by my psychologist.

Femke was easy to work with. She was kind to me and reinforced my belief that I was getting better. My comfort with her methods left me wishing that she had been my therapist from the very beginning.

There were some new things as well with my hand therapy. The extended therapy sessions were done in a group of between three and six other patients and two physical therapists, all working together during a three-hour session.

I loved those sessions working with my hand! Each Monday, we had to say what our next goal was—what we wanted to improve and learn—something like being able to pick up a pen. After we practiced those tasks for two weeks, our results were evaluated.

I was concerned because my stroke happened before most of the other patients had experienced their issues, but they seemed to be quite far ahead progress-wise. At eight and a half months after my stroke, I could still do very little with my affected hand. My arm and hand continued to be spastic, so I set a goal of being able to drink from a diet soda can. Although I no longer drink soda now, it was still something I consumed back then.

As I sat with my left elbow on the table, I attempted to hold the can and move it up toward my mouth. I had to force my left hand open and place the can inside the hand as the spasticity snapped my fingers closed. I needed to master both balancing the can and moving it smoothly up to my mouth. I thought I was making a bit of progress, but one of my therapists, Jenny, was not impressed.

Since everyone else seemed to be making more progress than I was, even if they had just had their stroke, that must have meant theirs wasn't as severe as mine. When I saw them already able to tie their shoelaces, I guessed that they were in the category of patients who have the "normal" three-month recovery period, as if they were bouncing back from a bruised brain.

My situation was different and much harder. Through repetition, I had to reprogram my brain so that the neuroplasticity would kick in. My recovery was going to take time, but I loved the three-hour hand workouts at Klimmendaal with the alternating team of physical therapists, especially when it was Lisette and Herma. I'm grateful to Klimmendaal for that.

I was a bit envious of some of the other patients there. But even if they were making more progress than me, we took the time to encourage each other when something good happened. And we laughed a lot.

After seeing one woman, who was 10 years older than I, taking the two sets of stairs to get to the rehab room instead of the elevator, I became so inspired by her that I immediately began to take the stairs too.

Some of the therapists disagreed with the idea of working in group sessions and still believed therapy should only be done on a one-to-one basis. What was not always acknowledged was the special bond that developed between patients when they worked together and shared their healing processes. It might have been helpful if the clinic had also extended the group sessions to speech therapy. They could've employed one less therapist each week and saved the clinic some money. But more importantly, bringing aphasia patients together may have a positive effect, reinforcing notions like "We are in this together," and "What can I learn from other patients?"

I began to read about Edward Taub's constraint-induced (CI) therapy research.[1,2,3,4,5] Taub, a behavioral neuroscientist on the faculty of the University of Alabama, made his breakthrough research in neuroplasticity while working on the Silver Spring monkeys case.[6] The monkeys were used as research subjects. They were deafferentated on one side of the body, meaning that signals were prevented from traveling from one side of the body to the brain. By restraining the functional arm (the "good" arm) in the monkeys, he was successful in proving that the monkeys would begin to use the less-functional (affected arm) in response.

Wow, I thought when I read this. The monkeys actually began to feed themselves using the side of the body that was damaged instead of the restrained "good" side.

Taub's lab was reported in 1981 by Alex Pacheco of PETA (People for the Ethical Treatment of Animals) for unacceptable treatment of the subject monkeys. Almost all of the charges were eventually dropped. Taub's current clinic specializes in constraint-induced movement therapy for people with "learned nonuse." Reading about Taub made me fleetingly consider breaking my "good" arm so my stroke-damaged one would get better.

Back at Klimmendaal, one of my therapists, Jenny, began one of our sessions by saying, "We are going to do some tests with your hand." She had taken me to a room where a wooden suitcase was visible and instructed me to take large dice and put them on top. Using every bit of strength and concentration I had, I managed to raise my arm to a 90° angle. I must have looked ridiculous: the left shoulder as high as it can get, turning my arm inward (not an anatomically correct position). My hand was too spastic to release the dice.

Moving on to the next test, I discovered it was something with pins that I couldn't even reach with my finger. Jenny's response was impatient. "There's no use in bringing out more tests because if you can't do this task, the next ones are only going to be more difficult. I'll report your test results to the management."

She had known in advance that I would fail that test since she had been working with me every week. She offered me what I considered to be a look of fake empathy. I wanted to say, "Let's agree to disagree. Please allow me to continue being a part of this group. I have made some improvement in balancing my hand, and just because my hand hasn't recovered in X amount of time doesn't mean that my hand won't recover. It should be all about neuroplasticity now. Besides, Taub's constraint-induced therapy has proved to continue working for years post-stroke."

But I couldn't say any of those things. Jenny probably didn't know anything about Taub's research or neuroplasticity, either. So I just said, "Okay. Thank you."

That same week, I received a letter telling me that it was my last week at Klimmendaal. In fact, they had kicked me out.

During my last week, I gave out bracelets to my fellow patients that said "stroke survivor." The men received a black bracelet, and the women got them in different colors. They were very thankful, and we hugged for a long time afterward.

I was determined to find out which organizations offered CI therapy in Sweden and the Netherlands. I planned to book two weeks of it every three months. And luckily, I was also going to Sweden for another two weeks at Rehab Station.

It was nice seeing Emma and Sandra again. But one evening, I saw my friends from high school, and that felt absolutely magical. We met at Fia's apartment at Folkungagatan, and I was very nervous about seeing them. I almost peed my pants from the nerves!

What if they thought I had changed? What if they didn't recognize me? But they did recognize me, of course. Fia, Chamilla, and Åsa were there, but Liza and Anneli couldn't make it.

I hadn't laughed as much since my stroke as I did together with those ladies. Our sense of humor had always been a bit like dry British humor, and we made fun of ourselves with satire and sarcasm. We told jokes about every sort of subject with very little room for taboos. The fact that I could hardly talk created more opportunity for good-natured teasing. All through the evening, we laughed, giggled, howled, and even roared. I had such a blast that it still makes me smile when I write about it.

I went home with an awesome feeling—happy!

Chapter 19

The Road to Hana

They were all mad at me now.

"Why don't you just sit down in the wheelchair? We are in a hurry, goddamn it, and we're going to miss the flight this way!" Remco said.

I refused.

It was one of those wheelchairs you can borrow at the airport. I could somewhat understand their irritation. Maarten gently tried to push me down into the wheelchair while Remco held it behind me. But I managed to get my right hand in the perfect position on top of the back of the wheelchair, and that was enough to provide resistance. If anyone else in the airport was watching, it must have been a funny scene, but I just did *not* care.

The Schiphol airport in Amsterdam is an enormous one-terminal building. That makes the airport a popular hub since you always arrive in the same terminal that your connecting flight departs from. No bus or train transfers are needed. The downside of the one-terminal concept is that it could easily be a one-kilometer walk from check-in to the departure gate. At my walking pace, it would take at least 45 minutes to reach Gate D28. Murphy's Law also applied, since that was one of the furthest gates distance-wise.

At the time, I walked with a brace on my left lower leg up to the knee and with a cane in my right hand. Still, I had trouble with my balance, so my pace was slow. But I refused to sit in any wheelchair. It might sound as if I was simply being difficult with my family. But to me, it meant a great deal to stay out of that chair. I had been working my butt off over the past eight months to get myself out of it. So, I was not getting back in under any circumstances. Period.

It was the first day after my Klimmendaal episode, and I was completely done with the rehab clinic now. It was entirely up to me to get better from that point on. Remco had suggested that we, as a family, celebrate this in a way that had motivated me for the past months: We would go on a trip. It would be a graduation present to Maarten and a gift to me to help me "start living again in my new life." So, we were off to Hawaii!

That was so typical of Remco. Most people might have suggested that I allow myself a trip to someplace temperate and not too far away, like the south of Spain or Greece. But Remco loves doing the opposite. Instead of going somewhere easier and relatively close, he decided we would go to Hawaii for three and a half weeks over Christmas. I loved the idea of visiting four of the main islands.

Remco was great at arranging family trips. Since he worked for a tour operator back then, he knew when to book the tickets and hotels, and how to figure out where to get a discount for travel professionals.

While all this was going on, Elle (streetsmart as usual) managed to get a handsome guy in one of the airport golf carts to drive the two of us to gate D28. Remco, Maarten, and Madeleine had to run to catch up with us. We were all so excited that by the time we arrived at the gate in time, they had forgiven me for not getting into that wheelchair.

I was still taking blood thinners (clopidogrel) and cholesterol-lowering medication (simvastatin). I also wore compression socks during the flight because I have Factor V Leiden, a mutated form of human Factor V, which causes blood clotting.[1,2,3]

Many people would hear that additional piece of medical history and say, “That Factor V Leiden must have been the cause of your stroke!” However, in the hospital, doctors deemed that unlikely. Factor V Leiden is a rather weak risk-factor for thrombosis (blood clots), especially in its heterozygote form.[4,5] It’s primarily associated with thrombosis in the venous system within your lower body. Examples of that are DVT, deep vein thrombosis,[6,7] in the legs or a pulmonary embolism.[8,9]

In rare cases, a clot can form in the veins and then migrate to the arterial side, the upper body, and then cause a stroke, which one can interpret as thrombosis in the brain’s arteries. To find out if this so-called paradoxical embolization[10,11,12] had happened, the doctors needed to determine if I had a hole in my heart—usually a defect in the wall separating the atria or right and left heart chambers. That could have enabled a clot to pass from the venous or right side of the heart to the arterial or left side of the heart.[13,14] If that happened, a clot could enter the upper body’s circulation and end up in my brain. But the chances of having such a hole were quite small. A hole in the heart existed at birth in less than .5% of all babies, and 90% of those holes spontaneously close very soon after that. A hole in the heart was, therefore, not very likely.

An unclosed hole in the heart by adulthood is a condition called patent foramen ovale.[15][16]

In a stroke like mine, with an unknown cause, one of the specialists decided it was worth investigating. And in my case, finding such a hole would raise the suspicion that the clot causing my stroke was related to the Factor V Leiden, originating in the lower body. Information like that would determine what medication was required—an oral anticoagulant instead of antithrombotic agents such as clopidogrel.

A standard echocardiogram was done and revealed no defects. Soon after, the doctors followed that with a TEE, transesophageal echocardiogram.[17] That procedure was rather unpleasant since I had to swallow an ultrasound probe that was inserted through my throat to position it *behind* my heart. The contrast fluid that was injected would have passed from the right to the left side of the heart if there had been a hole, but the examination indicated no such problem. They saw bubbles, but no contrast fluid. I was now one of the 10% of all stroke patients who never received an explanation for why it had happened. Still, the doctors decided that it would be wise to keep me on blood thinners and cholesterol-lowering agents, even though I didn't have "bad" or high cholesterol. Without knowing what had caused my stroke, they preferred to stay on the "better safe than sorry" side of things. But I eventually stopped all medications.

It was a long flight, but I didn't mind. I had been looking forward to that trip for three months. I loved thinking back to the last time Remco and I had been to Hawaii, 18 years earlier. We were so in love back then. I was 24, and he was 31. On that trip, one particular day in January 1998, Remco saved my life.

We were on Little Beach, near Wailea, Maui. I had been fascinated watching three young women with boogie boards, who I assumed were born in the area. Thinking back on that vivid memory, they were impressive as they paddled out on their boards and rode the waves.

Whenever they saw a wave big enough, they would start paddling, their boards picking up speed, and either sit or come up onto their knees to ride the wave to the beach.

"I want to do that," I said to Remco. So the next day, we rented boogie boards at Snorkel Bob's and went back to Little Beach. Just as I had seen those girls doing, I casually walked into the water with the boogie board safety line attached to my left wrist and a rubber flipper on my right foot. I teasingly told myself that I felt like I was already a pro. The waves were somewhat higher than on the previous day, but I couldn't wait to get out there on my boogie board.

At first, I made steady progress. I learned how to get past the breaking surf and then speed up to catch a wave. I might not have been as good as the three young women I admired earlier, but I was doing reasonably well.

Suddenly, bigger waves came toward me, and one hit me head on, causing me to fall off the board. Churned beneath the waves, I felt like I was spinning around in a laundry machine with no chance of escape. Gasping for air, I managed to get to the surface, but the current was so strong that it dragged me further and further from the beach.

I knew I needed to stay calm. As I saw another wave coming toward me, I remembered to "duck dive" under the wave and then swam beneath it. Under the water, I needed to keep my shoulders in the correct position to hold onto the board, go down, and wait for the wave to pass over me.

I must have done that at least eight times and was beginning to feel exhausted. As the current continued to drag me away from the beach, I popped up between the waves, saw Remco, and called out as loudly as I could. He must've realized I was in trouble because he was on his boogie board and at my side in no time. He then managed to save us by instructing me how to swim back to shore.

I say "us" because two days later, we received joyous news: I was pregnant with Maarten! From that time on, I had a great deal of respect for the power of ocean waves—especially when Remco made fun of me for not going into the ocean anymore on that trip. *Those were the days*, I thought, smiling.

Now we were on our way to Maui, Kauai, Hawai'i, and Oahu. I looked forward to Maui the most, especially being able to experience a piece of paradise again on the road to Hana.

Although jetlagged with our body clocks out of sync, we got up at 4 a.m. on our second day. Off we went in our Jeep Wrangler. The road to Hana may only be 52 miles long, but it has an exhausting 617 hairpin curves and 59 one-lane bridges.[18] That makes the drive around two and a half hours long. Little wonder that the road is sometimes called "the divorce highway" as a result of those argument-inducing obstacles.

No one else was on the road at that hour, and we drove in darkness for the first 10 miles. "We'll see this part of the road on our way back, and there is plenty more ahead," Remco told me. When the sun was about to come up, we stopped to enjoy the sounds of birds calling, distant waterfalls, the ocean, and utter silence from any human sources. For a moment, I forgot the previous eight months of struggle. I felt alive!

By the time it was 7:45, we had already paused along the road several times. We then stopped at one of the most beautiful waterfalls I've ever seen, just 20 meters from the road. Remco and the children took a narrow path so they could swim under the waterfall while I took pictures. I was confident that this day couldn't be beat as the best day of vacation. But 24 hours later, I had to correct myself after another fantastic day. And I decided to throw away my walking cane and brace!

I sensed that my somewhat impetuous decision to throw them both away at the same time annoyed Remco a little. I had already been walking quite slowly with my cane and brace, and throwing them away meant I was really going at a snail's pace. But there in Hawaii, I felt no hurry. I firmly believed that I had made the right decision. *It's now or never,* I thought. *Let's see if I survive this.* I knew I was up for the challenge.

I had been reading a lot of the research on neuroplasticity at the time, and it seemed to me that "survival" was an essential part of it. If I could trick my brain into believing that the only way to walk and survive from here on is without the cane and brace, wouldn't that be the path forward?

The first two weeks of walking without those aides were horrible. Not only did I move like a snail, people also stared at me. As I walked, I leaned (sometimes precariously) to the left side. I couldn't get my toes up, and I was struggling to not over-bend my knee. The children were not amused to see me walking this slowly. But I wholeheartedly believed in the most recent science: Through repetition, doing something consistently again and again, I could force neuroplastic changes in my brain. That would allow me to walk normally again—soon.

In more primitive times like the Stone Age, when there were no specialized canes, no braces, and certainly no wheelchairs, people may have recovered more quickly in certain cases because they had to survive. Otherwise, they could die from factors like starvation or exposure to the elements.

Taub's research found that monkeys could move their affected hand quite quickly again when it was necessary to feed themselves. If a skill was essential for survival, the brain freed up the required space for that skill. However, a modern lifestyle can sometimes get in the way of this incredible process. In his

TED talk "How brain plasticity can change your life," Michael Merzenich observes: "We pave even the path of our countryside, so that every footfall is certain, so that there can never be a challenge to moving across the physical environment."[19]

Believing that I should challenge my personal status quo by walking without the cane and brace, doing the opposite of what Merzenich mentions in his talk, I thought to myself, *I should start walking on grass, stones, and beaches.* I began to walk barefoot as soon as I could because I read somewhere that walking barefoot improved balance and proprioception.[20,21,22,23] Proprioception is the awareness you have of and get back from your limbs.

I have to warn you, please do not do this at home without assistance from a physical therapist!

At any rate, I imagined that the cane and brace were not invented yet, and that put me in survival mode. In the beginning, it was quite hard. I came close to giving up many times, primarily when my foot was too tired or I had difficulty bringing my toes up. I could only flex my foot about two centimeters, less than an inch, with a significant amount of concentration. If I was tired, I couldn't manage to do any of it. When I began walking without a brace, I could only get my right toe up, nothing else. But I hung in there. Three weeks later, I had slowly begun to get the hang of it. That doesn't mean I walked perfectly. Not at all! It was more like, not every single person came up to ask if "I was alright," just a few. (-:

If I hadn't taken that "rebel" standpoint, I may never have been able to walk freely again. I got so excited about my new success that I published about my stroke and follow-up achievements on Facebook and Instagram. Now everyone I knew, even distantly, had learned about my stroke.

It was a relief to get it out there. Maybe it took me almost nine months to share the news about my stroke because I felt ashamed somehow. I still don't know why it took so long for me to do that. But I probably first had to deal with and move past the feeling of failure in my life. I had finally reached a point where I was not ashamed anymore. The stroke had become a part of who I was.

My mind was already wandering off, though, to what I was planning to do next.

Run.

Chapter 20

Jumping

It was all up to me now—whether or not I would recover and how much recovery I would achieve.

I already felt moderately confident about being able to walk reasonably well for a stroke survivor, but maintaining my balance while coping with a blind right eye was still a significant issue. I bumped into things all the time. I was also dealing with a plate and 16 screws in my right leg from my fall the year before the stroke, and that previous injury had left a lingering pain that I sometimes felt while walking. I had been relying on my right leg more than my left since the stroke. But at that moment, I couldn't care less about those aches and twinges since I was finally walking without a brace and cane!

It might take me five or six years, but I believed I would walk normally again. It was time to set up a team to guide my recovery. I needed a physical therapist, a speech therapist, and a gym membership. Femke, one of my therapists at Klimmendaal, had contacted a speech therapist that she knew. "His name is Sander," she said. "He's good, and you're going to like him."

She was right. I did like him. We met every Friday for half an hour. The first time, I told him that my goal was to speak normally again. He didn't give me the look of pity I had seen too often. Instead, he said in a very straightforward way, "Ok, we'll work on this goal."

Unexpectedly, I encountered numerous obstacles when I began to look for someone to provide constraint-induced movement therapy (CIMT), which you will remember from the story about Taub's monkeys. CIMT[1,2,3,4,5] was impossible to find, in the Netherlands at least. As it turned out, the Dutch medical system only provided it for children. When my sister Isabelle tried to contact a Swedish CI therapist, they said they couldn't offer it either. I had a Swedish passport, but I was also a registered citizen of Germany. Trying to laugh through my frustration, I suggested, "Just send me the bill!" But they said no and that it was due to bureaucratic reasons.

Still flitting around my brain was another issue: I had to decide whether or not I was going to break my right arm. Every person I shared this idea with thought I was crazy. Continuing to believe that I needed to enter "survival mode" as part of my healing process, I was confident that breaking my right arm would jump-start me in that mode. My brain would be forced to make use of my affected left arm and hand to perform simple but necessary tasks like eating.

I didn't care about people's default reactions, and I had already realized the importance of developing my own methods. I was convinced that I had to think outside the box and do what felt right for me, even when I met resistance from those around me. Recovering from a severe stroke was about overcoming challenges. Nobody could make those necessary improvements for me, so I needed to rely solely on myself. If that meant I had to break my right arm, so be it. As I thought about the list of things that I wanted to learn again, I knew I would have to be smart about it and take it one step at a time.

Inspired by a story from Norman Doidge's book,[6] I thought that perhaps I should start crawling again, like a baby. I had already realized that learning to use my left foot for walking again was easier than relearning to use my left arm. My brain had no choice but to make use of the affected leg. Thousands of steps every day was enough repetition to get there. When crawling, I would have to rely on both my arm and leg for support, so I was forced to make use of my affected left side.

Reading up on the brain taught me that there is always a competition of "cortical real estate" which, in my case, my right arm was easily winning from my left. Even though I was born left-handed, my left arm would just hang there, letting my right arm do all the work. All the neuroplasticity I had engaged up to this point was used to teach my unaffected right hand. Since the stroke, I learned to do everything with my right hand, buttoning and unbuttoning my shirt, eating, writing, all of it.

I imagined that my neurons were firing and wiring together to make my unaffected right hand better in performing all tasks. So, how was I going to make it stop doing that and create improvement in the left hand instead? I didn't have an answer just then, but I hoped CIMT was a solution.

Being accepted for any CIMT program was going to be a daunting task. I learned that I needed at least some functionality in my left hand to build on. Even when I found a therapy practice that would consider my application, I couldn't meet their basic requirements. I had failed all the tests that required me to bend my thumb and index finger together. That motion was the most essential first step toward picking something up, and I couldn't do it.

My challenge would be finding a way to develop those basic skills on my own. I had a goal now, and it was an excellent first step. I spent an entire week planning my training while I tried things out to see what would and wouldn't work. As I ordered stuff online, trying to find tools that could be useful, I came up with several ideas for exercises that might eventually help me achieve my goal. At one point, half our living room was filled with exercise equipment (cue unhappy husband!).

I started playing table tennis, a.k.a. ping-pong. I had been quite good before my stroke, so I was convinced that my brain must have some of my former moves still hardwired into it. Since we had a ping-pong table at home, it was indeed worth a try. I couldn't hold the paddle at first because it was too heavy. Unfortunately, ping-pong proved to still be above my entry-level skills at that moment.

As an alternative, I came up with the idea to hang a tennis ball on a rope in the middle of an open door. I could hit it with a different, lightweight paddle in my affected hand.

At the beginning of my ping-pong adventure, I must have looked like a poorly programmed robot. My arm was still so spastic that I rarely hit the ball when it swung in my direction. Attempting to hold the paddle in my hand for more than 30 seconds was futile. After those brief seconds, the paddle would fall out of my hand without me feeling a thing. Still, I continued to believe that it was a start.

I worked at it for about 30 minutes at a time. At first, my sessions consisted of trying to hold the paddle while also trying to hit the tennis ball for 30 seconds. When the paddle fell out of my hand, I was so exhausted from the effort that I needed a five-minute break.

After three weeks with almost no improvement, I was about to give up, but I didn't.

The obstacle is the way, the obstacle is the way, the obstacle is the way, I would tell myself over and over again. *Marcus Aurelius, thank you for your wisdom.* The Stoics helped me persevere for those first three weeks, and soon after that, I began to see glimmers of improvement. I was able to hold the light paddle for about 40 seconds at a time, and my arm extension was a full five degrees more. To an outsider, these improvements would hardly be noticeable. But to me they were huge, motivating me more than ever. *Neuroplasticity, here I come!*

As you read this, you might be wondering how I could get so excited about such a small improvement. For me, the answer is simple: I had been learning all about the brain and the nuances involved in recovery. It takes time to reprogram the brain. It takes thousands of repetitions and countless small improvements that build upon each success. The motor map in my right brain had been destroyed, and the sensation in my left arm and hand was down to almost zero. It would be a long process, and I knew that. Recovery of my arm and hand was like a puzzle. *It may take 15 years,* I thought.

After six months of consistent effort, I replaced my light paddle with a standard ping-pong paddle. By then, I could hit two balls in a row while the tennis table was up on one side. That hadn't been an option six months earlier, so it was evident that my hard work had begun to bear fruit.

Encouraged by that progress, I continued to practice and purchased a box of 500 ping-pong balls on eBay. They were cheap balls from China, thin and easily broken. I couldn't have cared less. As soon as I felt that my hand and brain were up for the task, I increased the rigidity of my stance and firmed-up my grip. But progress doesn't always proceed in a straight line. There were days when my hand became so spastic that I couldn't hold the paddle at all. Other times, my hand was so tired that I couldn't hold it for more than five seconds. When that was the case, I used duct tape to wrap the paddle around my hand.

Why did I choose table tennis? Weren't there better ways to recover, like golf, boules, basketball, painting, or even playing an Xbox or PlayStation? I'm not a scientist, but for me, there was a clear and well-thought-out set of reasons for my choice of table tennis.[7,8,9,10]

I wanted to train my arm and hand to select a response rapidly from the countless alternatives of where a ball might be coming from. This was because

There were also other reasons.

First, I had read that table tennis could improve a person's balance. Staying balanced and being able to change direction quickly is key to being successful in table tennis.

Second, it improves coordination. Following the ball as it moves quickly toward you helps develop hand-eye coordination.

Third, it stimulates different parts of the brain. By anticipating an opponent's shot, or in my case, the ball bouncing off the table tennis wall, a player makes use of the prefrontal cortex for strategic planning.

Fourth, the aerobic exercise from the physical activity of the game stimulates the hippocampus. This part of the brain happens to be responsible for long-term memorization of facts and events.

Furthermore, table tennis keeps your brain sharp. *Alzheimer's Weekly* found, after a series of preliminary clinical studies in Japan, that table tennis remarkably increases blood flow to the brain. A measurable increase in motor skills and cognitive awareness were results.

My sixth and final reason for choosing table tennis was that the cerebellum (little brain) is known for its important role in motor memory. I didn't get my stroke in the cerebellum. Thus, I reasoned that my motor memory had to be intact. Since I have always been very competitive, I could visualize how I played table tennis with my left hand before my stroke, and make use of that visualization in my rehabilitation.

I got a so-called tennis glove to stick the racket in my hand instead of holding it. But the glove was too heavy for me. I felt like I was in a trance when I played and hated that I could only last for five minutes before my hand couldn't hold the paddle anymore. I also had no one to play against. That would surely have brought out my competitive instincts, but I didn't blame anyone for not wanting to play with me. I was too slow and could only hit about 1 in 20 balls coming my way.

When I ran out of energy and my hand was tired from holding the racket, I began to crawl on the floor with a brace on my left hand, separating my fingers. Then, after I had exhausted myself from crawling, I would sit quietly and read. I learned that left and right brain hemisphere coordination was boosted by crawling, although it was distressing that the left part of my body still just hung there limply.

Gross motor skills and fine motor skills are part of a baby's physical development. Those stages of development are activated by crawling. Gross motor skills are larger movements a baby makes with its legs, arms, and entire body. The fine motor skills used by the hands, fingers, and toes enable babies to balance, grasp things, and move items to their mouth. All of those skills develop further when they learn how to write, tie their shoelaces, and button their clothing, and are a direct reflection of their advancing higher cortical development.

What I read confirmed my gut feeling that I needed to move like a baby as part of my recovery. With a grin on my face, I imagined the staff at Klimmendaal treating stroke patients by teaching them how to crawl and pick up things from the floor before they were allowed to relearn walking. I firmly believed that such training, despite being a bit embarrassing, would have been better than urging patients to time their walks around the block—over and over again.

Since I knew crawling was also good for the development of hand-eye coordination and balance, I began consistently crawling over the next seven months for two hours each day. But in spite of all that work, my left arm continued to move to the outside of my body's core, while the right arm moved correctly, aligned in parallel to my core.

My chiropractor and functional neurologist who you'll meet in another chapter, Arjan Kuipers, explained later that I had been trying to crawl at too early a stage in my recovery. He played an essential role in my further improvement when he set up "pre-crawling" exercises for me.[11, 12, 13, 14, 15]

Without realizing it, some of my other trial-and-error efforts had been done too early as well. When I wondered how I could use my left hand while reading, I thought, *Use braille!* I bought some large wooden alphabet blocks with letters and corresponding braille dots on them. It was not a coincidence that I chose braille.[16] I had already studied it.

Gripped, I read that for blind people, touch activates not only the tactile area of the parietal lobe but also a part of the occipital lobe in the back of their head, which has to do with vision. A blind person reading braille experiences activation of both the tactile area and the visual area of the brain. This brain activation may cause a heightened sense of touch in blind people. However, in reading braille, the brain must not only perceive the shapes of the characters, it must understand those shapes as a language. A blind person reading braille probably (hypothetically) uses the same language areas of the brain as a sighted person does, such as the temporal lobe area above the ear called Wernicke's area.[17]

I felt stimulated by this information because I thought it might somehow help improve my speech as well. Italians have an expression: *Tutte le strade portano a Roma* ("All roads lead to Rome"), meaning there are many different ways to reach the same goal. What I also knew about brain neuroplasticity was that there were several ways to achieve the same goal. I needed to reprogram my brain to use different paths to be able to speak in order to achieve my goal. Unfortunately for me, since I couldn't feel the letters yet, reading braille was out of the question.

I soon stopped going to the gym I had just joined. It was the closest to me, only 10 minutes away in a nearby village-sized city. I knew quite a lot of people who used that gym and felt uncomfortable going there after my stroke.

One day while I was using a leg press machine, an acquaintance came up to me and said,

"Hello, Linda. Is that you?" I nodded. "How are you?" she asked.

I didn't have time to reply "fine" because she kept talking, saying, "I heard you had a stroke. That's terrible! And it must be awful for your children. How is your husband dealing with all this? It must be terrible for him too!"

Unable to cut in and answer her barrage of questions, and thanks to my limited speech, an awkward silence followed. I just turned around and ignored her. The third time something similar happened, I began to cry and then was angry with myself for crying. I wanted to scream at them, "Why don't you say something encouraging, like how wonderful it is that I keep fighting and that I will manage to get over it?"

All people had to say was "That's so terrible!" and "Isn't it awful?" and blah blah blah. I was overwhelmed immediately. Of course I knew it was dreadful to deal with the aftermath of a stroke. I was living that reality every day. So, why remind me of that? For all you reading this book who happen to be "acquaintances" of stroke survivors, I have some advice. Speak in a positive and encouraging way, will you?

I never went back to that gym again.

Luckily, I had Bart working with me once a week. Bart is a physical therapist who graduated in 1984 in the Netherlands and then went to Germany and got a degree studying orthopedic manual therapy. He was a big guy with grey hair, a broad chin, and friendly eyes. I knew him from our previous work together when he treated my broken leg and knee.

He was always friendly, and we laughed a lot. Bart also complained, rather often, about the insurance companies. He called all insurance companies "thieves." I agreed with him by that point. My insurance company had denied all my claims, and I had to pay for most of my rehabilitation myself.

I asked him tons of questions about different exercises and the brain, and he answered as best he could. One time, I asked him about the trampoline in our yard. "Do you think I can jump on the trampoline?" I asked.

"No, it's too dangerous now. You don't have the stability and balance to do that yet, but maybe in a year," Bart answered.

"Ok," I said.

With a smile on his face, he left for the day saying, "Until next week."

As soon as he was gone, I went out to the yard and made a beeline for that trampoline.

Chapter 21

Falco

"Happy anniversary!" they shouted while I blew out the candles. It was April 8, 2017, exactly one year after my stroke. Remco, the children, and I had just finished a wonderful dinner at The Duchess in Amsterdam. Afterward, we ate cake at Karin's beautiful apartment. As I mentioned before, Karin had been a big-shot lawyer who decided to change her life drastically after she experienced burnout. Remco's cousin Lauren, Karin's daughter, owned the best cake bakery in town. Always made to order, no two cakes were ever identical. Our special cake was round, about 40 centimeters high, champagne-colored, topped with flowers, and it read, "Stroke Survivor - One Year." It was a masterpiece that smelled flowery and fruity, and tasted delicious!

Madeleine had drawn a picture for me. It said, "Mama, I love you. You are soooo sweet." Seeing her drawing made me laugh, but I also had tears in my eyes.

Remco said, "It was a heck of a year, but I'm glad it's over. I figured out a nice gift for you, but you'll have to be patient. You'll get your anniversary present in a few weeks," he continued. I posted my "One Year Post-Stroke" story on Facebook and Instagram. What can I say? It was a great anniversary!

I put Remco's gift out of my mind for several weeks. Then he came home one evening and said with a smile, "Your anniversary present is outside." *Really? What did he get me?* I wondered. *A new bike perhaps?* I went out and there it was, posh grey, not too big, and aerodynamically curved. It was love at first sight. Since the roof was down, I could see the luxurious black leather upholstery inside. "It's a BMW 228i convertible," Remco said.

I was stunned! Gasping for air, when I could finally say a few words, what came out was, "Thank you, but I'm not sure I remember how to drive again."

"It has an automatic transmission. You've come a long way, and in no time, you'll learn to drive again," Remco said. "I bought it from a BMW dealer in the south of Germany. It was their showroom model, so it looks new, but it's not new. I ended up getting an excellent deal on it."

Remco was a natural dealmaker. He was patient, did his research, and negotiated effectively. He didn't get emotional and always managed to point out something to the seller, no matter how small, that might be his deal breaker. "What is the lowest price you want to sell this car for?" he would ask. Then he negotiated on that price.

Opening the door, I sat down in the driver's seat. The dashboard odometer read 24,018 km. Remco got into the passenger seat and said with a grin, "Let's go for a ride, then." After pushing the start button, I used my right hand to pick up my left hand and place it on the steering wheel—and off we went! I was scared at first since I hadn't driven for more than a year. We drove around a large, empty parking lot, and I soon got the hang of it. Then we drove very slowly on the small, quiet roads in the village where we lived. Within one month, I was driving on less busy, smaller roads anywhere, but I still needed to be extra cautious since I had no sight in my right eye.

I loved driving that car! It was the best gift Remco could've given me at the time. I had begun to fully realize that I lost most of my independence due to my stroke. Now one year post-stroke, it had slowly become more of an issue. For the first time since my stroke, I felt independent again because I had the freedom to drive my own car!

Anyone who has survived a stroke will understand how important that self-reliance and liberty was to me. I thought of Jeroen, my new friend from Klimmendaal who had suffered a severe head injury after his bike was hit by a car. Jeroen loved cars, and it was his dream to drive a Porsche 911 again. I should get a hold of him in a few years to see if he managed to get his new driving license. Dutch driving rules required you to take a new test after a stroke. For me, German regulations applied, and my doctor had permitted me to resume driving.

I was so happy with that beautiful car and the freedom it gave me, especially in good weather when I could drive with the top down. It felt like a safe haven and private space, somewhere I could turn my Spotify playlist up to the highest volume and listen to The Rolling Stones, Talk Talk, and a bunch of SoundCloud songs on my phone like the Autograf Remix of Marvin Gaye's "Grapevine" and a song by Austrian artist Falco, called "Jeanny."[1]

The unappealing aspect of the song is the premise. It's the story of a maniac who kidnaps young girls. However, the moment after the newsflash about a missing girl, Falco sings the most powerful "laa" or "aah" sound I have ever heard. Singing along as loudly as I could gave me goosebumps each time. My remaining anger began to melt away during these bursts of sound as I blurted out the desperate "laa-laa" as if my life depended on it.

If I think about it from a psychological standpoint, it's highly likely that I identified with the missing girl Falco was singing about: "Jeanny, quit living on dreams / Jeanny, life is not what it seems / Such a lonely little girl, in a cold, cold world..." and then, in the German version, "*Sie kommen dich zu holen / Sie werden dich nicht finden...*"

I found myself reliving my anguished sense of helplessness when the hospital's neurologist kept me waiting for five and a half hours after my stroke, before Remco screamed at them to take action. Back then, I couldn't make a sound—but never mind. That was in the past now. Besides, I had that Jeanny girl to hang on to if I began to re-experience tough moments.

During the spring and summer of 2017, we took two trips: one to Ibiza for a week, then later to New England for two weeks. When I think back on it, I have mixed feelings about those trips. I do love Ibiza. It feels very familiar. I've been there at least 20 times, and it's where I met my husband, Remco.

The first few days were pleasant, staying in a hotel with Madeleine and Maarten, feeling relaxed and comfortable around my family. Then, during the second half of the week, we were invited to a large birthday party, and that's when things began to go downhill.

Remco's uncle Paul was going to celebrate turning 70 years old with a three-day party in his villa by the sea. I knew I would be seeing many old friends for the first time since my stroke, and I would probably meet new people. I grew increasingly uncomfortable due to my own inner desire to look "normal" in front of everyone who would be at the party.

There are many beautiful villas in Ibiza, but Paul's was extra special and luxurious. It had two swimming pools (one was an infinity pool with a sea view), a professional gym, cinema, fortified safe room, about 10 bedrooms, and a 200 m^2 living room with a 240° view of the sea beyond. Paul occasionally rented the entire property out to a variety of people. These included Barcelona footballers like Messi and Fabregas, and sheiks from the United Arab Emirates. The sheiks had their Ferraris flown into the island by helicopter!

The setting was perfect, the organization was superb, and the host was a member of the family. Why was I so anxious and uncomfortable?

The answer consisted of two short words: my ego. I wanted to show off, "Here I am, a year and a few months after my stroke, and now look at me!" That attitude turned the party into a disaster for me. As people came up beside me, not knowing that I'd had a stroke, they would begin to chat or ask me a question. I tried to respond, "I've had a stroke, and I can't speak fluently yet." But hardly anything came out. I was simultaneously sad and furious with myself for being in that position.

One evening, I even squeezed myself into a red dress and put low heels on. It had only been four months since I took off my brace and threw away my cane in Hawaii. In regular daytime clothing and shoes, I still could barely walk. I definitely couldn't walk in medium-high heels! Alarmingly, I stumbled and fell from the stairs onto the terrace next to the house. I was lucky to not severely injure myself. I was embarrassed.

When I think back on it now, perhaps things would've been different if I had already read *Ego Is the Enemy* by Ryan Holiday.[2]

Our second and much happier trip was to the US, to drop off our son Maarten in Cambridge, Massachusetts, so he could begin his first year at Harvard University. We timed our arrival for a week before Maarten needed to start his classes. All five of us would fly over and take a road trip through New England together.

When we reached Bar Harbor, Maine, we relaxed at the waterside and watched the small fishing boats bringing in their lobster catch. My favorite meal was soft-shell lobster, native to the area, which is more tender and sweet-tasting than hard-shell lobster.

We returned to Boston and Cambridge after that week in the sun with family. I had always loved that part of New England, especially the area around Harvard. Remco and I were both impressed with Maarten for being admitted to that prestigious university. Less than 5% of those who apply to Harvard are accepted, so we were proud of Maarten.

Could we afford the nearly $70,000 per year for the following four years? Usually, the answer would have been no. But we discovered it was possible, and I'll tell you why. As Harvard explains on their website, 70% of their students receive some form of financial aid. One hundred percent of Harvard students graduate debt free, and 20% of families from the lowest income bracket pay nothing at all toward their children's education, housing, and food costs.

Harvard's philosophy of nurturing their students involves intentionally selecting the brightest minds, the ones with demonstrable leadership potential. They are admitted unconditionally whether they can afford tuition or not.

How can Harvard afford to do this? The funds come from endowments made by former students, influential business people, corporations, and those who wish to encourage excellence in the lives of students without the funds necessary to gain access to such an influential university. When those funds are invested, the interest created allows for a generous scholarship program.

Harvard is not only the wealthiest university in the world, it's also affordable to any family who has a bright child with leadership qualities. They have the largest endowment in the world *and* the most extensive academic library in the world, with 60 miles of shelving! Harvard has also produced eight US presidents and 158 Nobel Laureates.

Maarten was welcomed warmly by the other international students and Dean Rakesh Khurana. They clapped for Maarten as he walked onto the premises, and it was a lovely, movie-like scene. A few days later, we helped Maarten get settled into his dorm. While shopping at Target, we bought him a mini fridge and some other feel-at-home stuff. It was actually the same day former President Obama helped his daughter Malia move into her dorm at Harvard. He humorously describes his feelings about it in an interview with David Letterman on Netflix.[3]

Two days after that, it was time for us to return home. Saying goodbye to Maarten was difficult, and we all hugged him with tears in our eyes. A mixture of dismay and pride, we were dealing with emotions that we knew most parents encountered. We left him behind on the other side of the ocean—our first child to leave the nest.

As we walked off the campus for the last time, I looked over my shoulder for a while. Maarten was beaming. *He will be alright,* I thought with a smile.

Chapter 22

The Functional Neurologist Who Didn't Want to See Me

That's what I need, I thought.

I had been watching videos on YouTube about how to reduce the stiffness in my shoulder, stiffness that I believed was due to a lack of movement. Whether it was wise or not, I was drawing my own conclusions about the need for a chiropractor to adjust my shoulder and neck, increase the blood flow in those areas, and create a healing form of inflammation.

A high-velocity, low-amplitude adjustment consisted of a fast stretch that caused relaxation in the muscles and the tissue around the joint that was manipulated. It also created more freedom of movement, more stability, and a reduction in discomfort due to improved feedback to the central nervous system and spinal cord. Perhaps the most important effect was the enhanced signal to the central nervous system and brain as well as the stimulation of the cerebellum and higher cortical centers in the prefrontal cortex (the most human part of the brain, located in the front of the head).

Maybe I was wrong to be impatient, but I felt like I was responsible for creating my recovery all alone. I was fed up with the negative attitudes and limited knowledge about essential topics like neuroplasticity that I encountered in some of the doctors and therapists I met so far. And I was tired of wasting time by visiting less knowledgeable sources.

So, I decided to be bold. I wrote an email and sent it out to 15 chiropractors in the Netherlands. It said something like, "Hi. I'm Linda, and I need someone to adjust my neck and help me with some other exercises. I'm recovering from a stroke right now. I have aphasia. By the way, I'm going for a full recovery. I need a chiropractor that also knows about the brain. If you don't know what neuroplasticity is, don't answer this email."

It was a daring and somewhat confrontational email, but it succeeded. From 15 email requests, I only received four responses. Three of them were not the right sort of answer, but one of them chose to refer me to a specific person—Arjan Kuipers.

His name wasn't on my list, but I sent him the same email I sent to the others. Then I did a web search on his name and discovered that he was not only a chiropractor but a functional neurologist as well. I found some of his videos on YouTube and learned that he had written two books: *Help! My Child Has ADHD/Autism* and *The Single Most Overlooked Problem in Back Patients.*

When I decided to find out the difference between a functional neurologist and a conventional medical neurologist, I discovered it lies primarily in their approaches to treatment.

A conventional medical neurologist typically focuses on the diagnosis of anatomical pathology and the application of pharmaceutical and surgical interventions to treat disease.

A functional neurologist views the nervous system as a moldable, changeable entity that can be affected in its function through different types of environmental stimulation. Neuroplasticity is the very core of a functional neurologist's clinical methodology.

Wow!

He had passed the initial test. I was going to be his patient, period.

Or was I?

In a conversation I had later with Arjan, he told me that he had been concerned about the wording in my blunt email, stating that I was "going for a full recovery." Fortunately for me, he was somewhat curious about me and agreed to an appointment. We've laughed many times about that awkward beginning to our friendship.

While driving to his office in Zutphen, I imagined what he would be like in person. From watching his videos, I expected a sympathetic person. The office was quite busy, and he walked by while I was talking to the receptionist. "I know you," he said.

Really? I wondered. *How does he know me?*

"Room number one," he said.

He came into the room, and after talking to him for a short period, I knew immediately that my intuition had been correct. He was kind and understanding. I couldn't say very much at the time because of my aphasia, but he was patient with me. When he found out that I was Swedish, he started speaking to me in Norwegian. I was stunned and raised my eyebrows. He explained that his fiancée was Norwegian. "Okay," I said.

"Now I am going to do some tests with you," he said. It may be easier for me to turn this over to Arjan to explain the tests he did, so Arjan's story of our first meeting follows below.

Well, at least her aphasia is not as bad as I thought, was the first thing that came to mind when I heard her make reasonable conversation with the receptionist. Linda had made it clear beforehand that we should contact her by email and not by phone because of her impaired speech. I later found out that she had been practicing her speech for several hours every day, first thing in the morning, which had greatly improved her ability to speak.

After talking with Linda for some time, going through her history and asking what she had done so far to gain back lost function, it became evident that she was both highly intelligent and had done what almost no patient had ever done. She had taught herself more about the brain and neuroplasticity than most doctors and other healthcare providers knew. Also, she had gone all out in her efforts to recover from her stroke and wasn't settling for the limit set by healthcare providers on the time frame within which recovery should take place.

The testing on Linda's first visit included a lot of standard medical and neurological testing as well as more specialized functional neurological testing to assess the status of her brain and nervous system. This included testing balance, coordination, sensation, strength, and the function of the nerves that emerge through the skull (cranial nerves), especially eye functionality, which tells a lot about the different networks and areas in the brain.

I also examined her spinal and postural stability to find out what could be done for her left shoulder and upper back. It became evident that her shoulder, neck, and upper back discomfort was a direct effect of the abnormal posturing caused by the stroke. Shoulder, neck, and upper back discomfort is often seen after a stroke of the middle cerebral artery (with resultant spasticity and loss of function in the right or left arm). Otherwise, Linda was in good condition, and it showed that she had been training a lot to improve her spinal stability.

During the testing of Linda's eye functionality (how the brain directs the eyes) something remarkable happened. For this test, Linda sat on a high swivel chair. She wore a pair of infrared goggles that enabled me to see what happened with her eyes while spinning her to the right and left (she was sitting in the dark and unable to fixate with her eyes). This is called vestibular-ocular reflex testing and assesses different parts of the brain stem and cerebellum (little brain). In one part, we test what happens to the eyes when the spinning stops. Typically, a counter-movement is seen in the eyes, which should be equal on both sides.

While I was talking Linda through the testing procedure and asking her what she was experiencing, her voice suddenly stopped mid-sentence. It looked like she was unable to speak for 5-10 seconds after the first round of spinning had stopped. The post-rotation effect seemed to disrupt the coordination of her speech, indicating that integration at the brain stem level was not optimal. This part of the brain stem also plays a vital role in inhibiting (suppressing) spasms and lowering too-high muscle tone in the flexor (bending) muscles of her arm and wrist.

The initial testing showed that although Linda had suffered a major stroke, there was a lot to work with. Major parts of the networks connecting the damaged higher brain centers (outer cortex, deep nuclei) to the brain stem and cerebellum were still intact and could be used in regaining function. Other than that, Linda had been taking good care of her brain—psychologically, sleep-wise, and through nutrition and exercise.

Feeling relieved by that first encounter, I was also intrigued. I had so many questions! Even though I had a basic level of knowledge, I immediately wanted to know more about the specifics, such as why I continued to be so spastic in my arm and hand.

It was clear that Arjan was rushed for time in his busy practice, so I decided to try another approach. Sending him an email, I wrote, "Hello Arjan. I have been watching a few of your videos on YouTube, and I'm impressed with your knowledge. Maybe you could have coffee with me sometime after work since the limited time we have in your office is not enough for my questions? Best regards, Linda."

I got a positive response, and a few weeks later we met for tea. Finding a way to get around my lack of ability to speak in long or complicated sentences, I would write something on my phone and then hand it to him to read. I also had a few long questions prepared beforehand, for example:

"Sometime after my stroke, I got immense neuropathic pain. It was not like that at the beginning after my stroke. But it got gradually worse. None of the medicine worked. One of the medicines got me down from levels 8-9 to 5-6. But it affected my

REM sleep and made me drowsy. At one point, I hadn't slept in three nights, and because the pain was so bad, I wanted to kill myself. Then my son ordered a book called *Neuroplastic Transformation* by Michael Moskowitz. That was also when I learned about Norman Doidge's books. It took me three and a half months to get the pain down from 9 to 0 (with hard work!). But I know from my own experience that neuroplasticity works.

"Now I come to a question for you. My biggest problem is the spasticity in my arm. Where does spasticity come from in the brain? I know it originates from a damaged motor cortex in the brain and is taken over by the spine (and in my theory, the amygdala has something to do with this). If I understand better how spasticity works, then I can design a method to reprogram the brain.

"Where does the process 'I am going to move my left arm' come from? Where does the hypertonia come from? You said back and forth talking between the brain's hand and arm homunculus, thalamus, and cortex before action is put out to the muscles (the so-called efference copy[1,2,3,4,5,6] that takes place in the cortico-ponto-cerebello-thalamocortical loops).[7] Is it this movement that brings spasticity hypertonia (the 'wrong signal') down to the cerebellum and brain stem and eventually the spine? I guess what I would like to know is, where does the 'wrong' hypertension signal occur?"

"I was thinking of breaking my right arm. I thought I should do that to give the left arm a signal, 'You've got to go to work now,' based on Taub's CI therapy."

Waiting to see what would happen after I handed my phone to him, I was a little nervous about his possible reaction. *Is he going to think I'm some kind of stroke nut who is a bit mentally unstable? Is he going to laugh in my face at my crazy ideas?*

He didn't say a word, at first. Instead, he grabbed the notepad and pen I brought with me and started drawing. As he drew, he explained spasticity and the nervous system. This is what he said:

"Basically, what happens when a signal is sent out from the outer layers of the brain to move muscles in your arm (corticospinal and rubrospinal activation through the pyramidal tracts), a second signal is sent through different tracts (the extrapyramidal tracts). This is to make sure that there is a balancing act taking place where the muscles are activated. The second signal makes sure that the flexor tone is kept under control. This is important because there are very strong reflexes at the spinal level, which unchecked cause the flexor (bending) muscles to take over. This results in, for example, an inward rotation of the shoulder and a bent arm.

"Because both of these tracts were damaged during the stroke; the result is spasticity of the arm and a spastic posture of the affected arm because of the strong spinal reflexes that are not under control anymore. There are, however, strong influences from the brain stem reticular formation (groups of nerve cells in the brain stem)[8,9,10] and from the cerebellum[11,12] that have a regulatory effect as well (through the vestibulospinal and reticulospinal tracts).[13,14,15,16,17,18,19,20,21,22] In your case, these tracts are still intact but dysfunctional because of the scrambled and lost signal from the damaged brain parts. This is also the area that made your voice disappear for a moment after the spinning during your testing."

Then, in a second drawing, he explained why I shouldn't ever break my right arm. This is what he said about that:

"That is not what you are going to do, and I'm not even going to go into that other than, I understand why you're saying it. First of all, you can get complications from that fracture. You do not want to change the right arm's representation in the left brain. Even if it is suppressing the function of the counterparts on the right side, it is also keeping

Let's start with the "mind" portion of this mind-body connection. Remember at the beginning of the book when I told you I was getting terrible sleep? Yes, my husband snored. But I was also well-known for being a worrier.

Most of you know that you can't fall asleep when you have anxiety and stress. So, what was I worried about? I was constantly fretful about my business, my children, if people liked me, what people said about me, and many other things.

I read somewhere that "worriers die young," and I was not planning to be one of those people, especially since I had started to appreciate life more now and was so grateful for all my family and friends. I also enjoyed the little things more often, like watching the sunset and walking through the woods. So, how could I stop worrying?

I knew that it was never going to be clear cut, and it took almost a year for me to achieve the results I wanted. But believe me, it was worth it! By then, I knew that you could change your brain, but it requires patience and doing specific exercises every day.

As always, I began with my nose in a book, doing research. I can recommend the following resources to help you get out of your headspace and into your dream-space:

- *How to Stop Worrying and Start Living* by Dale Carnegie [9]
- *The Tools* by Phil Stutz and Barry Michels [10]
- *The Power of Now* by Eckhart Tolle
- *Ego Is the Enemy* by Ryan Holiday [11]
- Optimize, an app by Brian Johnson [12]
- Robin Sharma's course from Mindvalley Quest

And, of course, I still had several books on stoicism and many other resources that I took inspiration from.

I learned from these materials how to effectively turn off the non-stop "on switch" for the stream of thoughts that ran through my head and kept me from getting the sleep that I badly needed.

Meditation

Research shows that when meditation is done in the morning, it acts to improve your sleep in the evening.[13][14] I began by meditating each morning for 10 minutes with an app called Headspace.[15] I started to notice changes within two months. But it took me a full year for meditation to truly accomplish a state of "active rest"—not completely asleep, but a state of completely resting my mind. Training such as this leads to improvement in getting the "off switch" to work effectively.

Tolle's book *The Power of Now* was also helpful.[16] I began to listen to my breath while thinking of "nothing" as I prepared to fall asleep. Far from the ultra-short 10 seconds when I first began, I was able to think about nothing for up to 10 full minutes after I had practiced every day for a year.

Let me tell you one thing: If the brain gets bored while thinking about nothing, you get tired. And eventually, you will fall asleep from that boredom! I can happily share that it even worked when I woke up in the middle of the night. Instead of entertaining my brain by thinking about people or problems or what-ifs, I willed myself to listen to my breath and think about nothing.

Think about it this way: If you are in "Go, Go, Go, Go!!!" mode all day long, do you think you can lay in bed at night and tell yourself that you're going to go to sleep? Good luck with that! Some people can, but I am certainly not one of them.

By practicing the off switch during the day and doing my nighttime rituals, which I will talk about later, I was able to sleep soundly at night when I most needed to.

I also used ASMR. ASMR stands for "autonomous sensory meridian response."[17,18,19] Wikipedia states that "ASMR signifies the subjective experience of 'low-grade euphoria' characterized by 'a combination of positive feelings and a distinct static-like tingling sensation on the skin.' It is most commonly triggered by specific auditory or visual stimuli, and less commonly by intentional attention control."

On YouTube, I often listen to "Affirmation Meditation" from Maria to enable these sensations in my mind and body. Her soft, whispering voice gave me pleasant goosebumps on my skin, and what she said was very encouraging. Even though I didn't really believe her words in the first weeks, I eventually started to.

That's how the brain works, I thought. *It adapts to everything!*

No More Negative Self-Talk

The next step I took was to stop any negative self-talk. Let me give you an example of a conversation I would've had with my ego before I made this commitment to change the messages I was sending to myself:

Linda: I wonder if they liked me. I was pretty introverted and shy during dinner...

Ego: Are you kidding me? Of course they don't like you, because you didn't contribute anything useful. You were silent almost the entire time. They won't ever ask you out again!

That's how I had conditioned myself to think and react in the past. If I received a compliment, I would change the subject or respond in a way that indicated a lack of self-respect. Now I have disciplined myself to not care about what others might think about me. With an attitude of "it is what it is," I acknowledge that I have no control over what other people may or may not think (stoicism). I manage to analyze the things happening to me, and then I ask myself, "Can I do something about this situation?" If I can't, then I "switch off" and don't allow myself to worry about it. Again, stoicism.

Moving on to the body, you'll remember that mitochondria aren't just energy generators, and they have a dual purpose. Either they produce energy or go into defense response, the cell danger response (CDR). The more you activate cell defense, the more the energy mode is switched off. You'll hear about that in a later chapter.

Mitochondria regenerate and repair while you are sleeping.[20,21,22,23] If you don't get enough quality, restorative sleep, then your mitochondria are more likely to go into defense mode as opposed to energy mode. I needed to optimize my circadian rhythm and sleep patterns for my mitochondria to be less fragile.

I created a *ritus*, the Latin word for ritual. If I sound like I'm trying to be overly intellectual with this word, feel free to ignore it. I just thought it was a cool word! So, what did my *ritus* consist of?

Light Exposure

First, I began to expose myself to bright light in the beginning of each day. In the summer, I went outside without sunglasses on. In the winter months, I used a bright daylight therapy device. Keep in mind, however, that the sun is always the better option.

Second, I needed to block blue light exposure after sunset.[24,25,26] I installed f.lux, a blue-light blocking software (it's free) on my computer, and I always had my blue-light blocking glasses with me.

Also, our skin has light sensors built into it and can, in some ways, see the level of light surrounding it. Therefore, it is necessary to keep light out of your sleeping environment. I installed red or yellow light bulbs in my bedside lamp and bought blackout curtains that prevented light intrusion from outside sources.

I also implemented a "digital sunset" when all electronics were turned off three hours before I went to sleep. The only exception was when I was wearing my blue-light blocking glasses in the evenings. It was somewhat of a relief to say goodbye to my perfectionist self and getting lost in non-stop reading and searching on the internet.

Food

For a complete discussion of food, see the next chapter. However, I'll mention one thing here: intermittent fasting. I fasted overnight for up to 14 hours, three or four times a week. These time spans are essential for autophagy—ridding your body of damaged cells and renewing it. Toward the end of the day, your body should begin to relax and restore itself, not have to digest a huge meal.[27,28] So, I started to eat dinner earlier and breakfast, later.

You might respond that you're used to eating late at night and don't think you can eat any earlier. What if I offered a counter-argument? Evidence indicates that enhanced autophagy delays aging *and* extends the life span! Have I gotten your attention now?

To optimize your autophagy level, take a slow-and-steady approach as you progressively move your mealtime to earlier in the evening and later in the morning. Remember to transition slowly.

Exercise

I began to exercise first thing in the morning. There was plenty of time to get up and then work out doing high-intensity training. I had already noticed that I was never able to work out after 6 p.m. because, by that time of the day, I was too exhausted. Moving exercise to the morning is good for your circadian rhythm.[29,30,31] This is because exercise keeps your temperature elevated for at least four hours. When you cool down, however, your body releases the hormone melatonin, and that makes you tired and sleepy.

If I exercise at 7 o'clock at night, that means I won't cool down until 11. I didn't want that. Don't exercise too late in the day!

Temperature

Temperature plays an integral role in circadian rhythm. We are wired to be firmly affected by external temperatures. Look back at the patterns of our ancestors. They stayed up for a few hours after sunset, sitting in the light of an open fire.

Firelight emits mostly red light and contains none of the artificial blue light that disrupts the circadian rhythm. The combination of the hormone melatonin and drop in temperature put those hunters and gatherers to sleep in a natural way.

My bedroom is a sanctuary—cool, comfortable, and completely dark. There is an optimal temperature range of 60°-68° (15°-20° C) that you should aim for in your bedroom.

Now in the evenings, I usually go for a walk with our dog (a Weimaraner) followed by some family time, and then I take a hot bath. Raising my body temperature with hot water and then stepping out into a cooler environment allows my body temperature to lower. That lowered body temperature sets the stage for deep and restorative sleep.

Luckily, I live in a village that is quiet at night. But if your own atmosphere is not so serene and you find yourself waking up to outside noises such as barking dogs, traffic, or carrying voices, try wearing earplugs or using a sound-masking machine that emits white noise or pink noise (you can even use your phone for this).

The *Ritus* Summary

I got rid of my personal sleep kryptonite: watching TV, using the computer, engaging in intense conversation late in the evening, exercising too late in the day, and eating big meals late at night. I kept my bedroom cool and completely dark.

Every one of these seemingly small and marginal gains, when combined and compounded, does add up, and they make a significant difference in the quality of sleep you are getting.

One more thing: What is the 5 a.m. Club, and how and why did I become a member?

I watched Robin Sharma on Mindvalley Quest.[32,33] In the section "Habits of Masters," I learned that being a "master" is all about your habits and rituals. It takes 66 days to wire in a new habit. Sharma says: "The secret of iconic performers and high-level achievers of excellence is not willpower, but the installation of the right habits." One of these habits is to get up at 5 a.m. I didn't consider myself to be an "iconic performer" at all, but I felt that it was essential to examine the habits of the best performers in any field of endeavor to help me recover from my stroke.

Why did I want to get up at 5 a.m.? Let's illustrate that motivation with a quote from one of my heroes, Richard Branson. I read on the Virgin website:

"I have always been an early riser. Like keeping a positive outlook, or keeping fit, waking up early is a habit, which you must work on to maintain. Over my 50 years in business, I have learned that if I rise early, I can achieve so much more in a day, and therefore in life."[34]

There you have it: When you get up early, you can achieve much more each day, just like Richard Branson!

I found it kind of cool to be a member of a club like that. I hardly ever came across people who got up at 5 a.m. But when I did encounter those people, there was a certain recognition between us—a particular kind of smile and unspoken question: "You're a member too?"

In the beginning, it was hard to get up that early, but it eventually became easier. After just two months, I was able to get up at 5 a.m. without using an alarm clock. I loved it!

I had found a bigger reason for getting up early, one that was more important than keeping late hours and then staying in bed all morning. I discovered that my sense of purpose in writing this book was greater than my need for entertainment at night.

Chapter 25

The Blue Zone

I first heard about Blue Zones[1,2] when I watched the documentary *The Human Longevity Project.*[3] A "blue zone" sounds nice, don't you think?

For me, the color blue represents both the sky and the sea and is associated with open spaces, freedom, and imagination. A "zone" is an area or stretch of land having a particular characteristic. I liked it even when I didn't know what exactly occurred in Blue Zones. But I would soon find out.

What is a Blue Zone? The term first appeared in the November 2005 *National Geographic* magazine cover story, "The Secrets of a Long Life" by Dan Buettner.[4] He identified five areas where this phenomenon occurs: Okinawa (Japan), Sardinia (Italy), Nicoya (Costa Rica), Icaria (Greece), and among the Seventh-Day Adventists in Loma Linda, California.

Buettner offers an explanation based on observations and data as to why these populations live healthier and longer lives. I definitely wanted to live a healthier and longer life, but how?

Using Icaria as an example, a 2009 study on the island revealed it to be the location with the highest percentage of 90-year-olds on the planet—nearly one out of three people make it to their nineties![5] Furthermore, Icarians "have about 20% lower rates of cancer, 50% lower rates of heart disease, and almost no dementia."

But why?

People inhabiting Blue Zones share common lifestyle characteristics that contribute to their longevity. A Venn diagram of the study highlights the following six shared characteristics among people that live in a Blue Zone:[6]

- Put family ahead of other concerns
- Smoke less
- Semi-vegetarian (the majority of food consumed is derived from plants)
- Constant moderate physical activity
- Social engagement (people of all ages are socially active and integrated into their communities, not on social media)
- Legumes commonly consumed

It made sense. We are all sitting too much, and we don't eat large amounts of vegetables.

With the steady rise of digital technology, sitting has become the most common posture in the workplace. Most desk workers spend an average of 10 hours a day sitting! Sitting can be extremely detrimental to your health, even more so than smoking, as some claim.

What they were eating in the Blue Zone sounded like Michael Pollan's philosophy of food. He states it perfectly in his Netflix special: "Eat real food that is unprocessed, unrefined foods in their natural state, mostly plants—because of the positive impact it has on human health and the health of the environment—and not too much."[7]

RFMP (Real Food, Mostly Plants)

I believed in this and started implementing it in my life. I was eating reasonably healthy before, but to go to the next level, I needed to not only shape up my eating habits but also alter the time I ate as well. This is not going to be a cookbook, but I will share information about how I began to eat and continue to do so today.

First, I'll tell you about intermittent fasting, a program that is applied for four days a week over 10-15 weeks a year. That is intermittent fasting or "mimicking fasting" as Dr. Valter Longo calls it in his book *The Longevity Diet.*[8,9]

Advocates of fasting claim that it can make you live longer, heal faster, and expand your energy levels. Is that just hype, or is there tested science that backs up those claims?

While most of the research to date has been done on animals, not humans, a major amount of existing research supports the health benefits of fasting. It has been shown to increase BDNF (brain-derived neurotrophic factor) levels and stimulate neurogenesis.[10,11,12,13] Fasting has been shown to improve biomarkers (short for biological markers) of disease, reduce oxidative stress, and preserve learning and memory functioning according to Mark Mattson, senior investigator for the National Institute on Aging.[14]

"There are several theories about why fasting provides physiological benefits," says Mattson. "The one that we've studied a lot, and designed experiments to test, is the hypothesis that during the fasting period, cells are under mild stress," he says. "And they respond to the stress adaptively by enhancing their ability to cope with stress and, maybe, to resist disease."

Wow, I thought. *Hormesis once again.*

"There is considerable similarity between how cells respond to the stress of exercise and how cells respond to intermittent fasting," says Mattson.[15,16,17]

What doesn't kill us, makes us stronger. That makes sense. The mild stressor makes the cells grow stronger, just like a muscle. If we refrain from eating for a while, that in fact stresses our cells, and cells get more resilient as a result.

If you think about it, the way we have developed and adapted in this world is quite remarkable. But nowadays, the fridge is always full of food and drinks, and most of us sit behind a computer or in front of a television all day. With a grin, I imagined a two-week "retreat" where you could go to be hammered with mild stressors. I bet you would come out quite hardened, and if you had enough time to recover after those two weeks, your body and mind would be stronger and more resilient. If there were such a place, I'd go twice a year!

You can fast in many ways, but I usually stick to a pattern of fasting for 13-16 hours each day, and I only eat during the remaining eight hours. I skip breakfast (the word breakfast means "breaking the fast") and have lunch at noon.

At the beginning of this new way of eating, I sometimes had a so-called bulletproof coffee, coffee with grass-fed butter in it (see Dave Asprey and his book *Bulletproof*) to keep me from feeling hungry in the morning. I love coffee, but I refrained from drinking "the real stuff" and instead drank decaffeinated coffee for six weeks to get past the addiction stage. Why did I choose to do that? Is coffee bad for you or good for you?[18]

Some health gurus tell us that coffee is terrible and we should stay away from it at all costs. Other specialists say it is a superfood loaded with all sorts of beneficial antioxidants and phytochemicals. So, which one is it?

First, you need to know what adenosine is. Adenosine is an inhibitory neurotransmitter that tends to make you tired and sleepy.[19] More adenosine means less energy. At night, it builds up and is one of the primary signals telling your brain it's time to go to sleep.

Caffeine works by blocking the action of adenosine. Coffee is addictive, and if you consume coffee every day, you can create "negative neurotransmitter adaptations." Ari Whitten describes this very elegantly in his Energy Blueprint program.

The brain might begin to believe that there is an adenosine shortage and, as a result, produce *more* adenosine! By blocking adenosine every day, you can create an imbalance in your brain's neurotransmitters. The vicious cycle: You need even more coffee to get through the day.

What to do then?

I drank coffee without caffeine for six weeks. Then I started to use it randomly, consuming caffeinated coffee on one or two days each week followed by five days of caffeine-free coffee. I have to tell you about the first time I drank coffee with caffeine after six weeks of drinking decaf. I was in the UK at the time, and I felt such an amazing kick from the caffeine. It was like WOW. The difference in sensation was quite remarkable. Now I have that regularly when I drink caffeinated coffee after a week of decaf. If you don't believe me, try it yourself!

Let's move on to what I ate—and still do. First, I shopped for organic fruits, vegetables, fish, and meat. I ate surprising amounts of vegetables, and I got a juicer for another way to add even more. By the way, I had never heard of or seen some of the vegetables I was eating and drinking. I basically grabbed every vegetable in the supermarket!

I knew that dietary phytochemicals are hormetic stressors, not just antioxidants. Scientists have discovered that plants don't actually want to be eaten, so they develop chemicals to keep animals from eating them. These chemicals in fruit and other plants are a natural "pesticide" (we're the pests). It activates a cellular response when we eat them.[20,21,22] That response helps protect us from phytochemicals and a full range of other types of stressors. I now knew that I needed to eat loads of vegetables to jump-start and maintain this cellular response in my body.

I also needed to take charge of my gut, known in recent works as the "second brain," after all those antibiotics I had taken to get rid of my Lyme disease (which I think was more likely a case of burnout). Recent studies show that your brain affects your gut health and your gut may even affect your brain health. The communication system between your gut and brain is called the gut-brain axis.

Neurons are cells found in your brain and central nervous system that tell your body how to behave. There are approximately 100 billion neurons in the human brain. Interestingly, your gut also contains 500 million neurons! They are connected to your brain through nerves in your nervous system. The vagus nerve is one of the biggest nerves connecting your gut and brain. It sends signals in both directions.

Which foods help the gut-brain axis? A few groups of foods are specifically beneficial for the gut-brain axis. Here are some of the most important ones:

Omega-3 fats: These fats are found in oily fish and also in high quantities in the human brain.

Fermented foods: Yogurt, kefir, sauerkraut, and kimchi all contain healthy microbes such as lactic acid bacteria.[23,24,25]

High-fiber foods: Nuts, seeds, fruits, and vegetables all contain prebiotic fibers that are good for your gut bacteria.[26,27,28]

Polyphenol-rich foods: Cocoa, green tea, olive oil, and coffee all contain polyphenols, which are plant chemicals that have a beneficial effect on your gut bacteria.[29,30,31]

Tryptophan-rich foods: Tryptophan is an amino acid that is converted into the neurotransmitter serotonin.[32] Foods that are high in tryptophan include turkey and eggs.

I want to add one of my favorites to this list: green bananas. **Green bananas** are also rich in tryptophan and contain a high amount of resistant starch and pectin, which have been linked to several health benefits.[33] As bananas ripen, most of the starches are turned into sugar.

The last thing I want to say about the gut: Challenge your microbiome![34,35]

What do I mean by that? Don't eat the same things every week. Also, incorporate more exotic dishes, for example, from India or Lebanon.

Why? Indian dishes, for example, are typically made up of meat and/or vegetables in a spiced sauce. The vegetables contain lots of minerals and nutrients, and turmeric and other spices (curry powder) have anti-inflammatory and other beneficial health effects. Lebanese cuisine is my favorite, with its fresh herbs, spices, and vegetables. It speaks for itself!

I'm not an expert on what to eat, and I hate fashionable diets of all kinds. I'll continue to stick to the ideology/diet of RFMP (Real Food, Mostly Plants) and the way that people eat in the Blue Zones. To be honest, I've changed it a bit to RFLP—Real Food, Loads of Plants—and I hope you don't mind!

Chapter 26

What doesn't kill us, makes us stronger.

"Holy moley!" the woman shouted. She was entering the shower I had just left, and it was turned to the coldest temperature. She was mad about that.

I always forgot to put it back to an average temperature after I went into the shower. "Sorry," I said. But I wasn't really sorry for her. I was taking a cold shower to stimulate hormesis, and she got a small piece of it. Perhaps that wasn't such a bad thing for her!

I mentioned before the quote from Nietzsche that titles this chapter of the book. For me, it sums up hormesis. To refresh your memory, hormesis is the concept of how temporary stressors work to grow your mitochondria. Hormesis[1,2,3,4,5,6,7] is the act of increasing the number of big, healthy, and powerfully resilient-to-stressors mitochondria in your body.[8,9,10]

I believe that hormesis is the key to becoming stress-proof not only on a physical level but also a mental one. Most people feel an increase in their levels of mental stress when they worry about something or feel insecure. I can only relate this to myself, but I had a feeling that I could better handle mental stress while I was going through a period of systematic mild stressors (hormesis). I guess hormesis forced me to "get out of my head."

Research indicates that the number of mitochondria in your body will shrink by half after 40-80 years of age if you don't engage in multiple forms of hormesis.

Why aren't doctors and health gurus talking about this?

You can eat the healthiest diet, reduce stress, sleep well, and so on, but if you do not make a habit of hormesis in your daily life, the number and resilience of your mitochondria will shrink, hence, you will get tired more often. Challenges or stressors are what works to create a robust and healthy body and brain. Harshness in specific doses is useful if you want to live a healthier and longer life!

We live in a pampered and spoiled era that we might describe as anti-hormesis. Food is available whenever we want it, especially junk food without life-enhancing phytochemicals.[11,12,13,14] We can run our offices and perhaps the world while sitting on our butts. We hardly ever go out of our comfort zone.

Our earliest ancestors, on the contrary, lived in a world where hunting and walking was part of their daily routine. Food and plants were not always available every day. That may have created a state of scarcity (fasting). They were also exposed to heat and cold, beneficial stressors that made our ancestors more robust and resilient.

After reading about hormetic activity, I decided to implement those principles in my life. Remember though: If you choose to do this, you must first pay attention to circadian rhythm and sleep, and change your food habits if necessary. Start gently, with the consent of your doctor. Too much stress can have the opposite of the desired effect.

Hormesis through Exercise

Sprint interval training wasn't for me since I couldn't run at that time, but I could use the Stairmaster to get high-intensity training, HIT.[15,16,17] I got on a Stairmaster for five minutes during the day—one minute at full speed, one minute of rest, and then I repeated it. Sometimes I returned to the machine several times during the day.

Why didn't I go for one, longer session per day?

Because in my carefully formulated theory, I reasoned that our ancestors didn't know ahead of time when they would need to run. Relating that to my Stairmaster use, I figured it would be best to do that level of activity for several days, two to three times per day, and then stay off the machine for a couple of days. That worked for me.

I tried other variations, doing four minutes of intense Stairmaster training once a week in bursts of 20 seconds of intense exercise and then 10 seconds of rest. I almost threw up afterward. I suggest that you don't try this at home without a physical therapist. Much later, I went running for 30 seconds, and then rested for 30 seconds. Yes, I can now run a little bit. It took me two years' practice to do this.

If you can't walk yet, try using a small trampoline. You can stand up (try to get one with a handle on it) or kneel on it, giving almost the same effect. Or, you can jump up and down a little bit while on your knees.

Hormesis through Intermittent Fasting

Intermittent fasting increases the neurogenesis of mitochondria, so I periodically did not have breakfast before I worked out for the first time during the day. The reason for that was to encourage mitochondrial biogenesis.

The word "periodically" is vital to note because your body adapts to anything. If you want the effect of mitochondrial biogenesis, you need to do it periodically as I did. Periods of intermittent fasting also work because it increases autophagy (cell recycling). Intermittent fasting should be followed by HIT (high-intensity training) exercise, and shifting back and forth between autophagy and building mode is key.[18,19,20] If you combine that with the circadian rhythm habits explained in the chapter titled "Sleep," you have a powerful way to increase autophagy.

And remember, increased autophagy keeps you young!

Hormesis through Xenohormesis

What doesn't kill *plants* makes *us* stronger as well. I talk about this in previous chapters, but let me elaborate.

Plants contain phytochemicals, which are beneficial for human health. How do these plants get phytochemicals? Through xenohormesis,[21,22,23] environmentally stressed plants produce bioactive compounds (oxidants) that can transfer stress resistance and survival benefits to the animals and humans that consume them. So, plants are not just antioxidants.

Hormesis through Hot or Cold[24,25,26,27]

Two or three times a week, all year round, I went to a sauna with an outdoor swimming pool. I went into the sauna for 15-20 minutes and, immediately afterward, went outside and got in the pool, even in winter. The pool contained warm water, but after I emerged from the warmth, I stayed out in the cold air for three minutes or more. I also took cold showers three times a week after learning that exposure to cold temperatures stimulates mitochondrial growth.

Immediately after my cold shower in the morning, I was so energized, I felt like I could rule the world. I also tried walking barefoot through the dunes when it was cold. My feet felt like blocks of ice while I was doing it, but afterward, they felt warm and pleasantly worn out. Walking on a beach covered with cold stones hurt quite a lot, especially in my left foot that lacked muscle tone. However, it resulted in a stimulating and long-lasting sensation, as if I could still feel the stones beneath my feet for hours afterward when I was sitting in the car.

Hormesis through Hypoxia [28,29,30]

In South Korea, there are women (some in their eighties!) who dive to catch seaweed and shellfish for food.[31] They hold their breath for about three minutes during these dives and are among the longest-living people on Earth.

Researchers in Russia and Ukraine have also been looking at the use of breathing methods to enhance health and performance. At present, IHT[32,33] (intermittent hypoxic training) is primarily known in the athletic world where it has been successfully adopted by athletes to improve their fitness and athletic performance. By using specific breathing techniques, your body can induce low oxygen levels in the blood, cells, and mitochondria. That way the mitochondria is trained to increasingly apply oxygen more efficiently and accurately.

I use some of these techniques while walking. As I walked in the forest near our home, I practiced holding my breath to see how many steps I could take before inhaling again. The forest was also on a hill, so my body was further challenged by going up that incline and giving my hamstrings a good workout. Also, when I practice yoga, I try to incorporate breathing techniques like pranayama to enhance the experience.

Most of us have a hormetic-free lifestyle, and that makes us fragile. When people get sick (other than inherited illnesses), they usually think that a visit to the doctor will solve the issue as long as they are given a prescription for some type of medicine. I do honestly believe that the medical profession is wonderful, but there is a big difference between the phrase "I am studying medicine" and the phrase that I would like to hear more often, "I am studying health."

My reluctance to feel comfortable about certain parts of the medical profession does not include people who work in the emergency unit of a hospital, research specialists, and those who have a sympathetic heart in their work.

Perhaps doctors should instead be teaching their patients about the circadian rhythm, hormesis and the gut-brain connection and its relationship to illness, and that antibiotics destroy the good bacteria that are important to your brain and immune system. Of course, I know that antibiotics are still essential for life-threatening infections—I have no questions about or issues with that. But our bodies also have many natural defenses that we shouldn't meddle with unnaturally. I think the pharmaceutical industry has far too much influence in the hospital.

I'm also aware that some people will think or say aloud, "Never mind, she's just a woman from Sweden who thinks she's going to change up medical practice. She doesn't even have a medical degree."

I have no illusions that I will be able to change that type of opinion about me. But I also wish some doctors were less rigid or stuck in their ways. It would help if they read more about the latest research outside of their limited fields of specialization instead of playing God. None of the doctors I met following my stroke told me about neuroplasticity. I had to read about it for myself! Instead, every single one of them told me the same thing, that hardly any recovery would take place after the initial six months from the time of the stroke. But enough about that.

Who do I have confidence in? I believe in those scientists who think that a lack of hormesis is making us fragile and prone to disease.[34] As parents, we do the same when we're too quick to rush to the medicine cabinet for a child with a fever. A fever, not surprisingly, indicates that your child is fighting off some kind of infection, such as a simple cold, the flu, or an ear infection. It is not an illness in itself. In fact, a fever may do some good. A study published in the February 2004 *Journal of Allergy and Clinical Immunology* found that children who ran a fever during their first year of life were less likely to develop allergies later in childhood than children who did not have a fever.[35]

And what about the disinfectant sprays and gels we tell our children to use? I was guilty of that, too, before I read that without exposure to dirt and germs early in life, the immune system doesn't learn how to control its reaction to everyday invaders such as dust and pollen. This obsession with disinfecting everything can lead the immune system to misfire later in life, initiating allergies and other illnesses. Our children are too clean for their own good.

Years ago when we lived in Amsterdam, I remember one-year-old Maarten sucking on one of the plastic safety handles inside the streetcar. I was immediately shocked and cleaned his mouth thoroughly when we got home. Now I realize that there may be an excellent reason why children seem so eager to stuff everything and anything in their mouths. It may be due to a natural urge and because it is good for the immune system.

It goes against the *Zeitgeist* (a German word for "our belief system") to think the way I do now, and that makes some people uncomfortable. I believe our *Zeitgeist* has to change. Surely it's better to not be inside all day and all night, in a perfectly climate-controlled room, but outside as often as possible, in the heat and/or cold.

I would like to finish with a question from the book *Antifragile* by Nassim Nicholas Taleb:

"If someone put you in a box, what is written on your box? Fragile or antifragile?"[36]

Chapter 27

Elle

I looked at her from the corner of my eye. She was sleeping with her head on my shoulder. She still looked so very young and perfect.

She had inherited her father's dark brown eyes and brown hair. But her face carried my features. We had heard that a thousand times. She smelled of perfume, a perfume I once wore, but I didn't remember the name.

Elle turned 18 a few months earlier after finishing gymnasium (high school) the previous year—an entire year ahead of time and with excellent grades. Now she had decided to take a gap year. Elle and I took a Lufthansa flight to Mexico City, mother and daughter traveling together. It was early March 2018, a month before my second stroke anniversary.

Elle had been sent to Mexico to work on her book. No, she's not a writer! She's a model for IMG Models,[1] and she was scouted through Instagram. IMG's scouting program is called We Love Your Genes. They scout a few girls every year from images uploaded to Instagram. In the summer before her 17th birthday, Elle had posted a picture on Instagram that was taken at a Swedish lake house.

It was a typical Swedish tradition during the summer to go swimming in the cold lake and then jump in the sauna after the swim. Elle is the kind of girl that never really wears makeup in day-to-day life. That Instagram picture is a perfect example of Elle as we know her—no makeup, a girly smile, big lips, dark eyebrows, and huge eyes.

IMG, formerly known as the International Management Group, is a global sports, events, and talent management company headquartered in New York. IMG Worldwide has more than 3,000 employees and has been part of WME since 2013. IMG Models, a division of IMG Worldwide, is an international model management firm with offices in New York, Los Angeles, Milan, Paris, London, and Sydney.

Although Elle had been scouted through Instagram about 10 times since the age of 14, she was not scouted by IMG until she was almost 17, a year and a half prior to the events in this book. She had come up to me many times before, flushed with excitement, telling me, "Someone wants to sign me up as a model. Should I meet with them?"

Each time, I looked at the Instagram messages and checked out the agency that had contacted her. So far, I had disappointed her each time with a "no." I would add, "Just reply to them in a friendly way, saying you are not into it now because you are too young." I then explained to Elle, "Let's wait for the big fish because sooner or later, they will come."

Most of those scouts represented smaller Dutch agencies that almost always have only one office. Why did I tell Elle not to do business with them? In the Netherlands, there is not much work available for models. Dutch advertising mainly uses typecast models and actors that either look quirky, typical for the region, or similar to an "average housewife." The small amount of work offered is mostly editorial for a few Dutch fashion magazines that also fill their pages with photos from other markets. As a result, most modeling agencies in the region have little work and their most lucrative source of income is from another source altogether: talent scouting.

Those agencies act as "talent scouts" in a country full of tall, pretty girls with high cheekbones who could perform well on overseas catwalks. Agencies sign up a large number of girls so they can get their 5% or 10% commission when a model takes off in another market like Paris or New York. Without ever providing the model any opportunity to get her career started in her home country, they succeed by introducing models to foreign agencies. Then they collect their commission for many years afterward.

Before the arrival of social media, they provided a start for many models in the Netherlands and added value to their work by going out on the streets to places like shopping malls and sports venues, actively searching for local girls with the desired "look" for becoming a model. Now those same agents can simply scroll through the internet and find girls on social media like Instagram. But the same social media sites are also accessible to the agencies in Paris, London, and New York, and that diminishes the local agency's added value. So, call them lazy or call them spoiled, they add little to a model's career.

Compare this to an amateur soccer club that receives a commission from every future transfer their soccer player makes if the player succeeds as a professional. Those clubs deserve their commissions. They fulfill their role as a local club, run by volunteers who are finally rewarded for training and caring for a young potential soccer star. Those sports clubs have earned their reward, but that doesn't apply to the modeling agencies in the Netherlands.

One day, just as I had told Elle, the big fish came along. When Elle was 16, she came to me again, this time even more excited than before. I read the message sent to her on Instagram by Jeni Rose, the vice president of IMG models. I gave her a look, saying, "Elle, this is the big fish we've been waiting for. So tell them yes!"

Elle was finally on her way, and her dream of becoming a model was taking a giant leap forward. Jeni Rose and her colleague Dominique (nicknamed "Dodo," the head scouting agent for IMG Paris) agreed to meet with all of us, parents too. A month and a half later, we were at the Hyatt Andaz hotel on the canals of Amsterdam. The meeting place was just a stone's throw away from the house where Elle was born, years before we moved to Germany. By the time this meeting took place, it was five months before my stroke. I could speak normally.

Sitting down at the table in the black chairs of the Andaz lobby, Jeni Rose looked familiar, but she said it first.

"I know you," she told me.

"You look familiar too," I said.

"I recognize you from Ford Models in Paris!" she continued. "I was working as a booker at Ford Models back then. You were one of our models."

"Wow, really!" I said. Twenty-five years had passed, so I was stunned that she recognized me after all that time. Being the head of scouting and vice president of IMG models, she must have seen hundreds of faces each day for years. That afternoon, I thought to myself that she must possess superior facial recognition skills. Since my life and interests are mainly about brain stuff now, I looked it up from a brain perspective while writing this chapter.

We all have dedicated areas of the brain that are used only for facial recognition, and humans look at faces differently than other objects. This is the brain's *configura* or holistic strategy of facial recognition. There is a term for these facial recognition geniuses, created in 2009 by Harvard University and University College London: a "super recognizer."[2,3,4] Research showed that about 1% of the population possess significantly greater-than-average facial recognition skills. The average person can remember about 20% of faces seen, but super recognizers score 80%. Jeni was apparently one of them. If she ever got tired of being a model scout and VP, she could always find a job at Scotland Yard, which is on the lookout for talent like hers!

The conversation took an informal turn, and we shared some memories of Paris from 25 years ago when I was living and working there. Then we talked about Elle. They thought she was stunning and wanted to represent her as one of their We Love Your Genes girls. Elle was beaming from ear to ear, but first, we all agreed that she would have to finish gymnasium. Elle's height was only 5'6" (168 cm) at the time, whereas a model should be at least 5'8" (173 cm). But Elle was still growing, and her height didn't seem to matter to them. She eventually grew to 174 cm.

A year and a half later, a few months before Elle finished gymnasium (high school), Elle, Remco, and I went to Paris to sign the contract. By then, it had been nearly a year since my stroke and just a month after I had thrown away my cane in Hawaii. I remember snail-walking to their large office in the eighth arrondissement in Paris. I still couldn't speak much back then, just a few words.

Even though Remco assured me that they had been very sincere and concerned during the two previous meetings they had while I was still in rehab, I was so nervous that I didn't want to go in. I was worried I would clumsily spill my coffee or stumble over a doorstep.

I shouldn't have worried. When we arrived, the whole IMG agency greeted us warmly. Jeni and Dodo were very interested in how I was doing and were both extremely understanding. I knew immediately that I could leave my daughter in their care. That night, they took us out for a celebration dinner and made us feel relaxed and welcome.

By the time Elle turned 18, she had finished school and taken a gap year to start her career as a beginning model. She had briefly been to Stockholm, then Hamburg. Now IMG decided to send her out to Mexico City to work on her book. That meant a model lived in a city for a while, working on editorial jobs. Being around for a more extended period gave a model more time to establish contacts. People that you worked with could suggest you for other jobs. But more important than referrals at that stage were tear sheets. That was essential. Those are printed editorial pages in high fashion magazines like Vogue, Elle, and Harper's Bazaar. Those magazines didn't pay much for photoshoots, but the reward was working with world-class photographers and makeup artists, enabling you to get the perfect pictures to build your portfolio.

Elle was ready for it. She would need to invest in her career since modeling is not very glamorous when you first enter the business. Like all entrepreneurs, you have to keep your expenses down, share a cheap apartment, work hard, and take every opportunity that comes along. Remco and I, both entrepreneurs, were helping her see modeling as a business, not some type of "princess" life. We continued to reinforce the message: First, you have to invest so that later you can reap the rewards.

We were convinced that Elle would do well in her first years, and after that, she would be ready to go to Paris, New York, or London. To get a working visa for New York, for instance, a model needs 50 tear sheets, in other words, 50 published pages of fashion or beauty shoots in respected magazines. At that point, she had none but was determined to get a few in the coming months in Mexico City. I was nearing my second stroke anniversary, and Remco suggested that I could help her get settled if I went with her to Mexico and stayed there for three weeks. Remco planned to take Madeleine over for a visit during the last eight days as their holiday. But for now, at that moment, Elle just sat with her head on my shoulder, sound asleep, all of 18 years old. I was filled with love for her, like all my children.

We were a bit concerned about her going to Mexico since the reputation of the country included drug killings, gang violence, and students that disappeared, never to be seen again. As a mother, you don't expect to take your daughter into a warzone, but how different the reality was.

We loved *Ciudad de México* (Mexico City)! The elevation is high, around 2,250 meters (7,300 feet) above sea level, and I could certainly feel it while we were out strolling through the streets. During the first few days, I couldn't walk for long periods and got out of breath quite easily. If I think about it in terms of the hypoxia hormesis I wrote about in the previous chapter, that state of being out of breath was good for me.

Remco had booked us into the Hyatt Regency in central Mexico City, in the lush and green area called Polanco, one of the more affluent parts of the city. I worked out every day in our hotel. Arjan had provided me with several new exercises during the previous two months. They were both new to me and challenging.

Arjan had given a lecture a few months earlier that I attended. The subject was "Better solutions if your child has autism or ADD." He had a large audience in attendance, and the lecture lasted for an hour. One part of his presentation especially caught my attention.

The subject was primitive reflexes.[5,6,7,8,9] Most children with either autism or ADD still have some of these infant-stage reflexes. He gave an example: If you put a finger into a baby's hand, the baby squeezes it. I immediately recognized that this was similar to the reflex in my left hand! Next, he showed an experiment where the bottom of a baby's foot was struck with a small rubber mallet. The baby's response was to stretch its toes instead of the toddler or adult reflex of squeezing the toes. Again, I recognized my own body's reaction. My left foot responded like a baby as I stretched my toes, while my right toes squeezed.

Arjan explained other primitive reflexes, some of which I had and some of which I didn't. The theory was that, if primitive reflexes were still in place, you couldn't develop the brain to its full potential. Those same primitive reflexes also needed to mature into other types of reflexes as a child got older. He then went on to talk about the "building blocks" that need to be in place for the brain to develop correctly. Arjan discussed the solution for overcoming those primitive reflexes: movement, especially a "pre-crawling" movement. This required the child to make the same physical movements that a baby would when it is in the stage before it crawls.

While on the 45-minute drive home afterward, I mulled over what I had heard at the lecture. Then, with thoughts running non-stop through my head all night, I dreamt about the possibilities. *What if that method could work for me too? What if it was a solution to my spasticity?*

I couldn't understand why that appealed to me so much. I had already done crawling exercises the year before. But they didn't give me the hoped-for results, and I recently stopped my crawling altogether. Maybe it had been too early to try crawling? Perhaps I needed to concentrate on pre-crawling instead? It was worth a try.

The next time I saw Arjan, I was so excited that I practically bombarded him with questions.

"Relax," he said. "I already gave you some pre-crawling and other exercises, but I can show you some more when I have time. I'm going to Norway tonight. When I get back, I'll send you a video about how to do the exercises that I think you're up for." And he did.

When he returned, he gave me some books as well, including *Reflexes, Learning and Behavior* by Sally Goddard[10] and *Functional Neurology* by Randy W. Beck.[11] I promptly and eagerly dug into both of them.

By now, you must be thinking that all I do is read, read more, and work out. Yes, I'm afraid this is true! In my new life, I get up quite early, 5 a.m., and don't watch television at night. Also, I didn't have to read every single page of most of the books I used for research to come to my conclusions. I learned that from my time in law school in my early twenties.

During all-nighters before an exam, I needed to read all those thick books included in the curriculum. So, I learned to be selective, to know what was necessary, and then I read that part of the book three times. However, in spite of repeatedly reading those sections, most of what I studied during those nightly sessions didn't stick for long. I retained very little of the information after passing my exams.

Now I know that sleep helps you imprint newly learned information in your brain. So, I can honestly admit that I didn't learn much from those years of law school, thanks to a lot of all-nighters.

I read each of the books Arjan recommended. I also used the videos he sent to guide me through the exercises. At first, I had problems with my arm. It continued to be so spastic that I couldn't move it. Arjan advised me to start imagining that

I could already move my arm, in other words, to visualize the successful movement before it arrived.

I knew that I was disciplined enough to do those exercises five times a day, but in the beginning, it was quite tedious. If I wasn't able to move my arm, even slightly, it became so spastic that it moved in every direction but the desired one. Then, I just held my arm in a static hold in the right position. What saved me from giving up was that I now had experience being patient. After six weeks, I began to see noticeable improvements. Three weeks later, I was sure about that—things were moving in the right direction. Thanks to the pre-crawling exercises, I was witnessing reduced spasticity in both my arm and leg on the stroke-affected side.

I was in the hotel's gym in Mexico City when I sent a message to Arjan on my phone. "The pre-crawling works! I'm not there yet, but I know it's working." Then I sent him a video that Elle had taken of me as proof of my progress.

He was enormously happy for me, and I could feel it. For almost two years, I had tried every type of exercise that I could think of, with minor, minor, *minor* improvement of 2% at most. Now, I had achieved a 10% improvement in two short months!

I messaged Arjan again: "We are onto something here."

He wrote back: "I think so too."

Elle was in the gym with me each day. She needed to do her own daily workouts and was excited to see me making so much progress. It was also wonderful to have that shared time since we are so much alike. Elle is quite easygoing, she works out a lot (just like me!), and she loves healthy food. We even had a favorite restaurant that we went to quite often.

Remco and Madeleine came for a visit over Easter, and we decided that the four of us would go on a road trip to the eastern coast of Mexico. Remco rented a car, and we took off toward Vera Cruz via Puebla.[12]

Puebla has stunning Baroque architecture. While nearby, we also visited The Great Pyramid of Cholula, the largest pyramid known to exist in the world today.[13] It was rediscovered in only the early 20th century. In 1910, authorities began the construction of a mental asylum at the base of a large hill. As development progressed, it became apparent that the "natural hill" was an ancient pyramid, built in layers. The astonishing structure had been forgotten for centuries as nature reclaimed the site and vegetation covered it over. Then, several hundred years ago, the Catholic Church commissioned the building of a large church atop what they thought was a hill.

We were in Vera Cruz for three days when Elle received the message that she had gotten her first job! She was quite excited, so we changed our plans and drove back to Mexico City right away. Two days later, after arriving back at our hotel, we were surprised yet again when Maarten walked into our room. As a surprise, he had flown in from Boston to see us all. We went out for dinner that night to celebrate my second stroke anniversary.

Days later, when we were at the airport preparing to return home, Arjan contacted me. He said he had an idea. "We need to tell other people about your progress with the pre-crawling." I could tell he was excited, probably because he had been rewatching the video we sent to him. It was proof of my progress, clearly seen in Elle's video. Just a few months earlier, I couldn't get my arm to move at all.

"I was thinking of a portal, a website where we could teach people about pre-crawling exercises and 'do it yourself' constraint-induced movement therapy for home use. I can record masterclasses where I lecture to educate people about the brain, and you can give master classes too, eventually." I reminded him that I couldn't talk yet, but he wrote back, "In two years or so, you will be able to talk well enough."

Rolling it over in my mind, I thought about the ideas Arjan had proposed for the entire 10 hours that it took to fly back home. He had even mentioned a name that he thought was suitable for the website. I immediately registered it when I came home: Brain.rehab.

Chapter 28

Brain.rehab

We were walking barefoot on the Veluwe[1] in the Netherlands. It's an area with vast sand drifts. A sand drift is a geographic area of shifting sand, gray hair-grass, and moss.

I liked it there, especially walking barefoot. After my stroke, the brain map[2] of my left foot must have been almost completely destroyed. As I started walking again, the brain map began to reform[3] but was still not sensitive enough. Going barefoot sent sensory signals that could improve its sensitivity and was also good for my balance.[4,5,6,7]

Arjan walked beside me, barefoot as well. It was our first meeting to discuss the company, Brain.rehab, that we were in the process of starting.[8] *What would it be like if all business meetings took place like this?* I imagined people from a bank walking barefoot down the dunes with the legs of their suits rolled up. I grinned at the thought of it.

That's the first thing I would implement if I ever became CEO of a bank. What most CEOs were unlikely to have known (and I didn't either before my stroke) was that walking outside in the sun, barefoot even in the cold weather, is suitable for the body's hormesis! They could add years of enhanced life and resilience to sickness to those working for them.

CEOs and their employees would be less stressed and could intentionally choose to go outdoors for that type of health break in the middle of the day. It would be good for their collective circadian rhythm, thus they would all be able to sleep better. Better sleep creates more productivity and should enable employees at all levels to produce at improved rates.

"What are you grinning about?" asked Arjan.

"Nothing" I said. I felt it was too complicated to try and find the right words to describe my imagination.

"We need to get it out there, this information that six months post-stroke is just the starting point for more recovery, not the endpoint," Arjan said.

"I agree," I replied, and then continued, "Look at me and my recovery. I made most of it long *after* six months had passed. I could maybe say 40 words after six months, but there were no complete sentences. My arm was useless, and I was walking with a cane and brace because I had just come out of my wheelchair." It took a while to say all of that. I was talking slowly, and the sound of my words was somewhat indistinct and unclear.

"I know," Arjan said. "It's a shame that they told you to only expect a few months and no further. I hear that from a lot of patients as well—six months, then that's it."

"Why do they say that?!" I was upset when I spoke again, and I almost stumbled over a clump of moss.

"I guess most therapists don't have the knowledge, and it takes time for cutting-edge knowledge to break through and become more widely known," Arjan answered. "It may not seem like it, but we are living in a period when knowledge about the brain goes super fast. Twenty years ago, all doctors were told that the brain is static, and if you lose some brain cells, you never get them back. We now know that is not true. We can change things by making videos of cutting-edge science, to educate them! Then they don't have to read; they just have to listen."

"Are you talking about Brain.rehab being used to educate therapists?" I asked. "I thought we were making a portal for brain-injured people."

"That's true, I'm just thinking out loud here. It will be a portal for brain-injured people, but I'm dying to educate caretakers as well. To tell you the truth, I'm fed up with some doctors and physical therapists. They are so far behind."

"I know," I said. "But don't you think medical neurologists might try to mock you because you're a functional neurologist? Don't get me wrong! You know an awful lot about the brain and the nervous system, more than anyone I know, including medical neurologists."

Arjan looked at me as he said, "I know, but don't worry about it! I'm specialized in applied clinical neuroscience and functional neurology. And yes, I am also board-certified in chiropractic and functional neurology. As long as I give scientific references for all I have to say in the masterclasses, they can ridicule me all they want, and they can ridicule all the scientists and professors that wrote the science I base my masterclasses on."

"I agree, you do translate science into plain English so that everyone can understand it. Sorry for saying that," I said.

"Don't worry about it. If the website takes off, it is mainly brain-injured people that we want as subscribers, people who have experienced a stroke or any other accident. We'll make it for them."

At that moment, the initial idea of Brain.rehab helping people with brain injuries started to take shape. In the next month or so, we defined our goals more thoroughly. Brain.rehab would be a portal of motivation, help, training, and education for patients with brain damage, for after they finish their first six months of rehab. We would translate the most up-to-date insights on rehab techniques into standard, understandable English for the people it matters to most: the patients who want to improve.

We could guide these patients and explain to them why specific techniques work better than others. We want them to understand that it is not only about exercise but also sleep, nutrition, and training the brain. We can refer them to useful books and help them take charge of actively reprogramming their brains.

Brain.rehab is going to be one of the essential tools stroke patients can use to improve. We cannot expect a stroke patient to suddenly begin reading complex medical books. We cannot expect them to figure everything out for themselves. We also know that it should be financially affordable to them.

Our Mission Statement:

Brain.rehab will help one million stroke survivors and brain-injured people in the next 10 years by providing low-cost online training and information for home rehabilitation.

Our Vision:

We believe that six months post-stroke is just the starting point for more recovery of lost function. Only a fraction of the insights gained from research on brain plasticity, brain performance, and brain optimization is currently used in stroke and brain injury rehabilitation.

Some Key Elements of Brain.rehab:

Masterclasses on brain function:

- brain plasticity
- oxygen and circulation
- optimizing glucose levels
- brain activation
- sleep
- water
- the second brain (gastrointestinal tract)
- good fats
- monitoring your circadian rhythm
- managing stress
- food for the brain
- energy management
- building blocks for brain optimization
- basic neurological development and primitive reflexes
- core exercises
- static stabilization of the shoulder
- pre-crawling exercises
- top-down and bottom-up approaches
- supercharging your brain at home

Rehabilitation protocols:

- Home-based CIMT and CIMT priming protocols

Antispasticity:

- Pre-crawling and pre-crawling plus, cross-crawl patterns and primal kinetic exercises
- Core stability from absolute basics to advanced, posture and breathing protocols
- Walking protocols, leg stability
- Head-eye vestibular and balance protocols, brain area-specific training

ALSO:

Brain news items, and testing and evaluation of new treatment methods such as low-level laser, transcranial magnetic stimulation, and QEEG.

We were silent for the rest of the walk. It felt good to know that I would be able to give something back to fellow stroke survivors.

I also wished that there had been something like Brain. rehab already in existence when I was getting out of the clinic.

Now, together with Arjan, I was going to design it myself.

I got goosebumps just thinking about it.

Chapter 29

Stay Away From Crabs

(or "We don't do crabs.")

What on earth does the title of this chapter stand for? You'll find out in a minute.

First, I'll talk about Marisa Peer.[1,2] Marisa Peer is a best-selling Amazon author and award-winning hypnotherapist[3] who has helped CEOs, royalty, Olympians, and hundreds of others overcome their phobias. When I watched "5 Mental Models of Super Achievers" on Mindvalley,[4] she essentially advised her readers to start the task that they hate the most first thing in the morning.

Marisa Peer is awesome. She is so cool and in control. When she was diagnosed with uterine cancer, she could've asked, "Why me?" or said, "I don't deserve this." She instead maintained an attitude of optimism and said, "I am not doing illness." She began an anti-cancer diet and changed her lifestyle. Those words showed that she was not a victim but in control.

"I don't do sick."

"We don't do victim."

"We don't do crabs." (I'll come to crabs in a minute.)

I had been thinking about writing a book about my stroke recovery for a while, but I couldn't seem to get started. I was procrastinating.

Marisa Peer gave an example from her life (before she became famous) of getting up in the morning, and the first thing she did was call magazines, trying to promote her work. She hated that. But she kept doing it. And at a specific moment, she realized that she didn't hate it anymore. She had become successful calling magazines and it had turned into a habit. This is the same technique she used to write her book. She started writing first thing in the morning.

Why am I telling you this?

Because I also used this exact technique to write this book, first thing in the morning.

At first, I hated it. My ego had stopped me several times with comments like: *Just don't bother, you're not a writer anyway!* or *Who do you think you are?* At other moments, I would think to myself, *Nobody is going to read your book anyway.* There were always plenty of reasons I could come up with to not write.

But a voice within encouraged me: *Even if you only make a difference in one stroke survivor's life, your book is worth writing.*

So I kept going! And after two months or so, I had developed so many ideas and angles to write about that I began to like the process of writing. In fact, I found it difficult to stop and started looking forward to it each day! But once again, it took me two months to feel that way, all the while getting up each day not wanting to write at all. If you can discipline yourself to do something every day for about two months, then it becomes a habit.

Now, what's that about crabs?

Let me explain. I was reading a book called *Man Up: How to Cut the Bullshit and Kick Ass in Business (and in Life)* by Bedros Keuilian.[5] Bedros coaches entrepreneurs who want to operate at an even higher level by becoming "disciplined entrepreneurs" and destroying any limiting behaviors that create bottlenecks in growth.

In his book, he wrote a chapter called, "I have crabs!" (which is kind of hilarious). He told a story about watching a fisherman fishing for crabs. There was a bucket next to the fisherman with a lot of crabs in it. He saw one crab that wanted to escape, and he almost made it. Bedros told the fisherman, "Put a lid on that bucket because crabs are escaping."

The fisherman calmly replied, "No need for a lid." Bedros couldn't believe what happened next. The ambitious crab was hurtling toward freedom when, suddenly, the other crabs grabbed his legs and pulled him back down! The scene resonated with Bedros about events and people in his personal life. "I also have crabs in my life!" he said. "They're trying to pull me down."

Crabs like the ones in this story are a metaphor for toxic people who bring you down. In every person's life, there is a spectrum of toxicity. Some people around you are mildly toxic (they can be an annoyance to you). Others are so toxic that you can feel hatred toward them or the urge to avoid these people altogether.

When you live in a negative environment with too many toxic people too close to you, it will rob you of your utmost potential! The reason is simple. Poisonous people drag you down with their limiting beliefs. You often have to work incredibly hard to counteract their effects. Life is too short to live with toxic and difficult people. I want to live a life where the people around me both support me and want the best for me, just like I do for them.

Motivational speaker Jim Rohn said, notably, that we are the average of the five people we spend the most time with.

Write down the hours that you spend with these people, your top five. Those are the ones who have the most influence on you.

I saw things more clearly now. I would choose to surround myself with positive, empowering people. No more negative or disempowering people around me. I needed to cut some people out of my life entirely, those that had stepped on my boundaries and principles again and again.

The discussion above does not mean that you should cut those people out after one or two mistakes. But everyone needs their own set of ethics and boundaries for peace of mind. If those problematic people continue to step on your hopes and dreams, push you (hoping that you'll change and do things their way), or completely ignore your belief system and are disrespectful to you, it may be time to cut them out of your life altogether.

Let me illustrate this from my own experience. I hate it when people talk badly about other people. My first cut was a person who did precisely that in a very sneaky way. Putting my newly acquired knowledge to work, after a BBQ, I cut this woman out of my life. I won't tell you who she was, but I can tell you that I had known her quite well for at least eight years.

There were not many people at this BBQ, and I knew everyone there. This happened about five months after my stroke, when I could go home from the clinic on weekends. She sat on the other side of the table, talking to my husband while her husband completely ignored me for the whole dinner. She just said hello and goodbye to me. That was all.

Later someone told me, "She has difficulties dealing with sick people."

That didn't make it better, but worse. My rebuttal was, "I'm not sick! I've had a stroke!"

She came to visit me once at the rehab center. But after I came home, she didn't visit a single time even though I lived close to her daily route to work. I kept my decision to myself. That was not a hard thing to do at the time since I could hardly speak.

I cried in the car on the way home from the BBQ. My husband and children asked what was wrong, but I couldn't say anything just then. To see each other in good times, to have a drink or a meal, that was one thing...but in bad times, she stayed away. Someone like that is not a true friend. And that is why I cut her out of my life.

How to recognize a toxic person?

Although they are incredibly charming at times, they feed off your energy. I later realized I always felt drained after meeting with her. I'm not an expert on toxic people, and for you, it is crucial to recognize your own set of toxic people. Just go on Google and type in "toxic people." There, you might get answers to your personal dilemmas with people like that. Further, I found that the characteristics listed below are included in almost every article about toxic people:

- They are manipulative and want others to do what suits them.
- They can be judgmental and talk badly about other people.
- They never seem vulnerable.
- They make you defend yourself.
- They are not caring or interested in what's important to you.
- They don't apologize.

- They can't handle critics.
- They begrudge.
- They lack real compassion but can pretend to have compassion if it suits them.
- They want to be the center of attention.
- They are pleasant and charming if the situation goes their way (usually when they are the center of attention).

For me, this means that toxic people, even though they are often smart, are not well developed and run their lives in sort of an animalistic way. They are in a low conscious state.

By now I had become a pretty good judge of character. Usually, this subjective judgment comes with age but has also been known to arrive spontaneously after a significant life event or injury. After my stroke, this development went into turbo mode. I quietly observed people because I couldn't speak to them. Even before my stroke, I didn't have many friends in Germany and the Netherlands. My hectic lifestyle with three children and their various activities, while working 50 hours a week, left me with no time to even go to the hairdresser without my laptop in tow. It also didn't leave much energy for friends. After my stroke, all this changed, rather remarkably, for the better.

I wanted to add more positive people in my life. But how? I couldn't talk normally. So how would I find people that wanted to hang out with me and get to know me? Believe it or not, there were quite a few.

There was one friend who lived just a few houses away and worked for my company. You'll remember Marianna from the second chapter. She was right there when I had my stroke. I started seeing her more often, and one time she said to me, "I've been going to this yoga class. I really like it, and maybe you should come as well." Before my stroke, I would have let that pass, but now I was seriously considering it, grinning at the mental picture of me standing on my head.

"Why not? Let's go for it!" I said. That would undoubtedly require me to get out of my comfort zone. But I'd also have a chance to meet some new women who could become friends.

Anne was the yoga teacher. I liked her straight away. She was 39, good looking, and had the same kind of humor as me, putting herself on the spot a lot. She had been taught some hard life lessons. She lived in Argentina for seven years, working hard and running her own company together with her husband. After several disappointments in Argentina, they moved to my hometown, Elten, and there she continued working too much.

She told me that when she had her first child, she was working for a client of hers that had an auction website, something like eBay. She could be up all night monitoring the site at peak periods so she could contact programmers on standby if necessary. She would do this from Germany for a client in Argentina, while breastfeeding her baby, Isa, and working for hours at her computer.

Then suddenly, one day, she'd had quite enough. She stopped working 60 hours a week and made a radical career switch, becoming a yoga teacher! We bonded almost immediately, as I did with each of the other 10-12 yoga friends. We were all 30-50 years of age and got along well together. I proposed that we take a trip together. All of them said "yes."

We went to Ibiza at the end of the summer of 2018—a girls-only trip like we hadn't taken since our teenage years. The week was a success, complete with a lot of laughter about silly jokes. We did yoga on the beach and watched the sunset. One perfect night, Anne gave a yoga class on the terrace of our house, under the stars!

How abundant my life is, now that I have real friends that practically live next to me. I was happy that I dared to be vulnerable, dared to approach them even though I could hardly talk.

Why am I sharing this with you? Because I know that while recovering from a stroke, you will need all the energy you can preserve. Prevent toxic people from stealing that precious energy from you. Stay away from crabs, and be vulnerable at the same time to kind people who want the best for you.

Chapter 30

Plateau – How You Learn to Love It

Things hadn't been working out relationship-wise between Remco and me. He was often in a bad mood over the last year or two, and he yelled at me quite frequently. Basically, he was temporarily toxic. "Temporarily toxic?" you might say. "Is that even a thing?" Yes, it is because I'm using it, and in fact, I invented it. I have my share in this too. I got up early and went to bed early, while he's a night owl, and kept my fitness equipment all over the living room.

Anyone can be toxic or unpleasant at times, and that includes me. I have been temporarily toxic on occasion. But when the people involved are not truly cruel or nasty and you know that it's a temporary condition, there is no reason to cut them out of your life. They are merely overwhelmed people operating under stressful circumstances, usually for a short period, at least in my opinion.

The most common reasons that cause people to behave in a toxic manner toward their loved ones include stress at work, burnout, or a state of depression. Remco was stressed at work and perhaps he could feel the beginnings of burnout.

Dealing with the multilayered events surrounding my stroke couldn't have been easy either—the stress and uncertainty of the stroke and my prognosis, driving back and forth to the rehab center each day for six months to visit me, me being suicidal, all worrying about the successes and failures of my recovery, and fretting about the impact on the children and on him. I knew that it had taken a toll on him and my entire family.

Keeping in mind what I shared in the last chapter (don't let negative people drag you down like a crab), it was also unfair for me to be dealing with Remco's bad moods while I was in the middle of my rehab. None of us were happy, and all of us were stressed.

Remco had a travel agency that he ran with his sister, but he eventually left his job. Once he had created that opening in his life for something new, I suggested that he go on a long trip to think things through and try to rediscover some joy in his life. In spite of his initial reluctance to do that, he finally agreed.

Off he went for seven weeks to Dubai, India, Sri Lanka, Singapore, and several other countries. And when he returned, he had regained a relaxed and joyful state of mind. Having a sense of space between the two of us for a while was also good. I liked my time alone with Madeleine, and I also enjoyed the company of my new friends.

I worked out intensely each day, like I never had before. But I might have worked out a little too much. While practicing running on the terrace of our house, suddenly, *boom*! I fell.

Marianna took me to the hospital. I learned that my left wrist was broken. Too bad it was my left wrist. If you remember from earlier chapters, I had wanted to break my right arm so I was forced to use my left hand, hopefully engaging my brain in some additional healing. You'll also remember that Arjan gave me firm instructions to not do that.

After my stroke, Remco sometimes sent me website articles from the German magazine *Das Spiegel*. One article, in particular, drew my attention. The author wrote that having a cast on your arm can change your brain in 16 days. [»1 »2 »3]

Under those conditions, the brain changes to enable the awakening of more neurons on the opposite side of the brain so they can deal with the fine motor movements of the free arm. It reminded me of the story I previously shared about Taub and the research monkeys.

I promptly sent the article to Arjan, and he understood immediately. He promised, "We will get you a 'real cast' for your right arm once you are out of that new cast on your left arm. But that means you have to sleep with the cast on as well," he said. I agreed.

He was referring to a CIMTH program that he had designed for me. CIMTH, which stands for constraint-induced movement therapy for home use, was do-it-yourself CIMT for patients once they have moved beyond their time in clinics. I will dive deeper into this in chapter 38.

In the hospital, I begged the doctor, with Marianna and Anne's assistance, to put a brace on my wrist instead of a cast. I didn't want my brain to change even more toward favoring my right hand and arm, and I reasoned that a brace would make that less probable. I got the brace, and the doctor told me to take it easy.

I should have listened to the doctor's instructions, but I didn't. After waiting one short day, I started to play ping-pong again, all alone with half the table tilted up. I was trying to beat two shots in one set with three shots done with my left hand. When I refer to a "set," I mean hitting the ball against the upstanding table and then again. I could already do it twice but not three times. My wrist hurt a little, but I thought I could handle it. I managed to cope with the pain until that night—a sleepless night—when I was startled by the level of pain in my wrist and arm.

I was ashamed at the thought of returning to the hospital. What was I supposed to say once I arrived? How could I tell them that I had completely disregarded what the doctor said?

Tamara, a friend and next-door neighbor, asked me over for coffee at her house the next day. When I arrived, she looked at my face and immediately asked what was wrong. I showed her my brace, said it was broken, and then told her that I hadn't been able to sleep because of it.

After admitting that I had been moving it too much, I told her I was worried I might have moved it into the "wrong angle" by ignoring the doctor's advice.

Tamara, who is Dutch, immediately called the doctor's assistant and explained, in perfect German, what was needed. Tamara was a cut-the-crap type of woman, and she promptly hauled me over to the hospital. The wait for my scan was quite short this time, and afterward, I had a long talk with a doctor. We knew each other from an earlier episode when I fractured my tibia and damaged my knee. She was the doctor who operated and inserted 13 screws and a plate into my leg and knee.

I heard her when she told me to take it easy. She also explained that I couldn't run because of the previous injury to my right knee and leg. I thanked her and realized I could stop putting so much pressure on myself. It wasn't only the stroke that had damaged my ability to run. It was also the surgery.

You won't ever see me participating in a marathon in the future, but I continue to do a little running on occasion, only 1000 meters or so. However, over the next few weeks, I finally took it easy. And the time off gave me time to think about progress and setbacks.

The latest episode with my broken wrist was one of several setbacks I experienced since my stroke. Should we call them plateaus or stagnation?

If your recovery has stalled[4,5] or is even backsliding (like my latest broken wrist), you need to regard this retrogression[6] as a *plateau* in the learning arc. A weak person might give up in misery, but a strong person persists. I wanted to be one of the strong ones.

The only way to move past the plateau is to engage your body in manual transmission next time, not automatic.

What do I mean by that?

You have to do different activities! It may also be time to look for more progressive training that will move you to the next level.

Look for something you haven't done before, like swimming or Nordic walking. About a year and a half after my stroke, I started Nordic walking.[7,8,9,10] When I began, my left arm was cramped and spastic, and it continued that way for the next four months. Then, after I began to do the pre-crawling exercises from Arjan, my left arm was almost in a normal posture after just six months of using the exercises. I found that I could make a cross-crawl movement when I walked. A cross-crawl movement is when you bring your left arm and right leg forward, and then do the opposite with the right arm and left leg.[11,12,13] I continued that way for the following three months, and then, voila! I could walk with Nordic walking sticks!

My current routine includes walking three kilometers with Nordic sticks, four times a week. Since I dig into the forest floor while propelling myself forward, my triceps are getting a good workout too.

If you want to try this, start with the pre-crawling exercises, lying down, such as cross-crawl. When you can handle that, head out for Nordic walking. Remember though, do the pre-crawling very slowly (in slow motion) because you activate more neurons this way.

Performing that cross-crawl movement builds the bridge between the right and left hemispheres. Electrical impulses and information can then pass freely between the two portions of the brain. This bridging function is essential for physical coordination as well as intellectual activities such as learning languages and reading. More importantly, cross-crawl patterns are hard-wired in the spinal cord and thus (most often) not affected by a stroke. They are a great tool for your rehab.

Moving on, have you tried swimming regularly? I started swimming one and a half years ago, and at first, I could only stand or lie in the water. Then I progressed to swimming on my back with the right hand holding my left hand under my back. After seven months of that, I was finally ready to attempt a normal swim.

In the beginning, I absolutely sucked at it. But eventually, after spending six months on the pre-crawling exercises, I got the hang of it. I can now swim normally for 20 meters.

I'm dead serious: If you are going to do well in every stage of your recovery, "Embrace the suck," as an elite soldier would say.[14,15,16] That means that, if the situation is terrible, deal with it anyhow.

Don't be "arambhashura," a Sanskrit word describing to someone who is a hero in the beginning but not at the end.[17]

Instead, be a hero all the way to the end.

Chapter 31

Claire Wineland

In law school, whenever I received a question in class from the professor, I remember being so shy that my face got red. I got the answer right most of the time, but I hated speaking in front of a group of people.

Why, then, did I choose to study law? Surely I knew that a lawyer had to speak out loud in court all the time?

I can honestly tell you that I don't know why I chose law. Maybe it was because my sister did or because I didn't want to become a doctor or dentist like my brothers. Or perhaps it was because my father, who died a few years ago, was tough, and he obsessed about my grades at school. A 5 was the highest grade in Sweden back then, and he only ever accepted a 5. I'm not angry with him for that. He taught me discipline, which has come in handy while recovering from my stroke.

In short, I'm afraid I'm one of those people who would rather receive the eulogy[1] at a funeral than give one (to paraphrase a line from *Seinfeld*). Eulogies are given as a part of funeral services!

So, why am I telling you this?

I'm sharing this because Arjan asked me to do a lecture with him at his office, with stroke survivors as the audience. "We'll also film it," he said.

He asked me to tell my story, specifically, where I was at six months after my stroke and where I am two and a half years after. He believed people needed to know that much more recovery is possible after the initial six months.

He was right about that. At six months post-stroke, I could speak maybe 30-40 words, but I still had no sentences. I was walking with a cane and brace since I had just come out of my wheelchair. My arm was spastic and useless. All the things I could do now, I learned after six months had passed.

Oh no, I thought. *I can't possibly give a lecture. Besides that, I can't even speak!*

The conversation with my ego went something like this:

First, my ego thought that I shouldn't do it because:

1. I'm not a public speaker (remember law school?).
2. Nobody would understand me (I have aphasia, apraxia, and dysarthria).
3. I couldn't possibly remember the text that I planned to say.

And so on...

But then, when I thought more deeply about it, I decided to do it anyway.

Why? I thought back to myself in my wheelchair, unable to talk, and hearing people tell me, "You have to learn to live with your handicap for the rest of your life since the six-month window has passed."

I would have loved to see someone else like me say: "That six-month window is bullshit. You can recover all throughout your life."

I was dying to hear those exact words! I had to learn it myself from the books that I read, PubMed, and cutting-edge research.

Maybe I could inspire someone to continue to work as hard as I did, so he or she could recover further. It was now or never to overcome my fear of public speaking. I needed to do this, even though it was miles out of my comfort zone. There was a higher purpose to it.

I thought about Phil Stutz,[2] author of *The Tools.*[3] He said, "Your infinite potential lay outside your comfort zone." If I'm supposed to feel fear and discomfort as I take this journey, then what the heck, I'm also curious about feeling my "infinite potential." When I read this, I nodded to myself and started feeling pretty excited about leaving my comfort zone more often. Giving a speech was one way to do that.

We are addicted to our comfort zones. Is there a rehab center for comfort zone addiction? I don't think so. I grinned when I imagined myself going to a rehab center that forced me to do everything I was afraid of.

Luckily, I practiced hard (I will get to the practice in a minute) during the two and a half years after my stroke. I went from not making a sound to now talking slowly but with mistakes and pronunciation errors.

I had aphasia, dysarthria, and apraxia.

Aphasia is a speaking disorder. According to Wikipedia, aphasia includes one or more of the disabilities that follow.[4]

Inability to:

- Comprehend language
- Pronounce, not due to muscle paralysis or weakness
- Speak spontaneously
- Form words
- Name objects (anomia)

- Repeat a phrase
- Read
- Write
- Follow or understand simple requests
- Speak in a grammatically correct fashion (agrammatism)

Also including:

- Poor enunciation
- Excessive creation and use of personal neologisms
- Persistent repetition of a syllable, word, or phrase (stereotypies, recurring utterances/speech automatism)
- Paraphasia (substituting letters, syllables, or words)
- Dysprosody (alterations in inflection, stress, and rhythm)
- Incomplete sentences
- Limited verbal output
- Difficulty naming objects
- Speaking gibberish

As you can see, aphasia comes in many forms. Right after my stroke, I couldn't speak at all. But after three months, I was able to say a few words. I forgot what things were called, what the names of various items were, so my sister Anne put up Post-its of the words, sprinkled all around my room, to remind me what a curtain or cupboard was called. This inability to name objects (anomia) was part of my life for a long time after my stroke, but it is getting much better now. I learned to write again (with my right hand) within five months. And I relearned reading after only three months.

Reading was still there somewhere in my brain, but it was blocked out when my brain was enormously inflamed for months after my stroke. That's my conclusion, anyway.

And I clearly experienced the following Wikipedia documentation about aphasia:

- Inability to pronounce, not due to muscle paralysis or weakness
- Inability to speak spontaneously
- Inability to form words

I didn't experience the rest of the symptoms on the list.

What about my dysarthria diagnosis? If I look at Wikipedia again: "Dysarthria is a motor-speech disorder of the motor component of the motor-speech system and is characterized by poor articulation of phonemes."[5] Phonemes are one of the smallest units of speech that can distinguish one word from another, e.g., the difference between "pin" and "pan."

In other words, it is a condition in which problems effectively occur with the muscles that help produce speech, often making it very difficult to pronounce words. I didn't have an extended form of dysarthria, just a little bit.

What about apraxia? Apraxia of speech is difficulty planning and coordinating the movements necessary for speech (e.g., potato, potato = totapo, topato). I had that for sure.

You might be thinking, *Wow, she really has a lot of speaking problems!*

You are right about that. But I did two things that set the stage for success:

1. I pulled the page containing the word "impossible" out of my *Oxford English Dictionary* and crumpled it into a ball.
2. I wrote on a piece of paper, "TED talk[6] in 2022" and put it on our fridge.

Guess why I did that? I was setting my goals high (TED talk), and I thought "impossible" was a word I should stay away from.

I had my own set of exercises for speech based on trial and error.

First of all, I warmed up in the following way, four times a week:

1. I applied a heating pad to my face (especially the left side). You can buy one on eBay or Amazon.
2. I massaged my face and stretched it.
3. I did some mouth gymnastics including rolling my tongue over the inside of my lips. For more examples, look on YouTube for "facial warm-up exercises."
4. Next, I took a sip of water to gargle with. Gargling contracts the back of the throat, which activates the vagus nerve motor functions (stimulating the soft palate, the fleshy area near the back of the roof of the mouth).[7]

Then, I began the actual practice session (most of these practices I designed myself). Each session, I did all of the following activities in different combinations:

1. I **read out loud** in different languages.
2. I created **"hypoxia hormesis"** by saying a sentence over and over again until I was out of breath.
3. Sitting in my car with my favorite music blaring, I **sang out loud** as hard as I can.
4. Say one word, for instance, "bed." Then come up with as many **translations** as possible into other languages.
5. I used Sander's (the speech therapist) advice to say three meaningless words, for instance, "tippa, tappa, toppa,"

first slowly and then faster and faster. I used a metronome app for this. A metronome is a device used by musicians that marks time at a selected rate by giving a regular tick.

6. I used a **peripheral nerve stimulator** called MiniStim on my tongue.[8,9,10] Through the use of electrodes on my tongue, it provides a tingling sensation.
7. **Practice whistling.**[11] It took me two and a half years to be able to whistle again.
8. I incorporated **balance exercises**. Why? Balance exercises are specific activities that help build muscle strength as well as improve the functionality of your vestibular system. The vestibular system is one of the basic sensory-motor systems. It controls equilibrium, balance, and body movement, and is also one of the influencing factors in auditory language processing. While researchers aren't entirely sure how it influence these processes, there is clearly a connection. Along with a lot of other stroke survivors, I have a vestibular dysfunction from brain damage.[12] I also have auditory language processing difficulties.
9. Do you remember the **cross-crawling exercises** from the previous chapter? Performing these movements builds the bridge between the right and left hemispheres of the brain, allowing for electrical impulses to pass between the two, which is essential for physical coordination as well as higher brain activities such as reading and learning language.[13]
10. There's one more thing that I almost forgot. **French kissing** is an excellent way to stimulate the tongue, especially when half of the tongue is paralyzed! To do it without a partner, use your hand and simulate a French kiss against it.

These are the ten sets of exercises that explain why I could speak reasonably two and a half years after my stroke. You may remember that the doctors and therapists I saw at the hospital doubted that I would ever speak again since I couldn't make a sound following my stroke.

Later I added exercises I learned from a fellow stroke survivor named Paul Cummings. These were singing words (high and low), whispering, and talking with Mickey Mouse's voice. Paul is an extraordinary person who has chosen to help others overcome speech problems after experiencing them himself.

There is another thing that I began to do later, which also improved my speech. It's called N-Back,[14,15,16] and you can read about it in the following chapters.

Every once in a while, I put an ice cube in my mouth, and then I drank hot tea. I don't know if that "hormesis for the mouth" actually had any real effect, but there was no harm in trying it (do not do this with tea that is too hot).

I practiced my speech in the morning because I was too tired at night, which meant I was unable to speak clearly.

I also learned a lot from the video "Public Speaking 101" with Brian Johnson, available in his amazing Optimize app.[17] "Not to go for perfection but a connection with the audience," he said, quoting one of his mentors. I'm a recovering perfectionist, just like Brian Johnson, so I had a hard time with the idea of not giving a "perfect speech"—but I couldn't! My speech is not perfect at all, because I still have difficulty talking!

I also scrolled through YouTube for some inspirational talks I could learn from. And there she was. I stumbled onto a talk she gave at Klick Health MUSE New York.[18] Her name was Claire Wineland.[19]

She had oxygen tubes in her nose, and she spoke with a hoarse voice that still sounded so utterly alive. She began by talking briefly about the disease she was born with, cystic fibrosis.[20][21]

Cystic fibrosis, she explained, is a genetic disease that causes an overload of mucus (a thick liquid produced inside of your nose and other parts of your body). She explained that the mucus is like a "thick tar" coming out of your nose, lungs, and the rest of your organs.

Claire had already spent 3/4 of her life in the hospital. Cystic fibrosis is a progressive and consuming disease. When she was born, she received a life expectancy estimate of about 10 years. At the time of the recording, she was 18 years old.

She talked about how we need to change the way we treat sick people. How do we stop pitying them and start empowering them? There's so much disempowerment happening when you're sick. Others pity sick people, and so they begin to believe that they cannot be happy like healthy people. To share a quote from Claire, "I'm sick and probably always will be sick. And yet, I'm 100% content and happy with my life."

I recognized that too, but more from an intellectual point of view. Most people who didn't know me must've thought that, due to the severity of my stroke and extensive brain damage, I was left intellectually impaired because I couldn't talk.

But they were wrong! My brain functioned normally a few months after my stroke, even though I had difficulty speaking.

Concerning the inability to talk, I have to admit that I'm guilty of that type of reaction too. Before my stroke, I looked at people differently, especially if they were unable to talk.

Now I have compassion and see people through a different filter. There are times I think to myself, *I wonder if another Einstein is sitting right there.*

The lesson here is: Never judge anyone because of speaking impairment!

Claire Wineland died just a few years after the speech I watched on YouTube. I listened to it again and again, and also listened to all her other speeches. We may have been strangers in real life, but I felt enormously connected to her.

Just before I went out to speak to my own audience, I watched her video again. I was extremely nervous at first, but in the end, it went pretty well and I'm so glad I overcame my doubts and did it anyway.[22,23]

After my speech, I looked up Claire Wineland. I felt compelled to learn more about her life, where she lived, and what her hobbies were. Singing was one of her interests.

Claire was an American activist and author. Through her nonprofit organization Claire's Place Foundation, she worked to support and organize people with terminal and chronic illnesses and their families.[24] I knew she had died not long after her lung transplant, and then I saw the cause of her death.

The strong connection that I felt with her revealed itself.

She had died due to a stroke at 21 years of age, a blood clot that cut off blood flow to the right side of her brain.

Chapter 32

Stress

"I know it's already 2 now, but I wouldn't ask on such short notice if it weren't important! Can you and your husband come in this afternoon? OK, it's not a problem at 5 o'clock. Yes, about your daughter Madeleine. No, I can't say anything now. OK! I'll meet you here in the children's department then, around 5:30. Bye!"

The children's doctor hung up the phone. She had called me in the afternoon on Friday, April 11, 2014, to schedule an appointment that same day regarding my youngest daughter.

Looking back, it seems to me that this was the exact moment in time when my stressful life turned into a life of chronic stress. (If you're interested in what happened that day after the call I just described, reread chapter 15.) The emotional rollercoaster ride that we came to endure in the following weeks marked the start of my period of chronic stress.

It is essential to become better educated about how stress can cause devastating damage to the brain. Often referred to as the "silent killer," stress weakens the brain[1,2] and may cause it to shrink.[3,4] Stress also promotes brain inflammation,[5,6,7] upsets brain function, and leads to an increased risk of contracting Alzheimer's[8,9] and other inflammatory diseases. Stress makes people perform under par as well because it takes up space in their "working memory," thus leaving less memory available for the task at hand.[10,11,12]

Up to a certain point, just a little stress isn't bad since that is the body's standard mechanism for confronting the challenges of life. But once it goes further than that, it negatively impacts quality of life. Stress is the body's natural response to a specific set of stimuli, and it's designed to provide this necessary stress response. According to the CDC (Centers for Disease Control and Prevention), 90% of diseases have at least an element of stress that contributes to them.[13]

Stress can arrive in different forms, and those forms often overlap. Chemical, physical, and psychological stress can be distinguished by their origins.

Chemical stress sources include air pollutants, medicine, insecticides, specific food additives and preservatives, and certain cosmetic products.[14,15,16] These can cause dizziness, sickness, and headaches.

Physical stress[17,18] is any situation caused by overuse, injury, and illness. For example, broken or fractured bones, pulled muscles from a fall, sleeping disorders, allergies, overtraining, and nutritional deficiencies can all cause physical stress.

Psychological stress refers to the emotional and physiological reactions when a person confronts a situation in which the demands go beyond what he or she can handle.

There are also situations where different types of stress are related to the same event. As an example, think of someone who has developed back and shoulder pain, a form of physical stress, because his job requires him to pick up heavy boxes every day. Psychological stress, [19,20,21] for example, might also build up because of social pressure and calling in sick from work.

In my case, I had to deal with psychological stress because I was juggling a family and the demands of my professional life. That existing stress level increased as I worried continually about my daughter's health. Whether lifestyle-imposed, self-imposed or from unexpected sources, the ticking time bomb of stress factors exploded for me about two months later.

I went for a 20-km run that day. After my run, I felt awkward. I had a lot of neurological symptoms. Since I firmly believed that burnout was only for weak people, never me, my anxious search began. I felt compelled—pressured by my own perfectionist nature—to find a cure for the symptoms I had developed, ranging from tingling arms and head to sleeplessness. If I look back on it now, those symptoms were the forerunner of my stroke, which also happened on the second Friday of April, exactly two years later. My body was giving off ample warning signals, but I chose to ignore them.

In day-to-day practice, the brain deals with all stressors in the same way. Let's illustrate how your brain works. For instance, you may be walking down the street at night and see that a dark path is the shortest route to your destination. However, your brain detects a problem if you decide to take that route. The amygdala [22] (your emotional brain, responsible for making instinctive choices) steps in. The fight-or-flight response of the amygdala should kick in as you wonder if it's safe to go down that dark path. Your amygdala will then connect with the hypothalamus, the central part of the brain that has a variety of functions. One of its most important tasks is creating a link between the brain and the rest of the body through the autonomic nervous system (which has a sympathetic and parasympathetic part) and hormones. The nervous system coordinates the actions to be taken by transmitting signals to and from different parts of the body.

When the so-called sympathetic nervous system[23,24] activates a fight-or-flight response, it immediately increases the heart rate, shuts down the blood supply to the gut, and elevates the stress hormone cortisol.[25] The blood is diverted to the muscles because the body is preparing to go into battle while the immune system is simultaneously intentionally suppressed for a while. This is the function of the sympathetic nervous system.

When the danger has passed, the parasympathetic nervous system (also called the rest-and-digest system) takes over again. This is the part of the brain responsible for rest, replenishing nutrients, repairing cells, and regenerating—which is an expensive process metabolically. When your body is stressed, this is the procedure that unfolds, and this highly effective stress-response system has kept us alive for millennia. Your 21st-century body remembers its ancestral biological patterns. For that reason, it reenacts the same type of stress response it would have thousands of years ago, when a bear chased you.

When you are under chronic stress, like I was before my stroke, your sympathetic nervous system is repeatedly firing. I was in fight-or-flight mode for most of the day, and my parasympathetic nervous system never had enough time to rest, repair, and regenerate my cells. I was not aware of what could be heading my way health-wise, and I ignored my instincts and any flashing danger signs just as I had for years. Slowly but surely, I was reaching a state that was totally out of balance and on the verge of collapse.

If I had known how to at the time, I could have stimulated my parasympathetic nervous system, thus allowing me to regenerate. But back then, I was unaware of how to activate those procedures and encourage my body to begin healing itself. In the next chapter, I will explain how to do that.

If you want to reduce stress through better nutrition, you should consider reducing or completely cutting refined sugar out of your diet. A stressed body produces more cortisol, and cortisol is the hormone responsible for managing both blood sugar levels and stress. When your sugar level spikes, the body must release more cortisol to rebalance the blood sugar. Additionally, rapid increases in blood sugar levels can make you more anxious and stressed. Artificial sweeteners also have side effects that can lead to stress. Aspartame, for example, is found in more than 6,000 foods and drinks.[26,27,28] If I think back to my heavy consumption of Coke Zero, this was probably one more contributing factor to my body's overall lack of well-being.

We also know that stress creates a toxic environment for the microbiome in your gut. If you live in a constant state of stress, you create a toxic environment that suffocates the healthy bacteria that are meant to reside in your gut.

Lack of sleep will raise your stress level,[29,30] since it is entirely reasonable to get stressed about sleeplessness. The vicious cycle is then evident: "Lack of sleep also raises your stroke risk—even if you're relatively young and healthy." Research has found that those who cut back their sleep to less than six hours per night are at a fourfold higher risk of having a stroke compared to those who sleep seven to eight hours a night.[31,32]

I was one of those sleep-deprived people. I pushed my already fatigued brain to the limit, working more hours than I could handle, hardly ever taking time for myself. An added factor was that, a year and a half before my stroke, I took antibiotics for two and a half months because I thought

I had Lyme disease. In retrospect, I think it was straightforward burnout that I chose to ignore, although no one knows for sure.

By drinking Coke Zero all day as well as having a glass of wine at night, my gut had no time to recover from the antibiotics I was ingesting. The lack of sleep made it harder to get out of my increasingly depleted mental and physical state, and that added even more stress to my body. The doctors are still not sure what caused my stroke, but I'm relatively certain that all of those stress factors accumulated, compounded, and played their part.

Then, even in the months following my stroke, I was obsessed with the idea of doing rigorous and repetitive training for several hours each day. It allowed hardly any time to relax and feel refreshed. The Perfectionist Me thought, *If I work extremely hard, I will be out of this clinic in no time.*

That pattern of thinking was completely wrong, and I paid for it in the months that followed. My sleep was negatively affected by my stress levels when I was in recovery, especially with the limited timeframe that was counting down. Little wonder, then, that I was worried about every aspect of my life and the burden of my perceived recovery time limits. I was a sleepless workaholic.

Chapter 33

Unstress

Seneca, one of the leading Stoic philosophers, certainly got it right about 2,000 years ago when he said, "Our minds must relax. They will arise better and keener after rest." He wrote this in his book *The Shortness of Life.*[1]

This is easier said than done. In our current, hectic world, we must actively make the decision to relax our minds and then take the necessary steps to achieve this. So, how do you relax your mind?

There are many ways to achieve a peaceful and rested mind. Aiming for a good night's sleep is the first step. Add some pure enjoyment like a hobby or walk on the beach.

Let's move beyond the obvious options and on to other, more unusual ideas to help you relax.

I've spent the last two years researching this topic and experimenting through trial and error to discover ways to truly achieve relaxation. I can happily share that I have a more relaxed mind than I thought possible. In spite of my brain damage, I have a serene sense of clarity that was not part of my life before.

This state of mind does not happen from one day to the next. Like all processes in the brain, the processes that create a relaxed brain develop by adapting your habits incrementally. Sleep better, eat better, take the right supplements, do yoga, meditation,[2,3,4,5,6] work out, and spend time with family and real friends.

Before my stroke, I was always chasing things that I thought should be part of my reality, like wealth, success, and status. Going through a severe stroke shifts your mindset and focus. These days, I don't really care about the things I was chasing before. Friends, family, love, and life purpose are most important. My life is abundant when I'm with loved ones. I also sold my company and started a new one that is much more meaningful to me.

I must admit, I am still a beginner in this area. This means that I am not a specialist who has it completely figured out. However, you may be able to benefit from my experiences, so I'll share how I gave my parasympathetic nervous system a chance to recover from the self-inflicted stress I put it through for so many years. The lessons I've learned in the past two years might be beneficial to you or someone you know and shorten recovery time.

Emotional Stress

The first tool is meditation. Some people call meditation "an aerobic training for your brain, for your prefrontal cortex."[7] As I mentioned before, I did meditation with an app called Headspace[8] for 10-15 minutes a day. That worked well for a while. But after using it for a year and a half, I changed my meditation and began to get remarkable results.

I had watched a YouTube video called "Why you should forgive people that hurt you" by Vishen Lakhiani, the founder of Mindvalley.[9] Lakhiani talks about "40 Years of Zen," a program developed by biohacker Dave Asprey.[10] He hooked up a machine to the brainwaves of monks who had been meditating for at least 21 years, sometimes up to 40 years. A biohacking model crunched the results to help develop programming neurofeedback targets in meditation. Comparing the brainwaves of activities with the brainwave states of the monks revealed revolutionary results: Radical forgiveness is by far the most effective way to get a brain that is comparable to those monks in a short amount of time!

I looked up "useful forgiveness meditation" and found Ziva Meditation by Emily Fletcher to be quite helpful.[11] She has her own courses within the Mindvalley app. Also, Michael Beckwith's sessions on Mindvalley are a great resource.[12][13]

Forgiveness

Let's put the pieces of this puzzle together by linking it to our brain. What does forgiveness have to do with meditation? Two words (as I read on Emily Fletcher's website): grey matter.

Researchers discovered that the more grey matter a person has in his or her brain, the more likely that person is to forgive those who made a serious mistake.[14] Meditators turned out to have relatively larger volumes of grey matter, especially in their right hippocampus (the lateral lobe of the brain). Both orbitofrontal (the front of the brain above the eyes) and hippocampal (memory) regions have been implicated in emotional regulation and response control.[15][16] More grey matter in the brain has a high correlation with the meditators' ability to have positive emotions, emotional stability, and engage in more mindful behavior.[17][18]

With this information, I realized that I needed to forgive myself and others that had hurt me in the past. We have to do this using love and compassion. That means not only forgiving them but spending two minutes thinking about that person and how they hurt you. Picture them in front of you, and forgive them. Finally, hug that person (in real life or your mind). Your empathy allows you to understand why they hurt you.

Think of the person from a larger perspective. Hurt people hurt. He or she might have had failing parents as a child. They may have been abused or perhaps never truly loved. According to many studies, people who were hurt in their younger lives are more likely to hurt others later in life.

Maybe George Eliot was right when she wrote, "The highest form of knowledge is empathy."[19] George Eliot was actually Mary Ann Evans (1810-81), a woman using a male pen name, which allowed her to become one of the leading writers of the Victorian era.

I started forgiving small things first. I forgave the unknown guy that called out, "You stupid drunk!" when I wiggled out of a restaurant, unable to walk perfectly yet. The wiggling was caused by my stroke; I hadn't been drinking alcohol for a year and a half. In forgiving him, I had to imagine him having a mother who was drunk most of the time, and I must have reminded him of her, being there with my eight-year-old daughter.

Then I forgave the waitress who rolled her eyes while taking my order. It was evident that she thought I was stupid since it took me quite a while before I could pronounce what I was going to order. Who knows, maybe her boyfriend had just broken up with her, so she couldn't show any patience or understanding toward me.

I started to focus on specific things that may have impacted me more. I had to forgive one of the doctors at Klimmendaal for her behavior in a meeting regarding my brace. I was in the middle of trying to tell the doctors and brace maker that the foot brace I recently received did not fit at all. However, with a contemptuous look, she cut me off when I was halfway through my sentence, sneering, "Can you go to your swimming session now, Linda?" Perhaps she had a sick child.

It was time to start forgiving myself for quite a few things, too, like taking both of the children to daycare at such a young age. Maarten went at the age of six months, and Elle started when she was only two months. I had to forgive myself for not being at important family birthdays, for not being there when my brother and his wife came to visit me in Amsterdam 26 years ago, even though I said I would be. I had a list of things in mind that made me feel regretful.

Eventually, it was time to address the significant people and things that had wounded me. I had to forgive the doctor that kept me waiting for five and a half hours, even though I was having a severe stroke! Maybe she was too inexperienced in stroke treatment or not aware that young people can have strokes too. Perhaps it was difficult to see that I had a stroke in the initial CT scan. Maybe she didn't give me the MRI because she was ordered not to use an "expensive" MRI scan "so much?"

Despite sending the hospital several emails over the last few years, asking for a copy of the CT scan with my medical file, I have never received the CT scan picture. At this point, I have to take a deep breath and say, "Never mind."

Let's say it wasn't visible on the first CT scan. Did they keep me waiting because there was an emergency elsewhere in the hospital and that particular doctor was needed? Or did she try to return but got some bad news, perhaps something as extreme as her mother dying?

I have to admit that it was challenging to forgive her, and I had to come up with some creative excuses. But eventually, I succeeded in forgiving her. After that, I felt such a sense of relief. I didn't want to continue carrying the subconscious load of people that had hurt me over the years.

Before my stroke, I was highly sensitive to the behavior of others. Without meaning to, I retained in my subconscious the insensitive remarks and thoughtless actions of other people. I also made a remarkably successful effort to hide this sensitivity to the outside world. I have stopped doing that now and instead use "forgiveness meditation" regularly.

Stoic Philosophy

Stoicism taught me lessons about how to keep calm in this chaotic world. Not only does this philosophy teach us how to live well and become better humans, it can also aid in overcoming the difficult moments in life. Now I think "awesome challenge" as soon as things go in a different way than I expected. That means fewer worries. As I told you in a previous chapter, one of the main principles within stoicism is differentiating between things that are within our control and things that are not.

Crying

Indeed, crying does help get rid of stress.[20] The amygdala,[21][22] the area of the brain that controls emotional processing, sends a signal to the hypothalamus,[23] which connects your brain to your autonomic nervous system. The autonomic nervous system handles primitive functions that you usually don't control, like body temperature, hunger, thirst—and crying. Emotional tears contain an excellent natural painkiller called leucine enkephalin.[24,25,26] That's a good explanation for why you might feel better after a good cry.

In Japan, there's a communal event, "rui-katsu" (tear-seeking), when people get together to watch sad film clips and then cry to relieve stress.[27]

Chemical Stress

Enough about emotional stress—what about chemical stress? That can sometimes be caused by specific medication.[28,29] I believe that we should take as little medication as possible (of course, first consult with your doctor for his or her approval).

Natural Antibiotics

Last month, I got a bladder infection from sitting on a cold bench. A few years ago, I would have gotten antibiotics and begun to take them immediately. But not this time. I began to search for "natural antibiotics" on the internet. You may have heard that cranberry juice can help, but only if it's real cranberry juice, not the type of "cranberry drink" that is primarily apple juice with a small percentage of cranberry juice in it and a lot of added sugar.

As I continued my search, I found other foods that are considered "natural antibiotics."[30,31,32] These include honey, garlic, ginger, thyme essential oil, goldenseal, oregano, and many more. It worked! It took three weeks to get over my bladder infection in a natural way, but I will use this natural recipe if I ever get an infection again. Having learned the hard way that too many antibiotics can be devastating for your body's internal balance, I will only use antibiotics when absolutely necessary.

Food

Returning briefly to a few lines on food, I wrote about some of the more common stress-inducing foods in the last chapter. Now I will share what to eat to optimize your gut flora.[33, 34, 35, 36] Eat foods that are high in probiotics such as green bananas, kefir, vegetables, juice, and fermented vegetables and sweet potatoes that have been lying in the fridge for 24 hours.[37, 38, 39] Also, take omega-3 from krill oil, healthy fats, and natural sweeteners such as raw honey. Lastly, try to avoid all processed food and genetically modified food (I know this is difficult, but the payoff is worth it).

Physical Stress

Let's move on to physical stress.

Hormesis

Can you use "mild, short-lived stressors" to your body to become resilient to physical stress? Yes, I believe you can: Hormesis![40] Just as a muscle grows after you exercise and work out (when you give it enough rest), using hormesis, in my experience, makes me more resilient to stress. I have told you before what I feel like right after taking a cold shower—like "I own the world." That reminds me of what John Eliot says in his book *Overachievement*, that "the greatest performers eat stress like an energy bar."[41] I think I'll have to work on that!

My Ikigai

By discovering my "ikigai," I also found my biggest stress-reducer. This revealed itself when I read the book *Ikigai* by Hector Garcia and Frances Miralles.[42][43] What is ikigai, and what does it have to do with the parasympathetic nervous system?

Ikigai is Japanese and means "a reason for being." This word usually refers to the source of value in one's life or the things that make one's life worthwhile. My ikigai nowadays finds its cause in helping stroke survivors achieve their best recovery through the Brain.rehab portal.

What is the connection between finding your ikigai and helping your parasympathetic nervous system? It's not that difficult to guess. Finding your ikigai brings clarity.[44]

When I think about it, this is what I had been searching for before—not wealth and status, but a way to "matter" in this world. I'm determined to keep on doing that until I die, whether I get paid for it or not. And one more thing: Did you know that there is no word for "retirement" in certain Japanese dialects?

I've been thinking about *memento mori* a lot—in a positive way. *Memento mori* can be translated from Latin as "Remember (that) you will die."[45] The point of this reminder isn't to be morbid or promote fear but to inspire and motivate you and clarify your life's purpose. Coming so close to death, I've been given a second chance in life, and I'm committed to doing everything I can to not screw this up!

I'm determined that at my funeral one day, people won't give speeches to remember me like "She was always working hard in her business," or "You could depend on her being timely about answering her email," or any business-related qualities for that matter. Instead, I hope they will say, "She was a great, caring mother, partner, and friend, and she gave hope to and inspired many other stroke survivors."

There is no quick fix for this, and I know that. After my stroke, it took me two years to feel reasonably balanced. However, implementing the right habits will help you improve in small steps every day.

I have decided that my life should not be led in the same way as before, when I was living my life with my eyes closed.

I almost died three years ago.

Michael Bernard Beckwith,[46] the Zen meditation specialist I learned from on Mindvalley, calls these "kensho" moments. Kensho is an awakening that comes from a painful event in your life.[47] Living through this painful event helps you grow into a more complete human.

My stroke was an enormous kensho moment for me. I'm not (yet) able to eat my stress like an energy bar, but this second round in life has already opened my eyes wide.

And I really, really, really, really, *really* like what I see.

Chapter 34

Habits

Author and entrepreneur James Clear said, "The more you repeat a behavior, the more you reinforce the identity associated with that behavior."[1] The word identity was initially derived from a Latin word that means "being" and another that means "repeatedly." Therefore, "identity" is "repeated beingness."[2,3] Identity emerges from your habits.

"Wow, I'm glad it's still working. Lucky you!" a friend told me. She was referring to my left thumb that I could move a little bit. I had shown her, rather proudly, my recent ground-breaking move. *Luck,* I thought, *has nothing to do with it.* But I chose not to say anything. Instead, I just nodded. If she only knew!

Luck, realistically, does not exist. You see, most of the things that happen to us aren't random but instead products of our daily habits. I had worked *hard* on my habits, my exercise habits in this particular case, and it eventually paid off. I started with my shoulder, then upper arm, lower arm, wrist, and finally, my thumb. It took me two years and eight months to move my thumb one centimeter. Talk about a case of delayed gratification!

It was hell at times, all that training, the plateaus, and the doctors and therapists that said I would hardly recover after six months. But I'm proud of myself for proving them wrong. Arjan's pre-crawling exercises certainly had something to do with it, but I can't prove the direct link. And I still have a long way to go. Perhaps I will be fully recovered in 10 or 15 years. There's no need to think about that, though. Instead, I will enjoy what is happening now.

I still have research to do on several subjects, for instance, how to rebuild the brain map of my left hand. We usually think of maps as illustrating the space outside our bodies. But the body is also a space that can be mapped, and your brain needs this map to make sense of the world.

There is a 3D example of your brain's map of your own body called the "homunculus of man."[4,5] (Google that word and you'll see examples). It looks like a ridiculous alien with huge hands and lips. The homunculus represents the somatosensory cortex that maps out your body space, primarily based on movement information and touch but also other sensations such as pain. Your motor cortex, which commands your muscles to move, also has a body map (an equally ridiculous-looking homunculus).

A classical study of musicians done by Thomas Elbert and colleagues suggests that the maps in our brains change with experience[6,7]—specifically, with frequently-used parts of the map expanding into neighboring space, while underused parts shrink in cortical real estate. The musicians had increased cortical representation of the fingers of the left hand in string players. That's brain plasticity!

Reading this reminded me of the period when I had unbearable pain. If I understand it correctly, I managed to shrink the cortical representation of the pain maps through visualization of the pain maps in my head and body getting smaller and smaller. Result: zero pain.

By moving my thumb again and again, my brain will make the brain map of my thumb and the motor cortex of my thumb more "important" and stronger. Eventually (I hope), it will be an automatic movement, meaning I won't have to watch my thumb as I concentrate on moving it.

I still need to do more research about the most recent discoveries on these topics. During the past few years, I read that some cells around the affected stroke area are not dead but merely dormant and that the formation of new nerve cells (neurogenesis) is possible. With the correct type of stimulation, there might even be a possibility of either waking up those neurons or purposefully stimulating the formation of new neurons.[8,9] But I'll need to write a whole second book on that...

So, let's go back to the process of forming habits. Getting accustomed to daily habits was the only thing that kept me going after my stroke. I persistently stuck with my new routine for sleeping, exercising, eating healthy, and so on. Because of this, I went from hardly any results in the first year (I could walk with a cane and foot brace, but that was about it) to where I am now. I'm talking, walking, and can even run again.

How did I accomplish that? By putting the right habits in place!

During this period of research, I read several excellent books about habits, such as *Atomic Habits* by James Clear,[10] *Game Changers* by Dave Asprey,[11] and *Mini Habits: Smaller Habits, Bigger Results* by Stephen Guise.[12]

What is a habit anyway? A habit is a routine or practice performed regularly, and it is also an automatic response to a specific situation. One fundamental lesson I learned from these books is that seemingly small and unimportant changes in the beginning, can compound to become a remarkable change in your life, if you are willing to stick with them for years. I really liked that!

I thought about the tennis ball I hung in the door opening, the one I hit with a racket. Everyone thought I was crazy when I explained that I was doing it to relearn how to play ping-pong one day. But eventually, I did.

Being able to move my left thumb was a significant breakthrough. Breakthrough movements are often the result of many previous and consecutive actions.

The stages of progress with my thumb remind me of James Clear's example of bamboo. Bamboo plant[13] can barely be seen for the first five years of its life as it builds an extensive network of roots (my neurons) underground (in my head). Once the system has finalized and stabilized, the bamboo explodes into the air. My thumb may not have exploded, but it was now moving one centimeter! And the set of actions and habits I described before had made this possible.

If you manage to work on your good habits every day, they will combine and compound for remarkable results!

It is not easy to keep up with good habits, I know that. The results may seem drawn out and delayed, especially if you are a stroke survivor, since it may take years to see results. You'll need to have faith and continue to stick with it as you celebrate every small victory that comes your way.

How do we create good habits, and how do we lose bad habits? Many ideas are listed in the books mentioned above and in a variety of research papers. I'm going to suggest a few things that worked for me.

First, ask yourself this question: Who do I want to become with these new habits? (James Clear, *Atomic Habits*) This is called the "identity approach." Each action you take is a "vote" for the person you want to become. If performed regularly, it becomes automatic. Your brain does that to save energy and free up space for other things that may be more important. From the starting point, it takes approximately two months to form a habit. Researchers also suggest that "time and place" along with identity are essential when forming a habit.

Second, I'll share some of the habits I put in place for my post-stroke routine:

I exercise first thing each morning, and the result is that I don't have to think about it anymore. It has now become a habit.

Identity: sporty
Time: first thing in the morning
Place: in the basement

Next, I practice my speech in front of a daylight lamp

Identity: someone who speaks perfectly
Time: after my morning workout
Place: at the table with a daylight lamp

My day usually goes just like that. Sometimes, I mix my morning routines around, if I decide to something like writing first.

If you think it is too challenging to begin to form a certain habit, then take "mini habits" from the process. In the book *Mini Habits* by Stephen Guise, he suggests that it's the ultimate way to start forming habits. The author of that book couldn't get himself to exercise for half an hour. No matter what he tried, he couldn't make himself do it. Then he thought, *I'll just do one push-up. That's not so bad.* Doing that one push-up led him to think, *I could do two push-ups,* which led to three, four, and five push-ups.

The same concept can apply to taking a cold shower (initiating hormesis) for two seconds. You can do that, can't you? Then it leads to 10 seconds, and before you know it, you've done it for three minutes.

Maybe writing isn't your thing but you have a story to tell. If so, write one sentence a day—just one. I did precisely that when I began to write my book. I managed to write one sentence, then two, then three, and finally, I had created the first whole page.

Can you meditate for between 10-30 minutes at a time? If not, no problem! Take it slowly. Meditate for one minute instead of 10 minutes, and proceed from there.

Have you lost your ability to speak as a result of a stroke? If you have aphasia, you can begin by practicing one word (or sound).

If you have lost all your math skills after your stroke, then do one sum a day. I lost all my math knowledge on the day of my stroke. I didn't know what 1 + 1 was. Eventually, I got the basics back, but I used the resources of the Khan Academy to learn how to add and multiply again.[14] So, just practice one sum each day. That's how I got started on all of my habits. Make it easy for yourself, and build it up. But, you will need to be consistent and do it every day.

Afterward, some people might call it "an overnight success," but you will know it is due to the work you did in stages, slowly and surely, for many months before.

If you have problems with your working memory, use N-Back! Working memory is part of short-term memory.

The n-back test was introduced by Wayne Kirchner in 1958 to improve working memory. My suggestion to you: Get the N-Back app on your phone and use it every day as a (mini) habit.[15]

In *Game Changers*, I read about fluid intelligence. Working memory is critical to fluid intelligence—a concept developed by psychologist Raymond B. Cattell and later expanded on by John Horn.[16,17,18,19] Fluid intelligence is the ability to synthesize new information by solving problems without preexisting knowledge. Your IQ score measures your crystallized intelligence, the sum of your lifetime learning experience. You can raise your IQ, but it does not matter as much as your ability to process information through fluid memory.

Until quite recently, psychologists who studied intelligence all agreed that you could not increase your fluid intelligence. Then in 2008, scientists Susanne Jaeggi and Martin Buschkuehl found that young adults who practiced a version of the game also showed improvement.[20] After five weeks of practicing for half an hour each day, fluid intelligence within the subject group increased on average by 40%.

How does the game work? The game consists of randomly appearing numbers and words on the screen. For example, "1-N" implies that you have to remember the position of the item one turn back. And "2-N" means that you have to remember the position of the item two turns back, and so on.

Why am I telling you all of this? If you have aphasia and want to improve verbal working memory, this is a good tool. Create a mini habit of using it for five minutes a day. Speech rate and speech timing (how fast you speak) is based on your verbal working memory.

If you are willing to implement better habits, the sky's the limit for better changes in your life. All habits have something in common: They may be challenging to start and maintain in the beginning, but with discipline and practice, they can become almost second nature. You don't have to even think about it! It's like brushing your teeth every morning, you don't have to argue with yourself, "Am I going to brush my teeth or not?" You just do it, since it's a habit.

After my stroke, I was confronted with how vital habits are. I understood that if I was going to recover, I needed to create habits of reading about the latest research, doing the same exercises over and over again, practicing my speech, and several other daily things that I previously mentioned. Sometimes, I don't see any tangible progress for months. But I continue the habit, and eventually, boom! There is the result!

What about bad habits, things like binge-watching television, eating junk food, and staying rooted in limited beliefs? Using the identity approach worked like a charm for me. It's simple: Make a habit of NOT binge-watching television (gain knowledge by reading instead) and eating junk food (because you want to be fit). It's hard in the beginning, but hold out for just two months. Then it will have become a habit, and you won't have to think about it anymore.

Swapping out your limited beliefs through the right habits is crucial if you want to progress, especially in your recovery. Psychiatrists sometimes call this "writing in your best self diary."

For the last three years, I have done just that. When I talk about limited beliefs, I mean internal comments such as:

"I am not a writer."

"I cannot remember what I'm going to say in the lecture."

"I'm not good at math since my stroke."

"I will not get any better from my stroke after six months."

These beliefs are within you because some of them were taught to you by others and some you've taught yourself.

Whatever the source, unchecked, they can be devastating to your growth because they form an upper limit.

In the words of neuroscientist and best-selling author Robert Cooper, PhD, limited beliefs "derive from an embedded performance code from 2,000 years ago."[21] The brain wants to be safe and under control. It wants you to survive at any cost. Stay the same, if you want, and don't go out and do any "risky" activities. Your brain fears change, and it likes to keep you the same, safe person you have always been to conserve energy. Cooper calls this process engaging in a "downwire."

Upwiring requires much more effort and more risks. You have to aim your brain away from its comfortable default mode and steer it towards intentionally challenging choices (like giving a public speech, which was far outside my comfort zone) to support the kind of growth you want to achieve.

Our instinct is to do things in the same way that we always have (habit). This may work on a day-to-day basis, like driving the same route to work every day and not thinking much about it. But always converting to automatic behavior can be a detriment to innovative thinking.

Many people also begin to notice that their brains seem to be downwiring as they age.[22] But it doesn't have to be that way.

What if I had allowed my brain to always be in safe mode? I would not have taken the risky step of trying to walk without a walking cane and brace.

If I ask myself what the process of creating a routine of daily habits brought me during the last three years, the answer is simple: a lot!

Without the habits I formed, there would be no book (getting up at 5 a.m. to write).

If I hadn't started a habit of reading, there would be no book either. You get what you repeat. I learn from each new book I read. Not only that, I'm opening up to new ideas and learning how to see things differently. American businessman and philanthropist Warren Buffet said, "That's how knowledge works. It builds up like compound interest."[23]

Habits are the path to changing your identity. The most pragmatic way to change who you are is by changing what you do.

Be patient. If you have good habits, you are moving ahead. If not, change your bad habits. My practices of biohacking the brain to improve sleep, eat better food, and exercise brought me further than my doctors ever imagined. I have asked myself: Who do you want to become with these new habits? The answer: I want to do practically everything I could before my stroke, and become a more centered, happier human being.

What about you? What's the best script you can write for yourself? Who do you want to become?

I want to close this chapter with a quote from Aristotle, who got it right around 300 BC:

"We are what we repeatedly do. Excellence is not an act but a *habit*."[24]

Chapter 35

The Plastic Brain

"What's wrong?" I had called Arjan on FaceTime, and he could see by the look on my face that something was bothering me.

"Do you know Dr. Kandel?" I asked.

"Dr. Eric Kandel, the neuroscientist, and Nobel Prize winner?"[1] he responded.

"Yes," I said.

"Yes, I read all of his books. He's awesome, and a true hero, a pioneer of modern brain science," he responded. I was quiet. "Hello, can you still hear me?"

"Shoot," I said.

"Why are you asking about him?"

I explained to Arjan that I had been listening to fellow biohacker Dave Asprey's podcast, and Dr. Kandel was the interview subject. "Listen to the podcast," I said. Then I hung up.

The interview was about his latest book, *The Disordered Mind.*[2] When Asprey asked, "Does this mean when someone has a structural problem in his brain, that they are stuck? If you get hit in the head when you were a child and that part of the brain is not doing what it is supposed to do, is there any hope?"

Dr. Kandel answered, "If it's a child, yes. For instance, if you have damaged your left hemisphere, which is involved in speech, and if that occurs to you as an adult, you have something which is very unlikely to recover its normal function."

Arjan called me back. "Don't worry about it," he said. "He is a hero alright, but he is not an expert on stroke recovery."

"That's easy for you to say," I said, wiping tears from my face. "What if he's right? That I will never speak normally again?"

I was excited that my speech had improved by practicing every day and reading out loud. I thought my speech had also improved through playing N-Back. But I didn't tell people I was doing it because I only began two weeks before and wanted to feel confident that it worked before I recommended it.

If I could learn how to walk again, why couldn't I learn how to talk normally again? I couldn't understand it! Would I suddenly stop making improvements one day—even though I practice every day and practically see improvements every three months? I do understand that children have a much more moldable brain. But I had been eating incredibly healthy food and using the right supplements, I hacked my sleep, I have proper energy management, I hardly drink alcohol, and I use my own personally developed speech exercises every day. Why would it be "highly unlikely" that I got my speech back to normal again?

We will see, I thought. It took me two days to get over what I had heard the doctor say on that podcast.

Luckily, I was listening to an audiobook as well during that period, *Can't Hurt Me* by David Goggins.[3] David Goggins, two years younger than me, is an American ultramarathon runner, ultra-distance cyclist, triathlete, motivational speaker, and author. He is a retired Navy SEAL and former Air Force Tactical Air Control Party member who served in the War in Afghanistan and the Iraq War. If you read his book, believe me, you are cured of any self-pity.

I decided to convert my sadness into fuel and work even harder to recover my speech. My brain is plastic, after all, even though I'm 45 right now and not a child.

Until recently, it was believed that you were born with a set number of brain cells that could never be replaced and that you came into the world with a set level of intelligence that never changed. Now we know that's not true.

Neuroplasticity[4][5][6][7] is derived from two words: neuron (a nerve cell) and plastic (moldable).

The term may sound technical, but (to recap) it refers to your brain's ability to adapt to the environment. It's a lifetime process of reorganizing itself by forming new neural connections. Your brain is a continual work in progress. Although the brain can produce new brain cells and supporting cells, the brain cells' capacity to take on a new function when required and the capacity of the remaining brain structure to remodel and produce a new function are at the core of why you can regain lost function.

The sections below are a bit technical. If that's not your thing, just skip it and move on.

The concept of neuroplasticity has been around for at least 50 years. More than 100 years ago, Ramón y Cajal discovered the capacity of nerve cells to grow.[8] But it is only in the last 20 years that professionals have started to make full use of this potential.

Pioneers such as Taub, Merzenich, and Bach-y-Rita (inventor of the PoNS brain stem device for tongue stimulation) have shown that this concept can be used to great effect when you are dealing with a stroke or brain injury, regardless of the extent (see also the brilliant books about the brain's capacity to heal itself, written by Norman Doidge).[9,10]

Although knowledge of the brain's capacity to change is widely known, the majority of professionals working with someone after a stroke do not know enough to make use of its power or are bound to outdated rehab routines that just aren't cutting it when it comes to regaining lost function (see also the work of John Krakauer, *Broken Movement*).[11]

Let's start from the beginning. The period just after a stroke is literally a crisis situation where damage needs to be contained. The resulting lack of oxygen after stroke leads to oxidative damage and this, in turn, leads to reactive oxygen formation, which is the start of a downward cascade leading to massive damage and the death of neurons and their supporting cells. Inflammation results from a need to clear out damaged and diseased cells. This process must happen before healing and recovery can take place.[12,13]

At the borders of the affected brain areas, supportive cells start to form a barrier to contain damage and aid in the repair process started by inflammation. Glial cells, which are part of the brain's immune system, start to produce so-called cytokines, which are immune system messengers that initiate attacks against foreign material, like a dead neuron.[14,15]

Researchers also found that distant neuronal pools that are normally connected to the damaged areas become affected.[16,17] The brain is a collection of networks of neuronal pools (a group of neurons with the same function) that, in one way or another, connect to each other or have the potential to become connected. The connected neuronal pools become upregulated; they increase in function, most likely to counteract the effect of lost function in the areas affected by the stroke.

This has been observed close to the damaged brain areas as well as in more remote areas such as the brain stem, which is separately linked to much of higher cortical function. These areas literally prepare for what is about to happen. When neurons cease to exist, the axons (a branched extension coming from the neuron, which can travel over many centimeters to decimeters) that come off the neuron to connect with other nerve cells die off. This dying off of cells is called Wallerian degeneration.[18,19,20] The secondary effect that loss of function and death of neurons have on remote areas is called diaschisis.[21,22,23,24]

What I have not yet described is that, when an area becomes dysfunctional after, for example, a stroke, the opposite happens to the same area in the other hemisphere—it becomes more active.[25,26] This is probably a survival mechanism helping you recruit more functions and help from the unaffected side of your body. This is initially a good thing; after all, you have to learn to manage daily tasks again with altered functionality of your body.

However, you do not want this situation to persist for too long. Increased function on one side of your brain suppresses even further the already compromised function, in this case, in the damaged areas. Specific training of the affected body parts, whether speech, leg, or arm function, will help in regaining a more healthy balance.

After a stroke, big parts of the affected area are cut off from previously connected areas. This is largely dependent on the previous state and extent of the stroke.

Other things that have an effect on this outcome are:

- how well the brain was trained before the stroke
- how good the nutritional status was[27,28,29]
- how many mitochondria were present in the cells
- whether there was already a low-grade inflammatory process going on

All can play a major role in the immediate outcome of a stroke. These neurons often become isolated, and even if they survive, they are no longer connected to existing networks. Therefore—albeit alive—they do not have an immediate function any longer.

But there is good news as well. Bordering the walls of the so-called ventricular system,[30,31,32] (a cyst-like network inside your brain that provides vital buffering, protection, and balance for the brain's inner environment) are immature neurons that can migrate to damaged areas, which are usually more situated laterally to the ventricles. Once arrived in the affected areas, they can mature into neurons.[33,34,35,36]

At present, much research is dedicated to finding out how to stimulate these migrators (as well as dormant neurons that survive the stroke) to connect up to existing networks. Of particular interest are the supportive glial cells. They not only mediate the repair process and help contain damage around the affected brain areas by cooperating with astrocytes and other support cells, glial cells also have the capacity to change function and turn into neurons.[37,38,39,40] This is a recent discovery that opens many new possibilities. Supportive brain cells such as microglial cells,[41] astrocytes,[42] and oligodendrocytes[43] greatly outnumber neurons and are often still present in adequate numbers in the areas damaged by stroke.

What happens next in the ideal progression of repair (that is, a situation where inflammation subsides gradually) is that we see so-called neuronal sprouting[44] in the bordering areas. This means the surviving nerve cells start to grow out, stimulated by chemical factors from the damaged areas—a survival response. Much of this spontaneous growth is at random, but researchers also found that the new outgrowth from these neurons reaches and connects to functional areas.

For example, in a middle cerebral artery stroke (the most common), the primary motor cortex is affected in some way. This is the area from where you give conscious commands to initiate movement. The primary motor strip is interconnected and dependent on input from the somatosensory areas situated behind it and from input from so-called premotor areas and supplementary motor areas situated in front of the primary motor strip. All of these areas play key roles in the initiation and continuation of movement and are often not entirely wiped out by the stroke. The neuronal sprouting often reaches bordering areas and allows upregulation of function in these supportive areas, which often can lead to more recovery of lost function. Scientists have indicated that they frequently see increased activity and recovery of function because these areas start to take over tasks of the primary motor cortex.

How does it work? When stimulated or given a command, neurons (nerve cells) make more protein. These proteins not only make the cells more stable, but they can also be used to build nerve tracts, which is the growing of sprouts out of the nerve cell.

When areas in the brain are damaged by a stroke or injury (such as a blow to the head), surviving nerve cells and the healthy nerve cells bordering affected areas can start to take over function when stimulated to do a new task. Nerve cells can switch function because of the DNA inside the center of each cell. Each cell in your body has the complete body blueprint and, depending on where a cell ends up and the circumstances under which it has to operate, will take on different functions. All of the processes described up to this point are also called the neurostimulation phase of neuroplasticity (Norman Doidge described this in *The Brain's Way of Healing*). This is the first phase of neuroplasticity.

The first months after a stroke show the fastest and often most visible recovery. Much of this can be contributed to spontaneous recovery—the body's inbuilt capacity to heal itself and for the remaining neurons, supportive cells, and networks[45,46] to do their work. Usually, if the damage is not too profound, much recovery such as speech and the use of a leg or arm takes place even without therapy. Now, this is a point worth noting: Most help is also given in the first six months after a stroke. It is thus not strange that recovery can take place, after which a plateau usually is reached.

No offense to the physical therapists who are working for you to recover (in the first six months) since they are helping you stand and move your arm and so on. But I think it is likely that you maybe could have recovered to a large extent without having gone to the rehab clinic.

Another reason spontaneous and more rapid recovery takes place in the first months after a stroke is the recruitment of already existing networks of nerve cells with similar or slightly different functions. The brain has the possibility to make use of so-called redundant networks, which when not used often become dormant but still have the capacity of similar function to the damaged networks. These networks can, although often in a less controlled way, take over (some) lost function when stimulated precisely enough. A third reason change is more visible in the first months is that the chaos, depression, and brain inflammation caused by the stroke gradually settle down.

The above process of quieting down the chaos of signals after a stroke is part of the second phase of neuroplasticity; this is also called the neuromodulation phase. The second thing that happens, besides quieting down the chaos,[47,48] is the downregulation of the sympathetic nervous system.

After a stroke, the fight-or-flight part of your nervous system goes into overdrive to defend your body. It helps with the inflammation that is needed to clear out debris. It basically puts your body in survival mode. This is necessary in the initial first weeks but harms the repair process when it persists too long. You do not want your mitochondria to shut off into cell danger response,[49,50] or compromised circulation plus stress hormones going on in the system for too long.

We have to note that this is the ideal situation. The reality is that this often does not happen because of preexisting problems in the brain, such as an overly active limbic system, or poor brain health or nutritional status. The gradual settling down of chaotic and unguided firing within the nervous system after a stroke comes about when repair and recovery have first taken place, and when the appropriate timing and spacing of nerve signaling to vital areas and reticular activation system in the brain stem takes over again. They are scattered groups of neurons that play a major role in postural stability and muscle tone control. They also help the integration of brain networks and play a major role in the activation of higher brain centers. Proper function of these reticular areas[51,52] ensures alignment and coordination of the different networks so that they fire appropriately and in synchrony. Luckily, in most of us that have had a stroke(s), these areas are still intact and can be used for recovery.

The third phase in neuroplasticity is the so-called neural relaxation phase, where your nervous system literally has to recover from all the extra effort you have consciously and unconsciously put into repairing and redirecting function. This is the tiredness, fatigue, and lack of energy and drive that you probably have noticed, especially in the first months after your stroke. The tiredness does not just come from weak mitochondrial function; it often appears on top of that. Sleep, downtime, and recharging rituals are of the utmost importance when you are experiencing these symptoms.

The fourth and last phase of neuroplasticity is also called neural differentiation, when everything has settled down after the initial repair phase, spontaneous recovery, and the calming down of chaos within the central nervous system. It is the phase where the smoke clears, and you can assess the damage.

This is where the real repair starts to take place. The reality for you can be that this differentiation phase only starts when you are already many months into your rehabilitation. It is in this phase that nerve cells and networks can change into and adapt to new functions. What you have to understand is that although neuroplasticity is a gamechanger for recovery after a stroke or any damage to the brain, it is often a random event. If neuroplasticity does not take place in a directed and purposeful way, it will most likely not contribute much to further recovery.[53,54] This implies that you have to educate the areas where the brain has to change into a new function.

As I mentioned earlier, new research also shows that more neurons (nerve cells) survive than previously thought, but they become quiet because they are either in a state of shock, which causes the genetic material to switch into survival (quiet) mode, or simply not connected to a network anymore. Early repair and recovery from the initial shock situation (also called depression of cellular function) make function come back in some of these surviving nerve cells. Many researchers are currently looking into ways to reactivate and recruit these quiet dormant neurons.

Another discovery is perhaps even more exciting. Scientists recently found that supportive cells such as glial cells, which normally facilitate neurons and are part of the brain's immune system, can change into healthy neurons. Because these supporting cells are more numerous than brain cells, this potentially gives new possibilities as well.

There is a catch, though, with the brain's capacity to heal itself. To regain function, the brain parts that need to repair or reorganize have to be stimulated very precisely and with the right intensity. Specificity is the key.[55,56] What this means for you is that you will have to use what is not functioning, even if that seems impossible. Plus, it will take a lot of work—not just months, but possibly years. A very good example of how brain plasticity works is described in the chapter on constraint-induced movement therapy.

How do I personally encourage my brain plasticity?

I assembled a toolbox from what I read and immediately put the theory into practice, in the form of habits.

First of all, I create the perfect basis for the brain and nervous system to participate in optimal neuroplasticity in the form of:

- **The best sleep**, proper nighttime routines, perfect room temperature, no light, reduced blue light exposure (see the chapter on sleep)
- **Optimal brain nutrition**—think krill oil, alpha lipoic acid, N-acetylcysteine, curcumin, and blueberry extract, among others (see "The Blue Zone" chapter)
- **Increased energy levels by optimizing mitochondrial function**, e.g., increase mild, short-lived but intense exposure to stressors such as cold, heat, muscle strain, nutraceutical toxins, etc. (see chapters "The Biohacker Mom" and "What Doesn't Kill Us, Makes Us Stronger")
- **Reduced neuroinflammation**, one of the most overlooked problems after stroke and traumatic brain injury
- **Stress reduction** through optimal breathing, meditation, music, having a good time, and surrounding myself with supportive friends and family (see "Stress" and "Unstress" chapters)

Then, after creating the right basis for neuroplasticity, I specifically focus on retraining purposeful and correct stabilization before undertaking any more sophisticated movement retraining:

- **Core, shoulder, and hip stabilization** practiced to perfection, alongside or before any attempt is made to intensively retrain hand and/or leg/foot movement

I don't pretend to be an expert on neuroplasticity. But I have designed my life as a biohacker and will continue to try out everything to stimulate neuroplasticity. In fact, you can call me a "neuroplasticity guinea pig."

Dr. Eric Kandel used the words "unlikely to recover speech to its normal function." But he didn't say "impossible!"

I am going to do everything in my power to make it possible.

Chapter 36

Swimming Rats

Have you heard about the experiments by Professor Curt Richter[1] in 1957 that involved swimming rats?[2] As a Harvard graduate and Johns Hopkins scientist, he did a series of experiments that tested how long rats could swim in a bucket of water before drowning.

Dr. Richter discovered that, under normal circumstances, a rat could swim for an average of about 15 minutes before quitting (giving up) and sinking. However, if he rescued the rats just before they sank and drowned, dried them off, let them take a brief break, and then put the rats back into the same bucket of water, they could swim an average of 60 hours before drowning! Sixty hours! If a rat was *pro tempore* saved, it would survive 240 times longer than if it was not saved just in time.

Dr. Richter concluded that the rats were able to swim longer because they were given hope.

Maybe a worthier conclusion is that the rats were able to swim longer because they were able to extend their energy from the hope Dr. Richter provided.

You are also capable of much more than you previously thought, that is, if you are given hope.

However, do you have the energy to swim for as long as it takes? If you doubt it, maybe I can help. Previously, I talked about energy as it relates to biohacking and hormesis. I think hormesis is one of the most important things to do regularly to get more energy, but now I will discuss other things that improve your energy level. If you want to recover from a stroke, you need to optimize your energy so you have the strength and stamina to recover. An increased energy level is especially important to give neuroplasticity a chance to recover any lost function.

Your brain uses much of your energy.[3,4,5] After a stroke, it requires even more because it has to put in more effort for the same tasks. It is not as efficient as it once was. Recovery through neuroplasticity also takes more energy. The tiredness and fatigue you experience come from having to compensate all the time and the below-par performance of your mitochondria.

Improving energy levels will involve improving brain function in a structured way, reorganizing brain function as effectively as possible, and addressing the many issues that influence your cellular energy production. If you follow the advice laid out in the previous chapters about sleep and hormesis, you will have more energy. Some additional information follows.

Once again, skip the section below if you find it too technical or complicated.

All of the following have a significant impact on energy production:

- oxygen, circulation, and breathing
- glucose levels
- exercise

- circadian rhythm (daily biorhythms dictated by the sun)
- sleep habits
- water
- stress management
- hormesis (exposing your body to stressors over a short and repetitive period to build energy)
- toxins

Mitochondria appear to play a substantial role not only in energy production but also in immunity and inflammation. Your mitochondria are in either metabolic energy production mode or cell defense mode (also called cell danger response).[6,7,8] This on and off switching is the key to experiencing fatigue or not. Simply put, if you can keep your mitochondria in energy production mode, then you have energy. Anything that pushes the mitochondria into cell danger response makes you feel more tired (unless you have plenty of mitochondria you can use for energy production).

Fatigue is a situation where energy production in your mitochondria is shut off because they have gone into defense mode. For example, when you suddenly need to sleep a lot more, this can be a direct indication of a cell danger response in your mitochondria. Whenever mitochondria sense that viruses, bacteria, or toxins are trying to do damage or feed off energy production, they go into survival mode. That results in low energy.

The following can all cause fatigue because your mitochondria have gone into survival mode:[9,10,11]

- lack of sleep
- medication use
- excess body weight

- high blood sugar levels
- inflammation
- lack of exercise
- psychological stresses and adverse childhood events
- nutrient deficiencies
- lack of hormesis
- poor immune function
- toxins and leaky gut

Most of us have at least five or six of these factors present at any given time. Taking the most expensive supplements or even having the best diet alone will not help enough to improve energy levels when that is the case.

To be more precise, what are the most important triggers for your mitochondria to go into cell defense mode?

1. Blue light emitted by electronic devices at night or in the evening upsets the production of melatonin and your built-in biological clock.[12,13,14] Melatonin is a powerful antioxidant[15,16] protecting your mitochondria. At night, you recharge and repair your mitochondria, so you do not want to upset sleep by the wrong type of light.
2. Vegetable fats high in omega-6 fatty acids, like sunflower, safflower, soy, corn, and canola oils, are often used for cooking. These oils promote inflammation,[17,18,19,20,21] and it is better to avoid them. Inflammation is a significant cause of mitochondria going into defense mode.
3. Food intolerances. Many people have some form of food intolerance(s)[22,23] or even allergies to substances like eggs, dairy, gluten, soy, and nuts. It pays to eliminate any foods containing these substances for a while and then reintroduce them slowly.

4. Sugar is quite damaging to your body, especially high-sugar foods like sodas, candy, cakes, desserts, refined flour products in general, and processed foods. Damage to mitochondria probably only happens in products containing large amounts of sugar,[24,25] such as those named above. Naturally occurring sugars found in fruit and honey do not appear to have the same effect.
5. Advanced glycation end-products result from frying food containing proteins and fats (like bacon) at a high temperature.[26]
6. Food colorings, preservatives, and artificial flavorings. You can do without all of those, and some even have a strong carcinogenic (promotes cancerous growth) effect. They can make mitochondria shut down and go into defense mode.
7. Prescription and over-the-counter drugs. Many of these are damaging to mitochondria.[27,28,29] Long-term use is toxic to mitochondria. Medicines that have this effect include aspirin and NSAIDs, anticonvulsants, analgesics, anesthetics, antibiotics, cholesterol medication like statins, and steroids, for example, those found in asthma medication. You can ask your doctor if there are alternatives that are nontoxic or at least less toxic to mitochondria.
8. Lack of exercise. Now, this is an interesting one. We are biologically hard-wired to exercise. If we do not exercise and stimulate energy production in our mitochondria, our energy factories become dysfunctional. Also, the hormesis (exposure to stressors such as heat, cold, or high-energy exercise) caused by certain types of exercise will promote mitochondrial growth and energy production.
9. Over-exercising can produce a strong shutdown effect on your mitochondria. Going to the maximum at the gym

or running every day can have a detrimental impact on your energy production capacity.[30,31,32] Exercise smart and adapt it to your level of fitness. Make sure you build in an adequate number of recuperation (rest) days as well.

10. Psychological stress causes oxidative stress and damage in your mitochondria, period.[33,34,35]
11. Bacterial and viral infections want direct access to the mitochondrial energy source and will cause mitochondria to go into cell danger response mode.[36,37,38]
12. Insulin resistance causes constant oxidative stress damage inside our cells.[39,40] Too high blood glucose levels due to excess refined sugar in your diet will cause insulin resistance. As a result, the resistance this creates causes a toxic build-up of sugar outside the cells and the production of waste products inside the cell, all of which have a negative effect on the mitochondria.
13. Toxins in our environment are probably one of the biggest causes of mitochondrial dysfunction and even death.[41,42] Pollution in the air, exhaust from cars, and industrial fumes containing benzene and heavy metal traces are highly toxic. There are trace elements of insecticides and pesticides in our tap water as well as medicine residue. Chlorine and fluoride, both added to our drinking water, are also highly toxic to our mitochondria.
14. Fluoride, like that in most toothpaste, influences the metabolic levels of your body, among other things, because it is toxic to the thyroid gland. Decreased thyroid function has a direct effect on the number of mitochondria that are produced.[43]

So, what can you start doing right away to promote your energy production and shut down the cell danger response in your mitochondria?

1. **Remove all processed foods from your diet.** Processed foods contain bisphenols, phthalates (plastic additives), and artificial colorings,[44] and they promote insulin resistance. Start eating whole foods again and try to eat only what your ancestors would have eaten a hundred years ago. You should be able to identify what you eat, and if you can't pronounce the name of a food substance, you probably shouldn't consume it. Basically, if your great grandmother would not be able to identify a food in the grocery store, a food contains ingredients you cannot pronounce, or it has a long shelf life, do not buy it.
2. **Eat as much organic food as possible.** This helps you avoid chemicals like pesticides and herbicides that build up in our food.[45][46][47][48]
3. **Cut down or eliminate alcohol.** Alcohol is a well known mitochondrial toxin.[49]
4. **Install good quality water filters.** Pure water is hard to get these days. Our drinking water still contains many chemicals and traces of harmful substances like medication, fluoride, and chlorine byproducts.[50][51][52]
5. **Ventilate and purify the air in your house**, especially when you are living in industrial areas or a city. Whenever you smell gases or fumes, make sure to do this. It is a known fact that the air inside our house is often more polluted and dangerous for us than being outside.[53][54]
6. **Get rid of kitchen equipment that is full of chemicals**, like Teflon coated pans (can be highly toxic, especially when your pan is getting older) and cheaply produced ceramic-coated pans, which often contain heavy metals, etc.[55][56][57]
7. **Replace non-natural health and beauty products with organically based products.** Our shower products, facial

creams, perfumes and colognes, and other types of makeup are often riddled with all sorts of unhealthy substances. Hormone-disrupting chemicals that affect estrogen and testosterone levels, heavy metals, and other mitochondrial toxins are common in these products.[58, 59, 60, 61]

8. **Replace cleaning products with naturally based cleaning products.**[62]

When mitochondria go into cell defense mode, it's as if they are squeezed like a sponge. Many of the vital minerals and necessary nutrients are washed out.[63] These include magnesium, vitamin Bs, ubiquinol (COQ10), potassium, ATP, and ADP, to name a few. All of these play a major role in the energy-producing cycles within mitochondria. Losing these components is exactly how energy production is halted.

It is also important to note that damage to mitochondria is directly associated with aging.[64, 65, 66, 67] The more accumulated damage, the faster you age. That's something we don't want to happen, right?

So, what can you do to improve energy production, and repair and lower oxidative stress, besides removing all the factors that make mitochondria go into defense mode?

There are several ways to boost mitochondrial function, for example, eating foods that are good for your mitochondria (when you can tolerate them) and using compounds that build energy stores.

Foods that boost mitochondrial function include:[68, 69, 70]

- dark leafy vegetables
- shellfish
- fish eggs
- liver

- egg yolks
- avocados
- seaweed

Damaged mitochondria can be repaired, and there are specific foods and food components that can be used to do that. There is one element of the utmost importance for this, in particular, and that is phospholipids. In some studies, additional supplementation with phospholipids was responsible for a 40% reduction of fatigue in persons that were suffering from chronic fatigue.[71,72,73]

What foods contain phospholipids?[74] Raw eggs, fish eggs, krill, shellfish, and fresh, uncooked vegetables. You need to be aware that, when cooking these foods, the phospholipid content declines very rapidly. In addition to increasing these essential phospholipids in your diet (taking high-phospholipid krill oil is probably the easiest way), there are some other known boosters of mitochondrial repair and protection, such as phosphatidylserine and astaxanthin.

Astaxanthin[75] is a potent natural component found in some algae eaten by lifeforms like shrimp. Astaxanthin powerfully protects the mitochondrial membrane against oxidative stress and even increases oxygen uptake without causing the side effect of producing more reactive oxygen. Some krill supplements have both high contents of phospholipids and astaxanthin.

Why should we discuss toxins in the first place? Our governments and health agencies make sure we're protected from those, don't they? Well, yes. Up to a certain point, they make sure that you are not exposed to immediately dangerous levels of toxins in your everyday life.[76,77] That is where it ends though. There are many toxins in our environment that manufacturers and experts know are potentially dangerous for us. Because low levels do not pose a direct threat, they are allowed. Pollutants are everywhere—in your food, your house, the air you breathe, the soil, the clothing you wear, and in your daily care and cleaning products. I will outline the most important sources of toxins, detail how you can avoid them and lower the toxic load on your body, and explain how to detox and get rid of these toxins.

Almost all toxins will have a negative influence on energy production and your health. Toxins will promote inflammation in your body, dysregulate your immune system, and certainly have a negative impact on your energy production.[78,79] Many of them dysregulate the nervous system and, even worse, can cause cancer and a range of other diseases. Remember that when mitochondria perceive stress, they stop producing energy and instead, start to operate in cell defense mode (immediate cell danger response).

How much toxic material do we have in our bodies? According to researchers, quite a lot. Of course, this depends on your work, the country you live in, and whether you live in the mountains or the city. But the fact is, there are many studies of people who are not exposed to toxins in their work yet still have between 71-176 known toxins in their bodies.[80,81] That is staggering. This toxic load affects the way you feel and how much energy you have.

The most common toxins are heavy metals, for example, from car exhaust or gasoline fumes,[82,83,84] lead, thallium (10 times more toxic than mercury), and benzene.[85,86,87] Mercury and aluminum are pervasive toxins; mercury is present in a lot of products that have a white appearance, and aluminum is in most antiperspirants and deodorants.[88] In our vegetables and most processed foods, there are traces of insecticides, fungicides, herbicides, and if you are unlucky, you are even exposed to them when you live in the country or when your house or furniture has been treated for fungus like black mold. Exposure to fungus such as black mold produces aflatoxin, which can be found in trace amounts in our food.[89] Other common fungal toxins may be found in coffee. You can now purchase coffee on the internet that is certified as mold-free.

So, what can you do about this? Can you leave things as they are?

That's not a good idea, especially since our bodies are not made for the number of toxins we are exposed to nowadays. The toxic load we are expected to deal with is ever increasing. Because our primary detoxifying systems, the liver and skin,[90,91,92] cannot keep up with the number of toxins we are exposed to, most of them are stored.[93] Most toxins are fat-soluble and easily stored in our fatty tissues and organs.

It may be necessary to add detox-boosting and liver-supporting foods to your daily diet. In the end, having a lifestyle that includes the healthy consumption of clean food and avoiding toxins altogether is by far the best way to deal with these issues each day. With this in mind, you also have to make sure that your gut is healthy and you are not dealing with the consequences of a leaky gut as well. That would require an immediate solution, since toxicity in your body and a leaky gut are a terrible combination.

Now on to the good news! There are a lot of things you can do to reduce or even annihilate the effects of toxins.

First, make sure you eat lots of vegetables. This is a no-brainer. **Vegetables** not only contain a lot of micronutrients and chemicals that aid detoxification,[94] they also contain fibers that can bind toxins, making them easier to be removed by excretion. In addition, they provide the essential non-soluble fibers that build the diversity of our microbiome, which protects us from a host of diseases and plays an all-important role in the well-being of the rest of your body and brain.

Here are the other essential foods to help you detoxify:

1. **All kinds of greens and green juices.** The chlorophyll that makes up the vegetables and grasses in green juice is an excellent detoxifier.[95]
2. **Berries and cruciferous vegetables** like broccoli and cauliflower[96,97]
3. **Vitamin C-rich foods** like lemons and limes. They also help boost glutathione levels. This is the most important antioxidant in your liver and body.[98]
4. **Beets and Brussels sprouts**, which, prepared in the right way taste phenomenal (really)
5. **Herbs** that are useful include dandelion, milk thistle, artichoke, and turmeric (curcumin).[99,100,101,102]
6. **Liver from organically and grass-fed raised cattle or organic chicken** provides a lot of nutrients that support the liver.
7. Along with the food you eat, you can add **supplements** to boost and support liver function as well as detoxification. Milk thistle (especially the silymarin found in milk thistle) is one of the few products out there that can both repair damaged liver cells and protect the liver as well as support the detoxification pathways.

It took me approximately two years to feel this energetic, even though I'm now three years post-stroke. Of course I'm tired at night, but remember, I also get up at 5 in the morning and am still working hard on my rehab. You can improve your energy level too, by creating the right energy habits!

Of course, there are many diversities between humans and rats. But one resemblance emerges: We all need a boost of energy and hope to keep on swimming. My sincere ambition is to help give you some of that hope and insight throughout this book.

Chapter 37

Barcelona

"Nice shoes," Arjan said to me.

"Thank you," I replied.

I was looking proudly at my shoes. My first "real shoes" in the two years and ten months since my stroke! No hiking boots with a brace around my foot, no sneakers, but leather shoes with a slightly high heel. I was extra proud of that heel.

Like many women, I love to look tall, and I was fed up with always walking around in my sneakers. For almost three years, I had been diligently exercising my left ankle since I had no control over it and it moved around at random. Finally this past year, I got to a point where I could control it to some extent and allowed myself to wear "real shoes." Wearing those higher heels, I must have been above 1.8 meters tall. What's the fuss, you may think? I don't know—perhaps vanity.

We were headed to a dinner for the participants of a three-day course we were attending in Barcelona. It was held by Dr. Robert Melillo, one of the specialists on childhood developmental disorders in the US.[1] His areas of expertise include, among others: autism spectrum disorders, ADD/ADHD, OCD, dyslexia, as well as other learning disorders. As a clinician for 25 years, university professor, brain researcher, and best-selling author, his research led to the creation of Brain Balance Achievement Centers. These are after-school learning centers that offer a program of brain training, exercise, simple physical exercises, skills training, and dietary advice, which it says help children with developmental and learning disabilities.[2] To sum it up, Dr. Melillo's research is based on a wide variety of brain imbalances.

For example, in the case of autism, the two hemispheres of the brain are not functioning in balance with each other,[3,4] among other underlying mechanisms such as neuroinflammation.[5] There is one relatively "weaker side." Stimulation of the weaker side with whole-body reflex inhibition exercises involving music, laser, eye movements, vibration, and more are done in Brain Balance Centers. These methods aim to make the weaker side stronger, a practice called hemisphere-specific approach.

These children often have primitive reflexes. Primitive refl exes[6,7,8,9,10,11,12] are reflexes infants have, such as the Babinski reflex (when you rub the bottom of a baby's foot with a small mallet, the big toe goes up and the other toes flare out).[13,14,15] In a toddler, the reflex is already in its adult stage, so testing the reflex makes the toes curl down.

Primitive reflexes reappeared in my body after my stroke and are also seen in many other adult stroke patients.[16,17] Reflex inhibition exercises including pre-crawling can be done to get rid of these issues. Usually, primitive reflexes are suppressed by the development of the frontal lobes as a child transitions normally to the next stage of child development.

Researchers at Harvard have recently done a study on this topic, which produced some remarkably positive results in the children that took part.[18]

"How long have you known Dr. Melillo?" I asked Arjan while we were waiting for the lecture to start.

"I've known Rob about 18 or 19 years," he said.

"What's up with his tattoos?" I asked curiously.

"Rob has tattoos on both arms. Around the shoulder, there are the cell layers of the neocortex with the pyramidal cells that send signals to the hand. He also has depictions of different skulls indicating the evolution of humankind." Arjan replied, grinning.

Melillo wore a long-sleeved dress shirt and vest without a jacket, and I saw tattoos above his wrist. He also wore bracelets and rings. I could see he was a rebel, like me.

The room was filled with doctors, functional neurologists, and one or two people like me who had no medical background.

I loved the lecture! I sat with eyes wide open, soaking it all in like a sponge. Other speakers talked about low-level laser usage and how virtual reality games may assist hemisphere-specific treatment. I have to admit, though, we primarily went to Barcelona because of the laser therapy. It was known that transcranial low-level laser (light) therapy has a positive effect on brain injury.[19][20]

"I have an idea," I said to Arjan. "Why don't we set up a Brain.rehab center with all the cutting edge machines required to stimulate the weak side?"

His face lit up as he thought about it for a minute. "I like your idea. I love it, in fact. But first, we need to get a response from the investors."

We sought out investors when we decided to launch Brain.rehab, so we could engage on a full-time basis in making videos about the nature of the brain, therapy, treatment for brain injuries, and recovery protocols. But we hadn't yet received any answers from the investors we approached.

We knew there was a need for an online portal for stroke survivors and received a large number of responses from the announcement of the online program and the follow-up lecture we gave. We heard from people who were frustrated that there were no resources for those who were six months post-stroke—no rehab facilities and no online guidance or encouragement. Arjan and I both felt compelled to help those millions of stroke survivors and brain-injured persons get answers to their questions about recovery.

Throughout our weekend in Barcelona, we thought about the Brain.rehab centers, made lists of the equipment we would need, and then added some additional text to the business plan we had written:

Brain.rehab Centers

The Brain.rehab Centers will support patients who want additional cutting-edge treatments and paid personal assistance. The training centers offer state of the art technological therapies including light, sound, vibration, laser, virtual reality, physical strength conditioning, timing, and coordination therapy. All these can help stroke survivors recover further.

In the Brain.rehab Centers, we will make use of:

- laser devices
- interactive metronome systems for timing and rhythmicity
- Dynavision D2 coordination trainer
- virtual reality training

- vestibular training and integration gyroscope systems such as medical gyrostims
- VNG eye coordination measurement system
- head-eye vestibular training protocols
- CAPS balance and fall risk assessment systems from vestibular technology
- eye and coordination training systems like the NSI system
- QEEG, which provides live functionality pictures of the brain

"Now we wait and see what they say," said Arjan.

We both felt that we were on to something—something big! It had begun a year earlier when I messaged Arjan from Mexico City to tell him that using the pre-crawling exercises had created a significant improvement in my spasticity. Now here we were, a year later, planning to develop a Brain.rehab center.

There are so many interconnected issues that go unaddressed and so many unanswered questions in current rehabilitation practices and methods. We wanted to do better for stroke survivors looking for resources.

Spasticity and regaining arm, leg, and speech functions are not the only things stroke survivors have to deal with. There are also other difficulties, for example, synkinesis. Synkinesis is the involuntary movement of muscles or limbs at the same time that a voluntary action takes place.[»21 »22 »23 »24]

I woke up one morning, approximately two months after my stroke. I was lying in bed and began to yawn. As I looked at my left hand, I couldn't believe what I saw. My fingers were straight!

The issue of spasticity affects quite a lot of people after a stroke. For me, it was so bad that my fingers were clutched and rigid all the time. That's why I was so surprised to see my fingers outstretched and straight. Morning after morning, I yawned, stretched, looked at my fingers, and they were straight.

My son Maarten asked the doctors and therapists what the relationship was between yawning, stretching, and straight fingers, but none of them at Klimmendaal had an explanation. I didn't discover the answer until I met Arjan.

If you've had a stroke, you may have already experienced synkinesis. Wikipedia describes synkinesis as the "miswiring of nerves after trauma." This is manifested through involuntary muscular movements accompanying voluntary movements. For example, voluntary smiling will induce an involuntary contraction of the eye muscles, causing the eye to squint at the same time. In my case, coughing or sneezing caused my left arm and hand to make an involuntary movement. It is sometimes seen in children who move their tongue or jaw or grimace while drawing or practicing their writing. Either miswiring of the brain or immature developmental maturation usually lies at the root of these cases.

The ability to fine-tune movement is often lost after a stroke, even when the lower motor neuronal pools (groups of neurons that process information) that send signals to the muscles at the brain stem level and spinal cord level are intact. However, when connections from the cortex are lost, the tracts (bundled nerve fibers of the central nervous system) begin to degenerate. Nearby tracts that control facial or throat muscles can prompt a spillover signal that creates an incorrect facial or throat connection to arm and hand muscles. You might laugh and see your hand or arm move at the same time.

There are literally hundreds if not thousands of questions about issues like this after you've experienced a stroke. We really needed support to create a platform that could provide these insights to brain-injured people.

One Friday in February, I was sitting at Arjan's house, still working on the business plan. We had each worked hard on it, inserting as much detail as possible and coming up with additional ideas about how we could improve it.

We had already met with two potential investors, and it was a pleasant and productive meeting. We learned they receive approximately 600 proposals each year, and perhaps a tenth of them made it far enough to be granted a meeting. They gave us a shortlist—a handful of things that were "not clear" about our business plan.

Then on February 15, I got a phone call from one of the investors. I put the phone on speaker so Arjan could hear what was being said.

"Hello Linda, I have some good news to tell you. We will support your company Brain.rehab. We think it's an awesome company, and we also think you are going to help a lot of brain-injured patients!"

"Woohoo!" I couldn't contain myself. "Is it really true?" I said. "Thank you! Thank you!"

Tears were flowing down my cheeks.

Arjan was smiling. He hugged me and said, "This is going to be big, I can feel it."

Chapter 38

Main Subject Ignored

Is this how it's going to be? I thought while observing the two guys sitting opposite me.

These two fellows plainly ignored me. I sat with Arjan at a large table in a meeting room at their offices. Their company made individual adjustments to wheelchairs, hand braces, foot braces, and the like.

We went to this company to see if it was possible to make a "real cast" that I could use while doing the CIMT training. This way, I could circumnavigate breaking my good arm, the very thing Arjan was absolutely opposed to (chapter 22).

Arjan properly introduced me with, "Linda has had a major stroke. She cannot talk properly yet, but her thinking speed is beyond average." He continued, "We're here because we want to get a real cast for her right arm." Then he went on to explain about CIMT, why I wanted a real cast, and the cast characteristics: I needed to be able to sleep with it as well as get it off in case of emergency without having to use my left arm.

Arjan got their full attention for the next hour. We both came here for business, but they hardly looked at me at all.

For me, our first business meeting was unfolding into a disaster. The few times I tried to say something while Arjan attempted to turn their attention to me, they barely looked at me.

After the meeting, I was annoyed. It took me half a day to sort out my thoughts about the whole thing. Then I sent a message to Arjan: "I think this business meeting sucked, and I think you know why."

He wrote, "Because they ignored you?"

"Yes," I replied.

"Look," he answered, "We don't have to work with them to make your cast. Let's formulate it this way: We don't have to work with anybody that ignores you."

I agreed.

Before my stroke, I ran my own business for 15 years. Everyone listened to me. I certainly wasn't ignored!

I started wondering how other stroke survivors viewed this. Maybe a bank manager or CEO of a big company experienced the same: being ignored because you can't talk that well, even though nothing is wrong with your intelligence.

To all of you business people who can speak normally, just *listen*, will you? Just because somebody is having difficulty talking, don't ignore them! They may have the most valuable opinion of everyone, if you take the time to listen!

We never got the cast from them, but I will still get one for sure. I did have a normal brace, however, on my right arm when I did the constraint-induced movement therapy (CIMT) that Arjan designed for me.

He can best describe for himself how we came about designing our first CIMT program and contributed the rest of this chapter.

I asked Linda, "Do you know about CIMT?"[1,2,3] We were chatting over FaceTime.

"Yes, I do," Linda answered. "It is very intense and requires you to use your paretic arm instead of your good arm. I have an appointment at the Saint Maartens clinic to see if I can start a constraint-induced movement therapy program."

"Awesome," I said. "It is one of the few therapies that have proven to be very effective in improving arm and hand function."

Not long after this conversation, Linda learned that CIMT was no longer offered, aside from a modified version given during the first months of rehabilitation therapy after a stroke or head trauma—if you were lucky, that is. No CIMT was offered if you could not lift your wrist or extend your fingers by at least 10° without assistance.

Instead of accepting this situation, Linda began to search for it herself since CIMT had been proven to be effective after moderate and severe strokes, even years after the event. Linda's stroke happened one and a half years before she asked me this question. It turned out that, in the whole country, intense CIMT was still provided for children but not adults once they were out of the first rehabilitation period.

To put it mildly, we were both amazed and shocked by this. Why would they not provide a therapy that is proven effective? We will probably never know what the real reason is, but it might be because it would require a large number of additional staff members, thus costing more money. It's also very time consuming and demands high levels of motivation, an essential part of CIMT.

Not willing to settle with this lack-of-availability problem, we decided to construct our own version of this successful therapy, with a twist. This time, it should be possible to do constraint-induced movement therapy in the patient's home environment. We had to make it accessible for anyone that did not have access to CIMT for one reason or another but was willing to put in a lot of work on their own or with the aid of a spouse or therapist.

Looking through all the scientific studies done with constraint-induced movement therapy sparked a new idea as well: Why not make the CIMT even more effective by adding a priming protocol to enhance the impact of hours spent training? Many activities can be done to accomplish this, including mentally visualizing the movements,[4,5,6,7] improving the temperature of the paretic arm to speed up nerve signaling and feedback to the brain,[8,9] and electrically stimulating the muscles to help movement and feedback. These ideas could also include neurofeedback and specific hypnotherapy,[10] which also showed beneficial effects in a variety of cases.

This conversation is where the excerpt you're reading began. In the following paragraphs, I will tell you more about CIMT, how it started, where the idea comes from, what you can expect from it, the basic construction of the therapy, and how much effort and motivation it takes.

Edward Taub[11] introduced constraint-induced therapy (1980) after studying monkeys (see chapter 18) and later humans with paralysis after a stroke. He observed that even after the severe damage of a stroke, there is capacity left to recover function. He also observed that there is one big problem: After a stroke, you start relying more and more on using the good arm (or any other body part for that matter). This leads to the so-called learned nonuse of the affected limb. How does this work?

As you are probably aware, there is a connection between the right and left side (the hemispheres) of your brain. This bridge is called the corpus callosum.[12] When engaging in right arm activity, which gets its information and control from the left hemisphere, signals are sent to the opposite half of the brain, the right hemisphere. This signal is to inhibit (dampen or stop) activity in the arm control parts of the right half of the brain, and it ensures that the right arm can perform optimally and all brain control is super-focused.[13, 14, 15] However, there is one significant problem when you are dealing with the effects of a stroke on these areas: The function is already lost or compromised. Thus, using the properly functioning side further decreases the capacity for activity in the paretic limb.

This phenomenon is part of what Taub called learned nonuse of the arm affected by stroke or brain injury. The good news is that, although stroke or brain injury can wipe out whole areas in your brain, research shows that often many neurons and supportive cells (glial cells) are still alive but dormant after the shock caused by stroke or brain injury. Usually, there are still some tracts available to the arm, and the repair of damage through neuroplasticity that we have talked about before (see chapter 35) can take place. Also, there is a lot of redundancy in the brain,[16] which means there are networks and connections that have a similar function and can still be activated, even if they have not been used or did not function effectively before. Taub's solution was drastic yet simple in execution. You have to unlearn nonuse by restraining the good (still functional) arm or leg. Hence the name "constraint-induced therapy."

We designed a therapy where, for two or three weeks at a time, the good (functional) arm and hand were constrained for eight to ten hours a day. This forced the non-functioning arm to become more active again in tiny, incremental steps, much like a child when it learns to use his or her arm purposefully and in more complex ways.

This is how the idea of CIMT began. The idea of constraining the good arm originated even earlier. Sarah Towers described previous experiments (1940) where a similar process was already being used on monkeys.[17] Interestingly enough, like with many other pioneers, Edward Taub was initially ridiculed. He was even banned from progressing with his scientific studies. Now, however, he is seen as a pioneer in stroke recovery and celebrated among his colleagues.

So, how does CIMT work in practice? When CIMT began in the 1980s, the protocol was to restrain the good arm for eight to ten hours a day for the duration of two to three weeks. During this time, the stroke survivor consistently worked with a therapist. This often meant concentrated periods with a therapist in the rehab center. How severely the spastic/paretic arm was affected determined the type of exercise that was carried out.

Exercises could range from picking up a softball, if possible, to flipping over a wooden block and would gradually become more difficult. Later, the practice of CIMT became more varied in the duration of constraint. For example, in some facilities, the constraint time would be three hours a day and extend over a somewhat longer time period. More often than not, this is dictated by the therapist's availability. The presence of the therapist is required for obvious reasons. In the initial period after a stroke, just getting up and walking unaided can cause significant problems. Dexterity, or the ability to do anything with the affected hand and arm, is often absent at the start.

Another perhaps even more critical aspect is the motivation part.[18,19,20] The person helping you plays a big role in keeping you motivated enough to bounce back after the many moments of frustration. In most rehabilitation facilities, you would not be a candidate if you had a major stroke and are unable to lift the fingers or wrist to 10° unaided (like in Linda's case). However, we also know that even if much more work needs to be done to get results when not being able to perform the action previously described, and that perhaps the initial results may not be so great, constraint induced movement therapy is still one of the best ways to get function back.

The CIMT we constructed for the home environment is aimed at all levels of impairment. This means that the set of exercises will differ from person to person depending on the severity of the stroke or brain injury. Another important aspect is the type of skill set that the person partaking in CIMT wants to acquire.

At this point, you probably realize that constraint-induced movement therapy is hard work. What I have not told you yet is that, for your brain to use its capacity to change in the right way, you have to be very specific and purposeful in what you are doing. More importantly, every tiny movement needs to be repeated hundreds of times a day to obtain any result. Do not worry at this point if that seems like an impossible task both mentally and physically. That is precisely why this therapy came about.

On to the next obstacle!

Performing CIMT training in your home means that there will not be a trained therapist present to aid you, just the people in your surroundings or you by yourself. Again, **do not be afraid or give up at this point**. This explanation is written with the knowledge that CIMT home therapy is tough but possible, and it gives excellent results. One of the reasons why Brain.rehab came about (see chapter 28) is to do exactly this: go over the whole process step by step and try to tackle any objections or obstacles you may have. We also provide training videos and instructions, so there won't be any doubt about what to do. And yes, even the motivational part will be covered to some extent.

The major advantage of a CIMT rehabilitation protocol you can do at home is that it is extremely flexible and adaptable to your specific situation (not a generic CIMT program), and it gives access to exclusive (high-cost) training methods that would not normally be readily available. Another important factor is that you can do the CIMT home training more often. In the literature, we see cases and studies performed in a one-time situation, not repetitively. Again, this is most likely due to the time-restricted availability of therapists, and cost factors drive the decision in most cases. In our opinion, having the possibility to go through several rounds of CIMT for a period of years can make more progress attainable than what would typically be achieved. It also prevents the type of decline in any regained function that is often seen when the initial rehabilitation period is finished.

What can you expect from CIMT home training, other than knowing that it will be challenging and hard work? First of all, you cannot see this form of therapy as a cure-all or think that through CIMT alone you will get rid of your spasticity and be able to use your arm and hand as before. Instead, you should start by having an open mind to the possibilities it brings.

You've already learned that CIMT is one of the few forms of training that gets results. These results are dependent on your effort and persistence and, probably most importantly, your level of belief that you can and will make progress. One of the reasons why Linda wrote this book is to explain why and how you can also make progress after the first six months of initial rehabilitation. The first six months are just the start. Based on scientific papers on the subject and our personal experience, not make-believe or anecdotal evidence, it is very reasonable to think that you will make progress in regaining lost function when engaging in CIMT therapy. The extent to which lost function is recovered varies from person to person. It is also dependent on many factors ranging from the amount of damage done by the stroke to the basic circumstances you have created in your life (see previous chapters in this book).

With this knowledge, we decided to give it a shot and started constructing a home protocol for Linda that closely resembled the ones used in rehabilitation centers. This meant finding exercises Linda could do. Remember, at this point, she had suffered a severe stroke that left her with very little function and feeling in the left arm and hand.

The exercises included scooping rice with a big spoon or cup (which she luckily could hold when placed in her left hand), putting domino pieces on their side, and tracing big drawings with her hand and fingers, to name a few.

We began by instructing her family on what constraint-induced movement therapy would involve and how demanding it would be for them as well, for example, regarding going to the bathroom, getting the brace on and off, the frustration that would most likely result when no visible progress was being made, and what to do if nobody was home. Luckily, everyone was very motivated to help Linda out!

She would do the CIMT home program for two weeks straight with a minimum of eight hours constraint of her good right arm.

With this, Linda was double-challenged because she used to be left-handed. Let me explain. She is one of the few people that also had her dominant language center in the right hemisphere. Therefore, Linda developed aphasia and a left side that she was unable to use adequately.

So, how did the newly constructed CIMT home program work out for Linda? As well as could be expected! Linda was able to do most of the work herself, and she figured out ways to overcome the times when her good arm was needed. She would do her speech therapy and preparation protocol before the CIMT and then get going.

She was, of course, extra tired in the beginning. But the adrenaline surge from knowing that she was going to take a new step in her recovery kept her going. After the first five or six days, she hit rock bottom and was exhausted by the repetitive exercises and apparent lack of progress. Many of the exercises that we devised were, simply put, extremely difficult. But Linda pulled through and began to notice improvements such as being able to use her entire left arm more effectively while driving. As the feeling on the weak side continued to improve, she reported at the end of the two weeks that it was like having a left arm again. Objectively, it was very clear that Linda had regained not only improved feeling but also somewhat better and more refined control over her left arm and shoulder.

Linda had made another significant step in regaining lost function, and this was only the first of many CIMT home sessions that she has planned. Later, she would specifically focus the CIMT on her wrist and hand, another big challenge because control of the hand is the most tricky to improve after a stroke of the motor cortex.

Part of Linda's success during this first round of constraint-induced movement therapy was due to the fact that this therapy was not the only thing we were doing. Linda had already made significant lifestyle changes to support optimal brain recovery and function (see previous chapters). She also used additional techniques to improve feedback to and from the brain. This is what we call the priming part. This involved, for example, practicing the activities that she was going to do during the CIMT in her head as well as warming up the hand, arm, and shoulder to increase nerve conduction speed from the arm to the brain. All these factors came together to support Linda's success using CIMT.

Chapter 39

Linda 2.0

"The purpose of life is a life of purpose."

– Robert Byrne

"The greatest moments of our lives are when our mind or our body is stretched to its limit, in a voluntary pursuit, or in something both difficult and worthwhile."

– Mihaly Csikszentmihalyi

In the introduction of this book, I mentioned I had difficulty writing this because it went miles outside my comfort zone. I am an introvert who is carefully releasing my vulnerability to all of you.

I used to think, *I'll look like a wax statue in the "Hall of Failure"—right alongside my book—a book that's going to get tons of criticism.*

But I don't think so anymore. Now I just tell myself, *What the heck? It's a risk, but I'm going to take it anyway.*

It's not that I have suddenly become fearless. But I have learned to refuse to let my fear keep me from stepping into the unknown. Of course, the unknown is usually scary.

Remember, your mind is a creature of habit and operates based on fear. It continually scans your environment, looking for things to be afraid of, and it does this to keep you safe. In reality, though, giving in to fear doesn't make you strong and safe. It's just the opposite. Not taking any risks makes you weaker.

I call risk-taking "hormesis for the mind." If you can lose the fear of failure or criticism, you will start seeing enormous opportunities appear before you. They did for me.

Fear hijacks not only your creativity but also your cells, according to Dr. Bruce Lipton.[1] Bruce Lipton is an American cell biologist in epigenetics (the study of how the environment affects our genes) and a former researcher at Stanford University's School of Medicine. He's also the author of the book *The Biology of Belief.*[2] Dr. Lipton is best known for promoting the idea that environmental factors can influence gene expression.[3,4,5,6] This means that humans have a far more significant impact on their health than genetic research previously determined. You can't just blame genes for this or that.

As he experimented on stem cells, he put one cell apart in a dish and found that it divided every 10 or 12 hours. After a week, he had 50,000 cells. Every individual cell was genetically identical since they all came from the same parent stem cell.

Then he created three slightly different culture media by changing some of the components. A culture medium is a liquid or gelatinous substance containing nutrients in which microorganisms, cells, or tissues are cultivated for scientific purposes. In fact, he created three different synthetic versions of blood.

He put these three different environments in three different dishes. Each dish had portions from the genetically identical cells already in them.

As a result, in one of the dishes, the cells became bone cells. In another, the cells became fat cells. In the third dish, muscle cells.

Now he was left with a very profound question: What controls the cells' fate? Genes did not control the fate of the cells, the environment did! He concluded that as we change the composition (the synthetic version of blood), we also change the designation of our cells!

To quote Nobel Prize winner Elisabeth Blackburn,[7] "Genes load the gun, but the environment pulls the trigger."[8,9,10]

If I understand it right: Just because you have, for example, inherited cancer genes, it's worthwhile to do everything you can with your environment to counteract that, like eating incredibly healthy food, for example.

What changes the composition of our blood? Our brain does! What the brain and mind perceive, the brain reacts to by breaking it down into chemical compounds and electrical signals.

When you worry or feel anxious and uncertain about the future, that is, in fact, fear. Your brain's response to those worries is a release of stress hormones and inflammatory agents, putting you into fight-or-flight mode, a state of self-protection. Growth is also halted.

In contrast, when you perceive happiness and joy, your brain translates that into a response that releases dopamine, the pleasure chemical. Dopamine also enhances growth.

You can retrain your brain to feel joyful again. How? With the type of thoughts you consciously make. It sounds obvious, but positive thoughts make you happy, while negative thoughts make you unhappy.

Comments about yourself like "I'm too fat" are negative thoughts that make you feel like a loser or unworthy of anyone's time or attention. And "anyone" includes you.

"I am worried about... " is another type of negative thought that makes you feel anxious or depressed.

Often we are so preoccupied with the status quo that we forget we have the power to become the person we want to be (habits). Remember what I told you previously? Be in the constant pursuit of imagining being the best version of yourself, and create habits that support this accordingly.

Most importantly, treat yourself like someone you love.

I think about this quite often because, as you know, I was anxious and worried nearly all the time before my stroke, and I certainly don't want to fall into that mindset again.

For instance, I changed my environment by cutting out the crabs (people that bring negativity). I also decided that I don't want anyone in the "cheap seats" (again, crabs) who seem to think they have the right to hijack my life choices.

My dear friend and painting teacher, Liselotte, suggested, "Be like Teflon to people that hurt you with their words." Teflon is a coating applied to the surface of cooking pans to make it nonstick. So, to follow up on some very sensible advice: Don't let anyone else's words get stuck in your mind or your consciousness.

I have made must-do habits to eat healthy foods, practice hormesis, and encourage my parasympathetic nervous system to give it a chance to recover a little more every day. I also remind myself to get outside of my cozy comfort zone as often as possible. We can't grow or learn from the sheltered position of our comfort zone, remember?

Some people say, "Adversity is the best teacher," and it certainly was for me. I had worked myself silly and was continually striving for "success" as seen through the eyes of the world.

Money, status, and all of those things that society tells us are important, are not. I felt as if my soul was gasping for oxygen.

Instead of feeling satisfied with my life, I had a sensation of "unresolvedness." No matter how desperately I wanted to feel successful, accomplished, and valued by the outside world, my inner perception was unresolved and restless. Basically, I was looking for self-fulfillment anywhere.

I realize now that I had to hit rock bottom before things could get better.

Then I went on a self-examination tour. I took a good look at myself. I saw a sleepless workaholic that put way too much effort into extrinsic values (values outside myself).

I didn't like what I saw.

Following this realization, I decided that things had to change. I read and listened to hundreds of books, created a toolbox from what I learned and immediately put this theory into practice in the form of "trial and error" habits.

In this process, my entire value system shifted from extrinsic to intrinsic, operating from a position of internal reflection. That shift in perception means that I now consider the two strokes I've encountered to be "adversity training" that helped me build stronger "adversity muscles." It also helped me to regard most, if not all, of my challenges this way.

Stoicism has been a big inspiration for this dramatic shift in mindset. I am stronger and tougher than I have ever been. Instead of dwelling on why this is happening to me, I can calmly (most of the time) approach things from a more considered position such as, *Awesome challenge. How can I play my best cards here?*

Then I play them. And the more I do that, the easier it gets. It becomes a habit.

One of my goals in writing this book is to give hope to stroke survivors. If you are a stroke survivor and have lost hope, and you are somewhat depressed because of it, I'm talking to you now (apologies again if I appear too blunt).

Remember those swimming rats? They got their energy through hope. If you don't gain a sense of hope or inspiration from my book, that's fine. But if you follow the energy advice I gave you, you are at least going to have enough energy to swim!

I want you to take charge of your life. Even if you get help, in the end you are the only one who can do the work.

I'm sorry to say it, but nobody is coming to save you or make you happy. That's why I want you to come out of the "poopy pants mentality" (like I had in the first chapter of this book) and scratch out the word "fragile" written on the box you are in. Write "antifragile" on your box instead. Step out of the back seat of your car and get in the front seat, behind the wheel.

You need to be able to feel powerful and embrace your acceptance of the bad circumstances that have happened to you, whether you like it or not. Look at your story, and flip the pain you have endured upside down. Turn that pain into the fuel that ignites your positive power. That's what I managed to do, and I'm certainly not superhuman. Not at all! I was scared a lot of the time. Yet I managed to not pack it in and run away from facing those difficulties.

Cut out your excuses like "I can't do that" or "I'm too fragile, I had a stroke."

Stop acting "pre-dead" when you still have a lot of life to live. Don't give up and become a stroke statistic, for heaven's sake!

Create the right habits (food, exercise, energy management, hormesis) and use repetition again and again, until you become who you want to be. You need to become your habits!

It is only you who can do it. Take charge and prove those nay-sayers wrong. If you get stuck and aren't making progress in your rehab, you might need to step back a bit and do something like pre-crawling exercises, just like a baby. I believe that it's the only way to move forward again.

That reminds me of Jim Kwik,[11] the CEO and founder of Kwik Learning[12] and a leader in accelerated learning with online students of every age and vocation in over 150 countries. Kwik is a world expert in speed-reading, memory improvement, and optimal brain performance. I learned to speed-read because of him (yes, I hacked my reading too).

He was giving an interview with Mindvalley and told the following story:

> Jim spent a lot of time at his grandparents' house as a young boy, and they didn't have any toys for him to play with. The only thing available was an old typewriter. He became super fast at typing, tapping away at the keys with one finger from each hand. When he was old enough to go to middle school, they introduced typing classes. Of course, Jim was at the top of the class when he typed with two fingers.
>
> He proudly saw his name written on the blackboard as the student who was the fastest typist in the class. But not for long. The teacher taught all the students how to type with 10 fingers. He tried, but it felt awkward. His words per minute score dropped. Jim continued to type with two fingers while the rest of his classmates increased their speed typing with 10 fingers. Eventually, he was in the bottom 10% of the class.
>
> When he finally began to type with 10 fingers, to his despair, he became slower than ever—at first. But he continued to practice and soon caught up. Eventually, he was typing at the same speed as the other students.

What can we learn from this? Sometimes you have to step back and start over to properly learn something.

If you are stuck in your rehabilitation (I know most of you will be at some stage), go two steps back and work on your core stability. After that, you need to learn how to stabilize your shoulders and hips by holding them in a static position. Next, do the neuromotor (pre-crawling) exercises. Then we'll see how far you can get!

I've been doing this for nine months now. I have lost about 50% of my spasticity, and I can feel my arm and hand more. I am starting to move my fingers again too.

If any doctors or therapists happen to pick up this book, I want to say to you: Be careful not to shatter the hope for stroke survivors. I still don't understand why doctors and therapists set limits of six months instead of giving survivors realistic hope, but I'm no longer angry with them. They have their own challenges with administration, paperwork, and the time they are allotted to spend with each patient.

However, I do think that doctors need to practice a more holistic approach in their treatment of patients, one that addresses lifestyle, habits, exercise, and diet. Our current cultural paradigm dictates that we ignore health until disease develops. Then we receive medication to treat the symptoms of a disease instead of addressing the root of the problem: why the disease appeared in the first place.

I think you can postpone diseases by creating habits of hormesis, sleep, food, and mind training. I wouldn't trade the sharply focused and clear mind that I got from biohacking my brain for anything. Besides, I think that a lot of doctors have a limited belief in the brain's adaptability.

That makes me think of a funny story I read in *The Big Leap* by Gay Hendricks.[13] In his book, Hendricks tells a true story about events unfolding in the 19th century. Just as steam trains began to emerge and catch the public's interest, several prominent scientists suggested that the train speed needed to be limited to 30 miles per hour. The reason? They were convinced that people would explode if they traveled above that speed. It's hard to imagine that anyone could believe that, and fortunately, several people stepped in to prove the "expert scientists" wrong. Remember, these scientists were the hotshots of the time.

I need *you* to be one of those people that steps onto the steam train to prove them (doctors) wrong, like I did.

That's why, together with Arjan, we created Brain.rehab. It is my ikigai.

My passion for this cause is bottomless. I plan to be working for Brain.rehab for the rest of my life because I genuinely enjoy what I'm doing. I have fallen in love with the process, not the goal. That includes endless refinements, continuous improvements, and cutting-edge research that encourages us to build the best online portal for post-clinic brain-injured patients. I finally found my fulfillment, how to matter in this life, through helping others.

Earlier in the book, I told you that we had gotten investors for Brain.rehab. At first, we were enormously happy that we would have a substantial amount of money to jump-start Brain.rehab. But when the time came to sign the agreement, they wanted almost 70% of our company! They wanted control so they could sell the company later. Of course, we said no to that. We're not selling our ikigai! We took a deep breath and moved forward. Now we're doing it on our own, on a small budget.

If I look back at my life before my stroke, I was lost on the ladder of "success," lost in the need to behave in an acceptable way for fear of falling off.

From an early age, we're taught to believe that we are meant to climb this ladder if we wish to be perceived as "winners." We are also frequently exposed to commercial marketing that makes us believe we are not enough unless we have that new car, expensive piece of furniture, or latest skin cream. It's all part of the "I'll be happy WHEN..." lifestyle.

I used to think to myself, *I'll be happy when I sell my company in five years. Then I'll go on vacation, be more relaxed, and enjoy having the time to be a better mother.*

I was insane! That kind of "happiness" requires you to go at rocket speed all the time. It became evident that it was too much for me about three years ago, when I had my stroke.

I know now that happiness is achieved with a different formula altogether. The happiness formula can be a quiet moment, some time for reflection, a conversation with people you care about, or doing work that matters and is important to you.

Happiness comes from inside. It doesn't come by chance, it comes by *choice*. That's what my adversity taught me.

No illness is fun, and no one should feel compelled to be grateful for suffering. But, conversely, I have also learned that those who have suffered often live fuller lives because they understand the meaning of life. From my near-death experience, I truly understand how precious life is and that it can be taken away at any time. It's a sort of "gift" that many healthy people will never understand. That, I am grateful for. Yes, I am thankful that I had my stroke so I could learn this.

"Did she just say that she was happy she had a stroke? She must be out of her mind!" I can hear some of you saying those things, but that's fine, too.

Maybe you're right, and I am crazy. But I might never have gotten this far in my rehabilitation if I was still worried about being normal. My nonconformity made me who I am and put me where I am right now.

Do you see me as rather well adjusted? Well adjusted to what, a sick society? Maybe my weirdness is my greatest asset because real sanity rests in authenticity. If you think and live outside the mainstream, don't apologize for your eccentricity. Be a nonconformist and embrace it!

Remember, when you are out there biohacking your brain, learning, sweating, exercising, practicing hormesis, meditating, practicing your speech, and being antifragile as much as possible, I want to say just one thing to you: **You are not alone, fellow rebel!**

About the Author

Linda Rådestad is known for her nimble problem-solving and independent way to innovate. After a massive stroke at age 43, she became a professional biohacker and found her true purpose in life: to help those with a brain injury. She has now traded in her successful internet retail business for Brain.rehab, a company providing innovative home rehabilitation insights and training after stroke or brain injury. Linda currently lives in Cyprus, Sweden, and Germany. She can be reached at info@brain.rehab and followed at www.brain.rehab or @lindaradestad.

References

CHAPTER 1

Neuropathic pain

1. Colloca, L., Ludman, T., Bouhassira, D., Baron, R., Dickenson, A. H., Yarnitsky, D., Raja, S. N. (2017). Neuropathic pain. *Nature Reviews Disease Primers*, 3, 17002.
2. Cruccu, G., & Truini, A. (2017). A review of neuropathic pain: From guidelines to clinical practice. *Pain and Therapy*, 6(1), 35-42.

Esther Vergeer

3. Esther Vergeer. (2019). In *Wikipedia*. Retrieved September 5, 2019, from https://en.wikipedia.org/wiki/Esther_Vergeer

CHAPTER 2

REM sleep

1. Siegel, J. M. (2011). REM sleep: A biological and psychological paradox. *Sleep Medicine Reviews*, *15*(3), 139.
2. Feriante, J., & Araujo, J. F. (2018). Physiology, REM sleep. *StatPearls*. Retrieved from https://www.ncbi.nlm.nih.gov/books/NBK531454/

CHAPTER 3

Transient ischemic attack (TIA)

1. Transient ischemic attack. (2019). In *Wikipedia*. Retrieved May 5, 2019, from https://en.wikipedia.org/wiki/Transient_ischemic_attack
2. Sorensen, A. G., & Ay, H. (2011). Transient ischemic attack: Definition, diagnosis, and risk stratification. *Neuroimaging Clinics*, *21*(2), 303-313.
3. Khare, S. (2016). Risk factors of transient ischemic attack: An overview. *Journal of Mid-Life Health*, *7*(1), 2.
4. Coutts, S. B. (2017). Diagnosis and management of transient ischemic attack. *Continuum: Lifelong Learning in Neurology*, 23(1), 82.

Stroke

5. Yew, K. S., & Cheng, E. (2009). Acute stroke diagnosis. *American Family Physician*, 80(1), 33.
6. Khaku, A. S, Hegazy, M., & Tad, P. (2019). Cerebrovascular disease (stroke). *StatPearls*. Retrieved from https://www.ncbi.nlm.nih.gov/books/NBK430927/
7. Tadi, P., & Lui, F. (2019). Acute stroke (cerebrovascular accident). *StatPearls*. Retrieved from https://www.ncbi.nlm.nih.gov/books/NBK535369/
8. Musuka, T. D., Wilton, S. B., Traboulsi, M., & Hill, M. D. (2015). Diagnosis and management of acute ischemic stroke: Speed is critical. *Cmaj*, *187*(12), 887-893.

CHAPTER 4

Jill Bolte Taylor

1. Taylor, J. B. (2009). *My stroke of insight*. London, England: Hachette UK.
2. TED. (2008). *My stroke of insight - Jill Bolte Taylor* [Video file]. Retrieved from https://www.youtube.com/watch?v=UyyjU8fzEYU

CHAPTER 5

Thrombectomy

1. Filho, O. J., & Samuels, O.B. (2019). Mechanical thrombectomy for acute ischemic stroke. *Uptodate*. Retrieved from https://www.uptodate.com/contents/mechanical-thrombectomy-for-acute-ischemic-stroke

2. Ganesh, A., & Goyal, M. (2018). Thrombectomy for acute ischemic stroke: recent insights and future directions. *Current Neurology and Neuroscience Reports, 18*(9), 59.
3. Turc, G., Bhogal, P., Fischer, U., Khatri, P., Lobotesis, K., Mazighi, M.,...Fiehler, J. (2019). European stroke organization (ESO) - European society for minimally invasive neurological therapy (ESMINT) guidelines on mechanical thrombectomy in acute ischaemic stroke endorsed by stroke Alliance for Europe (SAFE). *European Stroke Journal, 4*(1), 6-12.

Right hemisphere

4. Bernard, F., Lemée, J. M., Ter Minassian, A., & Menei, P. (2018). Right hemisphere cognitive functions: From clinical and anatomic bases to brain mapping during awake craniotomy part I: Clinical and functional anatomy. *World Neurosurgery*, 118, 348-359.
5. Corballis, M. C. (2014). Left brain, right brain: Facts and fantasies. *PLOS Biology, 12*(1), e1001767.

CHAPTER 6

Aspirin in stroke prevention

1. Braslavsky, A. M. (2000). Aspirin taken right after a stroke may prevent a second one. *WebMD*. Retrieved from https://www.webmd.com/stroke/news/20000601/aspirin-after-stroke-helps-prevent-another#1
2. Maulaz, A. B., Bezerra, D. C., Michel, P., & Bogousslavsky, J. (2005). Effect of discontinuing aspirin therapy on the risk of brain ischemic stroke. *Archives of Neurology*, 62(8), 1217-1220.
3. Dalen, J. E. (2006). Aspirin to prevent heart attack and stroke: What's the right dose? *The American Journal of Medicine, 119*(3), 198-202.

CHAPTER 7

Park De Hoge Veluwe

1. De Hoge Veluwe National Park. (2019). Retrieved from https://www.hogeveluwe.nl/en

Klimmendaal

2. Klimmendaal. (2017). Retrieved from https://www.klimmendaal.nl/klimmendaal_revalidatiespecialisten.aspx

Dysphagia

3. NHS Inform. (2019). Dysphagia (swallowing problems). Retrieved from https://www.nhsinform.scot/illnesses-and-conditions/stomach-liver-and-gastrointestinal-tract/dysphagia-swallowing-problems
4. Philpott, H., Garg, M., Tomic, D., Balasubramanian, S., & Sweis, R. (2017). Dysphagia: Thinking outside the box. *World Journal of Gastroenterology*, 23(38), 6942.
5. Carucci, L. R., & Turner, M. A. (2015). Dysphagia revisited: Common and unusual causes. *Radiographics*, 35(1), 105-122.

Shoulder subluxation

6. Brosek, S. (2018). What to know about shoulder subluxation. *Medical news today*. Retrieved from https://www.medicalnewstoday.com/articles/321902.php
7. Vitoonpong, T., & Chang, K. V. (2018). Shoulder subluxation. *StatPearls*. Retrieved from https://www.ncbi.nlm.nih.gov/books/NBK507847/

Speech therapy

8. Logopedist. (2019). In *Wiktionary*. Retrieved May 5, 2019, from https://en.wiktionary.org/wiki/logopedist
9. Gerstenecker, A., & Lazar, R. M. (2019). Language recovery following stroke. *The Clinical Neuropsychologist*, 33(5), 928-947.

CHAPTER 8

Traumatic brain injury

1. Traumatic brain injury. (2019). In *Wikipedia*. Retrieved May 16, 2019 from https://en.wikipedia.org/wiki/Traumatic_brain_injury
2. Gerstenecker, A., & Lazar, R. M. (2019). Language recovery following stroke. *The Clinical Neuropsychologist*, 33(5), 928-947.
3. Hawryluk, G. W., & Manley, G. T. (2015). Classification of traumatic brain injury: Past, present, and future. In *Handbook of clinical neurology* (Vol. 127, pp. 15-21). Amsterdam, Netherlands: Elsevier.

Stockholm

4. Lonely Planet. (2019). Welcome to Stockholm. Retrieved from https://www.lonelyplanet.com/sweden/stockholm

CHAPTER 9

Syllables

1. Syllable. (2019). In *Dictionary.com*. Retrieved from https://www.dictionary.com/browse/syllable

Neuroinflammation after stroke

2. Shichita, T., Ito, M., & Yoshimura, A. (2014). Post-ischemic inflammation regulates neural damage and protection. *Frontiers in cellular neuroscience*, *8*, 319.
3. Fang, M., Zhong, L., Jin, X., Cui, R., Yang, W., Gao, S.,...Liu, T. (2019). Effect of inflammation on the process of stroke rehabilitation and poststroke depression. *Frontiers in psychiatry*, *10*.
4. Drieu, A., Levard, D., Vivien, D., & Rubio, M. (2018). Anti-inflammatory treatments for stroke: From bench to bedside. *Therapeutic Advances in Neurological Disorders*, *11*, 1756286418789854.
5. Gülke, E., Gelderblom, M., & Magnus, T. (2018). Danger signals in stroke and their role in microglia activation after ischemia. *Therapeutic Advances in Neurological Disorders*, *11*, 1756286418774254.
6. Perry, V. H., & Holmes, C. (2014). Microglial priming in neurodegenerative disease. *Nature Reviews Neurology*, *10*(4), 217.

Inflamed brain consequences and brain fog

7. Maier, S. F., & Watkins, L. (2012). Consequences of the inflamed brain. *The dana foundation*. Retrieved from https://dana.org/article/consequences-of-the-inflamed-brain/
8. \Xiong, Y., Mahmood, A., & Chopp, M. (2018). Current understanding of neuroinflammation after traumatic brain injury and cell-based therapeutic opportunities. *Chinese Journal of Traumatology*, *21*(3), 137-151.
9. Corps, K. N., Roth, T. L., & McGavern, D. B. (2015). Inflammation and neuroprotection in traumatic brain injury. *JAMA Neurology*, *72*(3), 355-362.

CHAPTER 10

Eyes and stroke

1. Pula, J. H., & Yuen, C. A. (2017). Eyes and stroke: The visual aspects of cerebrovascular disease. *Stroke and Vascular Neurology*, *2*(4), 210-220.

2. Bird, B., & Stawicki, S. P. (2019). Anatomy, head and neck, ophthalmic arteries. *StatPearls*. Retrieved from https://www.ncbi.nlm.nih.gov/books/NBK482317/

3. Lamirel, C., Newman, N. J., & Biousse, V. (2010). Vascular neuro-ophthalmology. *Neurologic Clinics*, *28*(3), 701-727.

Neuropathic pain

4. Neuropathic pain. (2019). In *Wikipedia*. Retrieved May 17, 2019, from https://en.wikipedia.org/wiki/Neuropathic_pain

5. Colloca, L., Ludman, T., Bouhassira, D., Baron, R., Dickenson, A. H., Yarnitsky, D.,...Raja, S.N (2017). Neuropathic pain. *Nature Reviews Disease Primers*, *3*, 17002.

Eye movement desensitization and processing (EMDR)

6. Shapiro, F. (2014). The role of eye movement desensitization and reprocessing (EMDR) therapy in medicine: Addressing the psychological and physical symptoms stemming from adverse life experiences. *The Permanente Journal*, *18*(1), 71.

Electrical muscle stimulation

7. Baron, R., Binder, A., & Wasner, G. (2010). Neuropathic pain: Diagnosis, pathophysiological mechanisms, and treatment. *The Lancet Neurology*, *9*(8), 807-819.

8. Armstrong, B. (2019). How to get fit using electrical muscle stimulation (EMS). *Scientific american*. Retrieved from https://www.scientificamerican.com/article/how-to-get-fit-using-electrical-muscle-stimulation-ems/?redirect=1

9. Porcari, J. P., Mclean, K. P., Foster, C., Kernozek, T., Crenshaw, B., & Swenson, C. (2002). Effects of electrical muscle stimulation on body composition, muscle strength, and physical appearance. *The Journal of Strength & Conditioning Research*, *16*(2), 165-172.

10. Karatzanos, E., Gerovasili, V., Zervakis, D., Tripodaki, E. S., Apostolou, K., Vasileiadis, I.,...Nanas, S. (2012). Electrical muscle stimulation: An effective form of exercise and early mobilization to preserve muscle strength in critically ill patients. *Critical Care Research and Practice*. Retrieved from https://www.ncbi.nlm.nih.gov/pmc/articles/PMC3321528/

Kindess

11. Einhorn, S. (2007). *The art of being kind*. New York, NY: Pegasus Books.

CHAPTER 11

Sleep and memory

1. Rasch, B., & Born, J. (2013). About sleep's role in memory. *Physiological Reviews*, 93(2), 681-766.
2. Potkin, K. T., & Bunney Jr, W. E. (2012). Sleep improves memory: The effect of sleep on long-term memory in early adolescence. *PLOS One*, *7*(8), e42191.

Gabapentin

3. Gabapentin. (2109). In *Wikipedia*. Retrieved May 18, 2019, from https://en.wikipedia.org/wiki/Gabapentin
4. Quintero, G. C. (2017). Review about gabapentin misuse, interactions, contraindications, and side effects. *Journal of Experimental Pharmacology*, 9, 13.

Gabapentin metanalysis

5. Wiffen, P. J., Derry, S., Bell, R. F., Rice, A. S., Tölle, T. R., Phillips, T., & Moore, R. A. (2017). Gabapentin for chronic neuropathic pain in adults. *Cochrane Database of Systematic Reviews*, (6).

Amitriptyline

6. National Health Service. (2017). Amitriptyline - for pain and migraine. Retrieved from https://www.nhs.uk/medicines/amitriptyline-for-pain/
7. Moore, R. A., Derry, S., Aldington, D., Cole, P., & Wiffen, P. J. (2015). Amitriptyline for neuropathic pain in adults. *Cochrane Database of Systematic Reviews*, (7).
8. Thour, A., & Marwaha, R. (2019). Amitriptyline. *StatPearls*. Retrieved from https://www.ncbi.nlm.nih.gov/books/NBK537225/

CHAPTER 12

Spinalis Rehab Station

1. Rehab Station. (n.d.). Retrieved from http://www.rehabstation.se/Rehabilitering/Om-oss/Other-languages/

Norman Doidge

2. Doidge, N. (2016). *The brain's way of healing: Remarkable discoveries and recoveries from the frontiers of neuroplasticity*. London, England: Penguin.
3. Norman Doidge. (2019). In *Wikipedia*. Retrieved May 21, 2019, from https://en.wikipedia.org/wiki/Norman_Doidge

The Brain that Changes Itself

4. Doidge, N. (2007). *The brain that changes itself: Stories of personal triumph from the frontiers of brain science*. London, Enland: Penguin.
5. BrainCoreOhio. (2007). *Dr. Norman Doidge, the brain that changes itself full show* [Video file]. Retrieved from https://www.youtube.com/watch?v=sK51nv8mo-o

Neuroplasticity

6. Shaffer, J. (2016). Neuroplasticity and clinical practice: Building brainpower for health. *Frontiers in psychology, 7*, 1118.
7. Voss, P., Thomas, M. E., Cisneros-Franco, J. M., & de Villers-Sidani, É. (2017). Dynamic brains and the changing rules of neuroplasticity: Implications for learning and recovery. *Frontiers in psychology, 8*, 1657.
8. Fuchs, E., & Flügge, G. (2014). Adult neuroplasticity: More than 40 years of research. *Neural Plasticity, 2014*.
9. Sharma, N., Classen, J., & Cohen, L. G. (2013). Neural plasticity and its contribution to functional recovery. In *Handbook of clinical neurology* (Vol. 110, pp. 3-12). Amsterdam, Netherlands: Elsevier.
10. Phillips, C. (2017). Lifestyle modulators of neuroplasticity: How physical activity, mental engagement, and diet promote cognitive health during aging. *Neural Plasticity, 2017*.

Taub

11. UAB Medicine. (2019). Constraint-induced therapy (CI therapy) - Taub Therapy Clinic. Retrieved from https://www.uabmedicine.org/patient-care/treatments/ci-therapy

Merzenich

12. Merzenich, M. (2004). *Growing evidence of brain plasticity* [Video file]. Retrieved from https://www.ted.com/talks/michael_merzenich_on_the_elastic_brain?language=en

Bach-y-Rita

13. Abrahams, M., & Winters, D. (2003). Can you see with your tongue? *Discover*. Retrieved from http://discovermagazine.com/2003/jun/feattongue

DNA

14. DNA. (2019). In *Wikipedia*. Retrieved May 26, 2019, from https://en.wikipedia.org/wiki/DNA
15. Sinden, R. R. (2012). *DNA structure and function*. Cambridge, MA: Academic Press.

Precise stimulation

16. Krakauer, J. W., & Carmichael, S. T. (2017). *Broken movement: The neurobiology of motor recovery after stroke*. Cambridge, MA: The MIT Press.
17. Russell, K. (2015). Helping hand: Robots, video games, and a radical new approach to treating stroke patients. *The New Yorker*. Retrieved from https://www.newyorker.com/magazine/2015/11/23/helping-hand-annals-of-medicine-karen-russell

Small wins

18. Amabile, T. M., & Kramer, S. J. (2011). The power of small wins. *Harvard business review, 89*(5), 70-80.

Michael Moskowitz

19. Moskowitz, M. H., & Golden, M. D. (2015). Michael H. Moskowitz, M.D., M.P.H. - biography. Retrieved from http://www.neuroplastix.com/styled-4/styled-4/mhm.html

Claes Hultling

20. Claes Hultling. (2019). In *Wikipedia*. Retrieved June 6, 2019, from https://sv.wikipedia.org/wiki/Claes_Hultling

CHAPTER 13

Michael Moskowitz

1. Moskowitz, M. H., & Golden, M. D. (2015). Shrink the map - (workbook page 13). Retrieved from http://www.neuroplastix.com/styled-2/page1/styled-22/Shrinkthemap.html
2. Moskowitz, M. H., & Golden, M. D. (2015). Michael H. Moskowitz, M.D., M.P.H. - biography. Retrieved from http://www.neuroplastix.com/styled-4/styled-4/mhm.html

Brain map

3. Roux, F. E., Djidjeli, I., & Durand, J. B. (2018). Functional architecture of the somatosensory homunculus detected by electrostimulation. *The Journal of Physiology, 596*(5), 941-956.

Neurons that fire together, wire together

4. Hebbian theory. (2019). In *Wikipedia*. Retrieved June 4, 2019,from https://en.wikipedia.org/wiki/Hebbian_theory
5. Langille, J. J., & Brown, R. E. (2018). The synaptic theory of memory: A historical survey and reconciliation of recent opposition. *Frontiers in systems neuroscience, 12*.

6. Kelso, S. R., Ganong, A. H., & Brown, T. H. (1986). Hebbian synapses in the hippocampus. *Proceedings of the National Academy of Sciences*, 83(14), 5326-5330.

Use it or lose it principle

7. Shors, T. J., Anderson, M. L., Curlik II, D. M., & Nokia, M. S. (2012). Use it or lose it: How neurogenesis keeps the brain fit for learning. *Behavioral Brain Research*, 227(2), 450-458.

8. Ackerman, P. L., Kanfer, R., & Calderwood, C. (2010). Use it or lose it? Wii brain exercise practice and reading for domain knowledge. *Psychology and Aging*, 25(4), 753.

9. Sun, Q. (2007). The missing piece in the "use it or lose it" puzzle: Is inhibition regulated by activity or does it act on its own accord? *Reviews in the Neurosciences*, 18(3/4), 295.

Neuroplastic Transformation Workbook

10. Moskowitz, M. H., & Golden, M. D. (2013). *Neuroplastic transformation workbook*. Sausalito, CA: Neuroplastic Partners, LLC.

Mental imagery and pain

11. Fardo F., Allen M., Elmholdt Jegindø E.M., Angrilli A.,and Roepstorff A. (2015) Neurocognitive evidence for mental imagery-driven hypoalgesic and hyperalgesic pain regulation. *Neuroimage*. 120: 350–361.

12. Berna C., Vincent K., Moore J. (2011) Presence of mental imagery associated with chronic pelvic pain: a pilot study. *Pain Med.* 12:1086–1093.

13. Berna C., Tracey I., Holmes E. (2012) How a better understanding of spontaneous mental imagery linked to pain could enhance imagery-based therapy in chronic pain. *J. Exp. Psychopathol.* 3:258–273.

14. Anderson M.C., Ochsner K.N., Kuhl B., Cooper J., Robertson E., Gabrieli S.W., Glover G.H., Gabrieli J.D.E. (2004) Neural systems underlying the suppression of unwanted memories. *Science*. 303:232–235.

15. Kosslyn S.M., Ganis G., Thompson W.L. (2001) Neural foundations of imagery. *Nat. Rev. Neurosci.* 2:635–642.

16. MacIver K., Lloyd D.M., Kelly S., Roberts N., Nurmikko T. (2008) Phantom limb pain, cortical reorganization and the therapeutic effect of mental imagery. *Brain*. 131:2181–2191.

17. Philips H.C. (2010) Imagery and pain: the prevalence, characteristics, and potency of imagery associated with pain. *Behav. Cogn. Psychoth.* 39:523–540.

18. Tracey I. (2010) Getting the pain you expect: mechanisms of placebo, nocebo and reappraisal effects in humans. *Nat. Med.*16:1277–1283.

19. Wiech K., Kalisch R., Weiskopf N., Pleger B., Stephan K.E., Dolan R.J. (2006) Anterolateral prefrontal cortex mediates the analgesic effect of expected and perceived control over pain. *J. Neurosci.* 26:11501–11509.

CHAPTER 14

Bananas are really berries

1. Petre, A. (2018). Is a banana a berry or fruit? The surprising truth. *Healthline*. Retrieved from https://www.healthline.com/nutrition/bananas-berries-or-fruits

Agency of recovery

2. Lysaker, P. H., & Leonhardt, B. L. (2012). Agency: Its nature and role in recovery from severe mental illness. *World Psychiatry*, *11*(3), 165.

3. Frost, B. G., Tirupati, S., Johnston, S., Turrell, M., Lewin, T. J., Sly, K. A., & Conrad, A. M. (2017). An integrated recovery-oriented model (IRM) for mental health services: Evolution and challenges. *BMC Psychiatry*, *17*(1), 22.

Aphasia recovery

4. The National Aphasia Association. (2019). Aphasia FAQs. Retrieved from https://www.aphasia.org/aphasia-faqs/

5. Kertesz, A., & McCabe, P. (1977). Recovery patterns and prognosis in aphasia. *Brain: A Journal of Neurology*, *100*, 1-18.

6. Hillis, A. E., Beh, Y. Y., Sebastian, R., Breining, B., Tippett, D. C., Wright, A. & Yourganov, G. (2018). Predicting recovery in acute post-stroke aphasia. *Annals of Neurology*, *83*(3), 612-622.

CHAPTER 15

Obsessive-compulsive disorder (OCD)

1. National Institute of Mental Health. (2019). Obsessive-compulsive disorder. Retrieved from https://www.nimh.nih.gov/health/topics/obsessive-compulsive-disorder-ocd/index.shtml

2. Hirschtritt, M. E., Bloch, M. H., & Mathews, C. A. (2017). Obsessive-compulsive disorder: Advances in diagnosis and treatment. *JAMA*, *317*(13), 1358-1367.

3. InformedHealth.org. (2008). Obsessive-compulsive disorder: Overview. *Institute for quality and efficiency in health care*. Retrieved from https://www.ncbi.nlm.nih.gov/books/NBK279562/

Growing skull fracture

4. Singh, I., Rohilla, S., Siddiqui, S. A., & Kumar, P. (2016). Growing skull fractures: Guidelines for early diagnosis and surgical management. *Child's Nervous System*, 32(6), 1117-1122.
5. Liu, X. S., You, C., Lu, M., & Liu, J. G. (2012). Growing skull fracture stages and treatment strategy. *Journal of Neurosurgery: Pediatrics*, 9(6), 670-675.

Lyme disease

6. Mayo Clinic. (2019). Lyme disease. Retrieved from https://www.mayoclinic.org/diseases-conditions/lyme-disease/symptoms-causes/syc-20374651
7. Biesiada, G., Czepiel, J., Leśniak, M. R., Garlicki, A., & Mach, T. (2012). Lyme disease. *Archives of Medical Science*, 8(6), 978.
8. Skar, G. L., & Simonsen, K. A. (2018). Lyme disease. *StatPearls*. Retrieved from https://www.ncbi.nlm.nih.gov/books/NBK431066/

Oxazepam

9. Oxazepam. (2019). In *Wikipedia*. Retrieved June 12, 2019, from https://nl.wikipedia.org/wiki/Oxazepam
10. Dinis-Oliveira, R. J. (2017). Metabolic profile of oxazepam and related benzodiazepines: Clinical and forensic aspects. *Drug Metabolism Reviews*, 49(4), 451-463.

CHAPTER 16

Lara Boyd's TEDx talk

1. TEDx Talks. (2015). *After watching this, your brain will not be the same - Lara Boyd - TEDx Vancouver* [Video file]. Retrieved from https://www.youtube.com/watch?v=LNHBMFCzznE

Multiple Sclerosis

2. National Multiple Sclerosis Society. (2019). What is MS? Retrieved from https://www.nationalmssociety.org/What-is-MS
3. Goldenberg, M. M. (2012). Multiple sclerosis reviews. *Pharmacy and Therapeutics*, 37(3), 175.
4. Ghasemi, N., Razavi, S., & Nikzad, E. (2017). Multiple sclerosis: Pathogenesis, symptoms, diagnoses, and cell-based therapy. *Cell Journal (Yakhteh)*, 19(1), 1

Parkinson's disease

5. Mayo Clinic. (2019). Parkinson's disease. Retrieved from https://www.mayoclinic.org/diseases-conditions/parkinsons-disease/symptoms-causes/syc-20376055
6. Massano, J., & Bhatia, K. (2012). Clinical approach to Parkinson's disease: Features, diagnosis, and principles of management. *Cold Spring Harbor perspectives in medicine*, 2(6), a008870-a008870.
7. Zafar, S., & Yaddanapudi, S. S. (2018). Parkinson disease. *StatPearls*. Retrieved from https://www.ncbi.nlm.nih.gov/books/NBK470193/

Harvard University

8. Harvard University. (2019). History. Retrieved from https://www.harvard.edu/about-harvard/harvard-glance/history

Botox to treat spasticity

9. O'Brien, C.F. (2002). Treatment of spasticity with botulinum toxin. *PubMed*. Retrieved from https://www.ncbi.nlm.nih.gov/pubmed/12569967
10. Lagalla, G., Danni, M., Reiter, F., Ceravolo, M., & Provinciali, L. (2000). Post-stroke spasticity management with repeated botulinum toxin injections in the upper limb. *American Journal of Physical Medicine & Rehabilitation*, 79(4), 377-384.

Stem cell therapy in brain trauma

11. Rolfe, A., & Sun, D. (2015). Stem cell therapy in brain trauma: Implications for repair and regeneration of injured brain in experimental TBI models. *PubMed*. Retrieved from https://www.ncbi.nlm.nih.gov/pubmed/26269908
12. Weston, N., & Sun, D. (2018). The potential of stem cells in treatment of traumatic brain injury. *Current Neurology and Neuroscience Reports*, *18*(1).
13. Watanabe, T. (2018). A review of stem cell therapy for acquired brain injuries and neurodegenerative central nervous system diseases. *PM&R*, *10*, S151-S156.

CHAPTER 17

Daily Stoic

1. Holiday, R., & Hanselman, S. (2016). *The daily stoic: 366 meditations on wisdom, perseverance, and the art of living*. London, England: Penguin.
2. Daily Stoic. (2019). Retrieved from https://dailystoic.com/

Stoicism

3. Stoicism. (2019). In *Wikipedia*. Retrieved June 14, 2019, from https://en.wikipedia.org/wiki/Stoicism
4. Pathak, E. B., Wieten, S. E., & Wheldon, C. W. (2017). Stoic beliefs and health: Development and preliminary validation of the Pathak-Wieten Stoicism Ideology Scale. *BMJ Open*, *7*(11), e015137.
5. Fabjański, M., & Brymer, E. (2017). Enhancing health and wellbeing through immersion in nature: A conceptual perspective combining the Stoic and Buddhist traditions. *Frontiers in psychology*, *8*, 1573.
6. Daily Stoic. (2019). What is stoicism? A definition & 9 stoic exercises to get you started. Retrieved from https://dailystoic.com/what-is-stoicism-a-definition-3-stoic-exercises-to-get-you-started/

Zeno the philosopher

7. Daily Stoic. (2019). Who is Zeno? An introduction to the founder of stoicism. Retrieved from https://dailystoic.com/zeno/

Meditations by Marcus Aurelius

8. Daily Stoic. (2019). Meditations by Marcus Aurelius: Book summary, key lessons, and best quotes. Retrieved from https://dailystoic.com/meditations-marcus-aurelius/

Discourses by Epictetus

9. Daily Stoic. (2019). Discourses of Epictetus: Book summary, key lessons, and best quotes. Retrieved from https://dailystoic.com/epictetus-discourses-summary-quotes/

Seneca's *Letters from a Stoic*

10. Daily Stoic. (2019). Letters from a stoic by Seneca: Book summary, key lessons, and best quotes. Retrieved from https://dailystoic.com/letters-from-a-stoic/

Byron Katie

11. Byron Katie. (2019). In *Wikipedia*. Retreived June 12, 2019, from https://en.wikipedia.org/wiki/Byron_Katie

The Obstacle Is the Way

12. Holiday, R. (2014). *The obstacle is the way: The timeless art of turning trials into triumph*. London, England: Penguin.

Quote by Marcus Aurelius

13. Daily Stoic. (2019). Quotes by Marcus Aurelius. Retrieved from https://dailystoic.com/marcus-aurelius-quotes/

Quote by Epictetus

14. Daily Stoic. (2019). Quotes by Epictetus. Retrieved from https://dailystoic.com/epictetus-quotes/

Quote by Seneca

15. Daily Stoic. (2019). Quotes by Seneca. Retrieved from https://dailystoic.com/seneca-quotes/

Quote from the Buddha

16. Hutyra, H. (2019). 108 Buddha quotes on meditation, spirituality, and happiness. *Keep inspiring me*. Retrieved from https://www.keepinspiring.me/buddha-quotes/

CHAPTER 18

Constraint-induced movement therapy

1. Peurala, S. H., Kantanen, M. P., Sjögren, T., Paltamaa, J., Karhula, M., & Heinonen, A. (2012). Effectiveness of constraint-induced movement therapy on activity and participation after stroke: A systematic review and meta-analysis of randomized controlled trials. *Clinical Rehabilitation*, 26(3), 209-223.
2. Kwakkel, G., Veerbeek, J. M., van Wegen, E. E., & Wolf, S. L. (2015). Constraint-induced movement therapy after stroke. *The Lancet Neurology*, *14*(2), 224-234
3. Thrane, G., Friborg, O., Anke, A., & Indredavik, B. (2014). A meta-analysis of constraint-induced movement therapy after stroke. *Journal of Rehabilitation Medicine*, 46(9), 833-842.
4. Physiopedia. (2019). Constraint-induced movement therapy. Retrieved from https://www.physio-pedia.com/Constraint_Induced_Movement_Therapy
5. UAB Medicine. (2019). Constraint-induced therapy (CI therapy) - Taub Therapy Clinic. Retrieved from https://www.uabmedicine.org/patient-care/treatments/ci-therapy
6. Edward Taub. (2019). In *Wikipedia*. Retrieved June 14, 2019, from https://en.wikipedia.org/wiki/Edward_Taub

CHAPTER 19

Factor Leiden V mutation

1. Factor V Leiden. (2019). In *Wikipedia*. Retrieved June 15, 2019 from https://en.wikipedia.org/wiki/Factor_V_Leiden
2. Kujovich, J. L. (2018). Factor V Leiden thrombophilia. In *GeneReviews*. Seattle, WA: University of Washington, Seattle.

3. Bertina, R.M (1997). Factor V Leiden and other coagulation factor mutations affecting thrombotic risk. *PubMed*. Retrieved from https://www.ncbi.nlm.nih.gov/pubmed/9299960

Heterozygote definition

4. Heterozygote. (2019). In *Biology dictionary*. Retrieved from https://www.biology-online.org/dictionary/Heterozygote
5. Lodish, H., Berk, A., Zipursky, L., Matsudaira, P., Baltimore, D., & Darnell, J. (2000). *Molecular cell biology*. New York, NY: Scientific American Books.

Deep vein thrombosis

6. Deep vein thrombosis. (2019). In *Wikipedia*. Retrieved June 14, 2019, from https://en.wikipedia.org/wiki/Deep_vein_thrombosis
7. Stone, J., Hangge, P., Albadawi, H., Wallace, A., Shamoun, F., Knuttien, M. G., & Oklu, R. (2017). Deep vein thrombosis: Pathogenesis, diagnosis, and medical management. *Cardiovascular Diagnosis and Therapy*, 7(Suppl 3), S276.

Pulmonary embolism

8. Mayo Clinic (2019). Pulmonary embolism. https://www.mayoclinic.org/diseases-conditions/pulmonary-embolism/multimedia/pulmonary-embolism/img-20006463
9. Bělohlávek, J., Dytrych, V., & Linhart, A. (2013). Pulmonary embolism, part I: Epidemiology, risk factors and risk stratification, pathophysiology, clinical presentation, diagnosis, and non-thrombotic pulmonary embolism. *Experimental & Clinical Cardiology*, 18(2), 129.

Paradoxical embolism

10. Paradoxical embolism. (2019). In *Wikipedia*. Retrieved June 14, 2019, from https://en.wikipedia.org/wiki/Paradoxical_embolism
11. Chant, H., & McCollum, C. (2001). Stroke in young adults: The role of paradoxical embolism. *Thrombosis and Haemostasis*, 85(01), 22-29.
12. Purandare, N., Oude Voshaar, R. C., Burns, A., Velupandian, U. M., & McCollum, C. (2006). Paradoxical embolization: A potential cause of cerebral damage in Alzheimer's disease? *Neurological Research*, 28(6), 679 684.

Heart, anatomy, and function

13. Sullivan, D. (2018). The heart: All you need to know. *Medical news today*. https://www.medicalnewstoday.com/articles/320565.php

14. Khan Academy. (2019) *Circulatory system and the heart* [Video file]. Retrieved from https://www.khanacademy.org/science/high-school-biology/hs-human-body-systems/hs-the-circulatory-and-respiratory-systems/v/circulatory-system-and-the-heart

Patent foramen ovale

15. American Heart Association, Inc. (2019). Patent foramen ovale (PFO). Retrieved from https://www.heart.org/en/health-topics/congenital-heart-defects/about-congenital-heart-defects/patent-foramen-ovale-pfo

16. Hampton, T., & Murphy-Lavoie, H. M. (2018). Patent foramen ovale. *StatPearls*. Retrieved from https://www.ncbi.nlm.nih.gov/books/NBK493151/

Transesophageal echocardiography

17. American Heart Association, Inc. (2019). Transesophageal echocardiography (TEE). Retrieved from https://www.heart.org/en/health-topics/heart-attack/diagnosing-a-heart-attack/transesophageal-echocardiography-tee

Road to Hana map

18. Guide of US. (2019). Road to Hana map. Retrieved from https://www.hawaii-guide.com/maui/road-to-hana-map

Michael Merzenich TED talk

19. Merzenich, M. (2004). *Growing evidence of brain plasticity* [Video file]. Retrieved https://www.ted.com/talks/michael_merzenich_on_the_elastic_brain?language=en

Barefoot walking advantages

20. Lindberg, S. (2018). Does walking barefoot have health benefits? *Healthline*. Retrieved from https://www.healthline.com/health/walking-barefoot#bottom-line

21. Hollander, K., Van der Zwaard, B. C., De Villiers, J. E., Braumann, K. M., Venter, R., & Zech, A. (2016). The effects of being habitually barefoot on foot mechanics and motor performance in children and adolescents aged 6-18 years: Study protocol for a multicenter cross-sectional study (Barefoot LIFE project). *Journal of Foot and Ankle Research*, 9(1), 36.

22. Hollander, K., De Villiers, J. E., Sehner, S., Wegscheider, K., Braumann, K. M., Venter, R., & Zech, A. (2017). Growing-up (habitually) barefoot influences the development of foot and arch morphology in children and adolescents. *Scientific Reports*, *7*(1), 8079.

23. Hollander, K., Heidt, C., Van der Zwaard, B. C., Braumann, K. M., & Zech, A. (2017). Long-term effects of habitual barefoot running and walking: A systematic review. *Medicine & Science in Sports & Exercise*, 49(4), 752-762

CHAPTER 20

Constraint-induced movement therapy (CIMT)

1. Peurala, S. H., Kantanen, M. P., Sjögren, T., Paltamaa, J., Karhula, M., & Heinonen, A. (2012). Effectiveness of constraint-induced movement therapy on activity and participation after stroke: A systematic review and meta-analysis of randomized controlled trials. *Clinical Rehabilitation*, 26(3), 209-223.
2. Thrane, G., Friborg, O., Anke, A., & Indredavik, B. (2014). A meta-analysis of constraint-induced movement therapy after stroke. *Journal of Rehabilitation Medicine*, 46(9), 833-42.
3. Kwakkel, G., Veerbeek, J. M., van Wegen, E. E., & Wolf, S. L. (2015). Constraint-induced movement therapy after stroke. *The Lancet Neurology*, 14(2), 224-234.
4. Physiopedia. (2019). Constraint-induced movement therapy. Retrieved from https://www.physio-pedia.com/Constraint_Induced_Movement_Therapy
5. UAB Medicine. (2019). Constraint-induced therapy (CI therapy) - Taub Therapy Clinic. Retrieved from https://www.uabmedicine.org/patient-care/treatments/ci-therapy

Norman Doidge's book

6. Doidge, N. (2016). *The brain's way of healing: Remarkable discoveries and recoveries from the frontiers of neuroplasticity*. London, England: Penguin.

The brain on ping-pong

7. Kloeffler, D. (2011). This is your brain on ping pong. ABC News. https://abcnews.go.com/Technology/brain-ping-pong/story?id=12721610
8. Biernat, E., Buchholtz, S., & Krzepota, J. (2018). Eye on the ball: Table tennis as a pro-health form of leisure-time physical activity. *International Journal of Environmental Research and Public Health*, 15(4), 738.
9. Guo, Z., Li, A., & Yu, L. (2017). "Neural efficiency" of athletes' brain during the visuospatial task: An fMRI study on table tennis players. *Frontiers in behavioral neuroscience*, 11, 72.

10. Miriam Stoppard Lifetime Ltd. (2019). Why playing ping pong is great for the brain and could help prevent dementia. Retrieved from http://www.miriamstoppard.com/news/playing-ping-pong-great-brain-help-prevent-dementia/

Pre-crawling exercises

11. Cimbiz, A., & Bayazit, V. (2005). Effects of infant crawling experience on a range of motion. *Neurosciences (Riyadh)*, *10*(1), 34-40.
12. Adolph, K. E., Berger, S. E., & Leo, A. J. (2011). Developmental continuity? Crawling, cruising, and walking. *Developmental Science*, *14*(2), 306-318.
13. Borer, K. T. (1995). The effects of exercise on growth. *Sports Medicine*, *20*(6), 375-397.
14. Goddard, S. B. (2002). *Reflexes, learning, and behaviour: A window into the child's mind*. Eugene, OR: Fern Ridge Press.
15. Butcher, K., VandenBerg, A., & Dodds, T. (2013) Why crawl? *Michigan State University extension*. Retrieved from https://www.canr.msu.edu/news/why_crawl

How braille activates the brain

16. Kloc, J. (2011). Reading braille activates the brain's visual area. *Scientific American*. Retrieved from https://www.scientificamerican.com/article/the-reading-region/

The language area of the brain

17. Binder, J. R. (2015). The Wernicke area: Modern evidence and a reinterpretation. *Neurology*, *85*(24), 2170-2175.

CHAPTER 21

"Jeanny" song

1. FALCO. (2009). *Falco - Jeanny (official video)* [Video file]. Retrieved from https://www.youtube.com/watch?v=Urw-iutHw5E

Ego is the Enemy

2. Holiday, R. (2019). *Ego is the enemy*. London, England: Penguin.

Obama describing dropping his daughter off at Harvard

3. games free fier. (2018). *Obama describes dropping daughter Malia off at college* [Video file]. Retrieved from https://www.youtube.com/watch?v=vjPUZWAq83M

CHAPTER 22

Efference copy

1. Niziolek, C. A., Nagarajan, S. S., & Houde, J.F. (2013). What does motor efference copy represent? Evidence from speech production. *Journal of Neuroscience*, 33(41), 16110-16116.
2. Jeannerod, M., & Arbib, M. (2003). Action monitoring and forward control of movements. *The handbook of brain theory and neural networks*, 83-85. Cambridge, MA: MIT Press.
3. Gyr, J. W. (1972). Is a theory of direct visual perception adequate? *Psychological Bulletin*, 77(4), 246.
4. Gallistel, C. R. (2013). *The organization of action: A new synthesis*. London, England: Psychology Press.
5. Miall, R. C., & Wolpert, D. M. (1996). Forward models for physiological motor control. *Neural Networks*, 9(8), 1265-1279.
6. Griisser, O. J. (1995). On the history of the ideas of efference copy and reafference. In *Essays in the history of the physiological sciences: Proceedings of a network symposium of the European Association for the History of Medicine and Health Held at the University Louis Pasteur, Strasbourg, on March* (Vol. 26, p. 35).

Cortico-ponto-cerebello-thalamocortical pathway

7. Palesi, F., De Rinaldis, A., Castellazzi, G., Calamante, F., Muhlert, N., Chard, D. & Wheeler-Kingshott, C. A. G. (2017). Contralateral cortico-ponto-cerebellar pathways reconstruction in humans in vivo: Implications for reciprocal cerebro-cerebellar structural connectivity in motor and non-motor areas. *Scientific Reports*, 7(1), 12841.

Brain stem reticular formation

8. Reticular formation. (2019). In *Wikipedia*. Retrieved July 7, 2019, from https://en.wikipedia.org/wiki/Reticular_formation
9. Jang, S. H., & Kwon, H. G. (2015). The direct pathway from the brainstem reticular formation to the cerebral cortex in the ascending reticular activating system: A diffusion tensor imaging study. *Neuroscience Letters*, 606, 200-203. doi: 10.1016/j.neulet.2015.09.004.
10. Moruzzi, G., & Magoun, H. W. (1949). Brain stem reticular formation and activation of the EEG. *Electroencephalography and clinical neurophysiology*, 1(1-4), 455-473.

Cortico cerebellar connections and recovery in stroke

11. Schulz, R., Frey, B. M., Koch, P., Zimerman, M., Bönstrup, M., Feldheim, J., & Gerloff, C. (2015). Cortico-cerebellar structural connectivity is

related to residual motor output in chronic stroke. *Cerebral Cortex*, 27(1), 635-645. Schulz, R., Frey, B. M., Koch, P., Zimerman, M., Bönstrup, M., Feldheim, J. & Gerloff, C. (2015). Cortico-cerebellar structural connectivity is related to residual motor output in chronic stroke. *Cerebral Cortex*, 27(1), 635-645.

12. Lee, J., Lee, A., Kim, H., Chang, W. H., & Kim, Y. H. (2018). Differences in motor network dynamics during recovery between supra- and infra-tentorial ischemic strokes. *Human brain mapping*, 39(12), 4976-4986.

Reticulo spinal tracts

13. KenHub. (2019). Reticulospinal tract. Retrieved from https://www.kenhub.com/en/library/anatomy/reticulospinal-tract
14. Baker, S. N. (2011). The primate reticulospinal tract, hand function and functional recovery. *The Journal of Physiology*, 589(23), 5603-5612.
15. Schieber, M. H. (2007). Comparative anatomy and physiology of the corticospinal system. In *Handbook of clinical neurology* (Vol. 82, pp. 15-37). Amsterdam, Netherlands: Elsevier.
16. Ten Donkelaar, H. J. (1976). Descending pathways from the brain stem to the spinal cord in some reptiles. II. Course and site of termination. *Journal of Comparative Neurology*, *167*(4), 443-463.
17. Takakusaki, K., Kohyama, J., Matsuyama, K., & Mori, S. (2001). Medullary reticulospinal tract mediating the generalized motor inhibition in cats: Parallel inhibitory mechanisms acting on motoneurons and on interneuronal transmission in reflex pathways. *Neuroscience*, *103*(2), 511-527.
18. Honeycutt, C. F., Kharouta, M., & Perreault, E. J. (2013). Evidence for reticulospinal contributions to coordinated finger movements in humans. *Journal of Neurophysiology*, *110*(7), 1476-1483.

Reticulospinal tracts in motor and postural control

19. Takakusaki, K. (2017). Functional neuroanatomy for posture and gait control. *Journal of Movement Disorders*, *10*(1), 1.
20. Deliagina, T. G., Zelenin, P. V., & Orlovsky, G. N. (2012). Physiological and circuit mechanisms of postural control. *Current opinion in neurobiology*, 22(4), 646-652.
21. Takakusaki, K., Chiba, R., Nozu, T., & Okumura, T. (2016). Brainstem control of locomotion and muscle tone with special reference to the role of the mesopontine tegmentum and medullary reticulospinal systems. *Journal of Neural Transmission*, *123*(7), 695-729.

22. Physiopedia. (2019). Reticulospinal test. Retrieved from https://www.physio-pedia.com/Reticulospinal_Tract

CHAPTER 23

Head Strong

1. Asprey, D. (2017). *Head strong: The bulletproof plan to activate untapped brain energy to work smarter and think faster—in just two weeks.* New York, NY: HarperCollins.

Dave Asprey

2. Dave Asprey. (2019). In *Wikipedia.* Retrieved July 12, 2019, from https://en.wikipedia.org/wiki/Dave_Asprey

Biohacking

3. Keulartz, J., & van den Belt, H. (2016). DIY-bio - economic, epistemological and ethical implications and ambivalences. *Life sciences, society and policy, 12*(1), 7.

Biohacking blog

4. BulletProof. (2019). Show your gut some love. Retrieved from https://blog.bulletproof.com/

Antifragile book review

5. Runciman, D. (2012). Antifragile: How to live in a world we don't understand by Nassim Nicholas Taleb – review. *The Gaurdian.* Retrieved from https://www.theguardian.com/books/2012/nov/21/antifragile-how-to-live-nassim-nicholas-taleb-review

Minding My Mitochondria

6. Terry, L. W., & Asala, J. (2010). *Minding my mitochondria: How I overcame secondary progressive multiple sclerosis (MS) and got out of my wheelchair* (2nd ed.). Iowa City, IA: TZ Press, LLC.

Khan Academy

7. Khan Academy. (2019). For every student, every classroom. Real results. Retrieved from https://www.khanacademy.org/

Energy Blue Print

8. Energy Blueprint. (2019). Want to overcome fatigue and get your energy back? Retrieved from https://www.theenergyblueprint.com/

Mitochondria

9. Friedman, J. R., & Nunnari, J. (2014). Mitochondrial form and function. *Nature, 505*(7483), 335.

10. Cooper, G. M. (2000). Mitochondria. *The cell: A molecular approach* (2nd ed.).2nd edition.. Sunderland, MA: Sinauer Associates. Retrieved from https://www.ncbi.nlm.nih.gov/books/NBK9896/

Adenosine triphosphate (ATP)

11. Khan Academy. (2014). *ATP: Adenosine triphosphate - energy and enzymes - biology - Khan Academy* [Video file]. Retrieved from https://www.youtube.com/watch?v=PK6Hmle2EAg

12. Bonora, M., Patergnani, S., Rimessi, A., De Marchi, E., Suski, J. M., Bononi, A. & Wieckowski, M. R. (2012). ATP synthesis and storage. *Purinergic Signalling, 8*(3), 343-357.

Cell danger response

13. Naviaux, R. K. (2014). Metabolic features of the cell danger response.

Mitochondrion, 16, 7-17.

14. Naviaux, R., Naviaux, J., Li, K., Bright, A., Alaynick, W.,...Wang, L. (2016). Metabolic features of chronic fatigue syndrome. *Proceedings of the National Academy of Sciences, 113*(37), E5472-E5480.

15. Naviaux, R. K. (2019). Metabolic features and regulation of the healing cycle - a new model for chronic disease pathogenesis and treatment. *Mitochondrion, 46*, 278-297.

Hormesis

16. Mattson, M. P. (2008). Hormesis defined. *Ageing research reviews, 7*(1), 1-7.

17. Hood, W. R., Zhang, Y., Mowry, A. V., Hyatt, H. W., & Kavazis, A. N. (2018). Life history trade-offs within the context of mitochondrial hormesis. *Integrative and Comparative Biology*, 58(3), 567-577.

18. Bárcena, C., Mayoral, P., & Quirós, P. M. (2018). Mitohormesis, an antiaging paradigm. In *International review of cell and molecular biology* (Vol. 340, pp. 35-77). Cambridge, MA: Academic Press.

19. Calabrese, E. J., & Mattson, M. P. (2017). How does hormesis impact biology, toxicology, and medicine? *NPJ aging and mechanisms of disease*, 3(1), 13.

20. Radak, Z., Chung, H. Y., Koltai, E., Taylor, A. W., & Goto, S. (2008). Exercise, oxidative stress and hormesis. *Ageing research reviews*, 7(1), 34-42.

21. Ristow, M., & Zarse, K. (2010). How increased oxidative stress promotes longevity and metabolic health: The concept of mitochondrial hormesis (mitohormesis). *Experimental gerontology*, 45(6), 410-418.

Effect of high-intensity exercise

22. Cipryan, L., Tschakert, G., & Hofmann, P. (2017). Acute and post-exercise physiological responses to high-intensity interval training in endurance and sprint athletes. *Journal of sports science & medicine*, *16*(2), 219.

Intermittent fasting

23. Pattillo, A. (2019). The truth behind what intermittent fasting does to your body. *Inverse*. Retrieved from https://www.google.nl/amp/s/www.inverse.com/amp/article/57625-what-intermittent-fasting-actually-does-to-your-body

Toxic phytochemicals

24. Kennedy, D. O., Wightman, E. L. (2011) Herbal Extracts and Phytochemicals: Plant Secondary Metabolites and the Enhancement of Human Brain Function. *Adv. Nutr.*, 32-50

Sleep, dangers of too little sleep

25. Colten, H. R., & Altevogt, B. M. (2006). Extent and health consequences of chronic sleep loss and sleep disorders. *Sleep disorders and sleep deprivation: An unmet public health problem*, 55-135. Washington, DC: National Academies Press.
26. Medic, G., Wille, M., & Hemels, M. E. (2017). Short- and long-term health consequences of sleep disruption. *Nature and Science of Sleep*, *9*, 151.
27. Krause, A. J., Simon, E. B., Mander, B. A., Greer, S. M., Saletin, J. M., Goldstein-Piekarski, A. N., & Walker, M. P. (2017). The sleep-deprived human brain. *Nature Reviews Neuroscience*, *18*(7), 404.
28. Nicholson, C. R. (2006). Importance of sleep: Six reasons not to scrimp on sleep. *Harvard health publishing*. Retrieved from https://www.health.harvard.edu/press_releases/importance_of_sleep_and_health

Dangers of artificial light

29. Cho, Y., Ryu, S. H., Lee, B. R., Kim, K. H., Lee, E., & Choi, J. (2015). Effects of artificial light at night on human health: A literature review of observational and experimental studies applied to exposure assessment. *Chronobiology International*, 32(9), 1294-1310.
30. Contín, M. A., Benedetto, M. M., Quinteros-Quintana, M. L., & Guido, M. E. (2016). Light pollution: The possible consequences of excessive illumination on retina. *Eye*, *30*(2), 255.

31. Al-Naggar, R. A., & Anil, S. (2016). Artificial light at night and cancer: Global study. *Asian Pacific Journal of Cancer Prevention, 17*(10), 4661.

CHAPTER 24

Charles Czeisler

1. Harvard Medical School. (2012). *Sleep deficit: The performance killer* [Video file]. Retrieved from https://www.youtube.com/watch?v=pNHcXmiYsBk
2. Charles Czeisler. (2019). In *Wikipedia*. Retrieved July 12, 2019, from https://en.wikipedia.org/wiki/Charles_Czeisler

Stages of sleep

3. Khan Academy. (2019). *Sleep stages and circadian rhythms* [Video file]. Retrieved from https://www.khanacademy.org/science/health-and-medicine/executive-systems-of-the-brain/sleep-and-consciousness-lesson/v/sleep-stages-and-circadian-rhythms
4. Colten, H. R., & Altevogt, B. M. (2006). Sleep physiology. *Sleep disorders and sleep deprivation: An unmet public health problem.* Washington, DC: National Academies Press.
5. Carley, D. W., & Farabi, S. S. (2016). Physiology of sleep. *Diabetes Spectrum, 29*(1), 5-9.

REM sleep

6. Leonard, J. (2017). What is REM sleep? *Medical news today.* Retrieved from https://www.medicalnewstoday.com/articles/247927.php
7. Peever, J., & Fuller, P. M. (2017). The biology of REM sleep. *Current Biology, 27*(22), R1237-R1248.
8. Purves, D., Augustine, G. J., & Fitzpatrick, D. (2001). *The possible functions of REM sleep and dreaming.* Sunderland, MA: Sinauer Associates.

How To Stop Worrying and Start Living

9. Carnegie, D. (1990). *How to stop worrying and start living.* New York, NY: Pocket Books.

The Tools

10. Johnson, B. (2015). *PNTV: The tools by Phil Stutz & Barry Michels* [Video file]. Retrieved from https://www.youtube.com/watch?v=ThIgZALR1HY

Ego Is the Enemy talk

11. Talks at Google. (2016). *Ryan Holiday: "Ego is the enemy" - talks at Google* [Video file]. Retrieved from https://www.youtube.com/watch?v=Ug414e-PCn4

Optimize app by Brian Jonsson

12. Optimize. (2019). Optimize every facet of your life. Actualize your potential. Retrieved from https://www.optimize.me/

Meditation and its regulatory role sleep

13. Nagendra, R. P., Maruthai, N., & Kutty, B. M. (2012). Meditation and its regulatory role on sleep. *Frontiers in neurology*, 3, 54.
14. Rusch, H. L., Rosario, M., Levison, L. M., Olivera, A., Livingston, W. S., Wu, T., & Gill, J. M. (2019). The effect of mindfulness meditation on sleep quality: A systematic review and meta-analysis of randomized controlled trials. *Annals of the New York Academy of Sciences*, *1445*(1), 5-16.

Headspace app

15. Headspace. (2019). Your guide to health and happiness. Retrieved from https://www.headspace.com/

The Power of Now

16. Tolle, E. (1999). *The power of now: A guide to spiritual enlightenment*. Novato, CA: New World Library.

Autonomous sensory meridian response (ASMR)

17. Autonomous sensory meridian response. (2019). In *Wikipedia*. Retrieved July 14, 2019, from https://nl.wikipedia.org/wiki/Autonomous_sensory_meridian_response
18. Poerio, G. L., Blakey, E., Hostler, T. J., & Veltri, T. (2018). More than a feeling: Autonomous sensory meridian response (ASMR) is characterized by reliable changes in affect and physiology. *PLOS One*, 13(6), e0196645
19. Lochte, B. C., Guillory, S. A., Richard, C. A., & Kelley, W. M. (2018). An fMRI investigation of the neural correlates underlying the autonomous sensory meridian response (ASMR). *BioImpacts*, 8(4), 295.

Circadian rhythm and cell danger response

20. Naviaux, R. K (2019). Metabolic features and regulation of the healing cycle - A new model for chronic disease pathogenesis and treatment. *Mitochondrion*, 46, 278-297.

21. University of Basel. (2018) Our circadian clock sets the rhythm for our cells' powerhouses. *Science daily.* Retrieved from https://www.sciencedaily.com/releases/2018/03/180306093116.htm

22. Naviaux, R. K. (2014). Metabolic features of the cell danger response. *Mitochondrion, 16*, 7-17.

23. Naviaux, R. K. (2019). Metabolic features and regulation of the healing cycle - A new model for chronic disease pathogenesis and treatment. *Mitochondrion, 46*, 278-297.

Blue light and sleep

24. Harvard Medical School. (2018). Blue light has a dark side. *Harvard health publishing.* Retrieved from https://www.health.harvard.edu/staying-healthy/blue-light-has-a-dark-side

25. Tosini, G., Ferguson, I., & Tsubota, K. (2016). Effects of blue light on the circadian system and eye physiology. *Molecular Vision, 22*, 61.

26. Hatori, M., Gronfier, C., Van Gelder, R. N., Bernstein, P. S., Carreras, J., Panda, S., & Furukawa, T. (2017). Global rise of potential health hazards caused by blue light-induced circadian disruption in modern aging societies. *NJP aging and mechanisms of disease, 3*(1), 9.

Nutrition and sleep

27. St-Onge, M. P., Mikic, A., & Pietrolungo, C. E. (2016). Effects of diet on sleep quality. *Advances in Nutrition, 7*(5), 938-949.

28. Frank, S., Gonzalez, K., Lee-Ang, L., Young, M. C., Tamez, M., & Mattei, J. (2017). Diet and sleep physiology: Public health and clinical implications. *Frontiers in neurology, 8*, 393.

Exercise and sleep

29. Kline, C. E. (2014). The bidirectional relationship between exercise and sleep: Implications for exercise adherence and sleep improvement. *American Journal of Lifestyle Medicine, 8*(6), 375-379.

30. Dolezal, B. A., Neufeld, E. V., Boland, D. M., Martin, J. L., & Cooper, C. B. (2017). Interrelationship between sleep and exercise: A systematic review. *Advances in Preventive Medicine, 2017.*

31. Wunsch, K., Kasten, N., & Fuchs, R. (2017). The effect of physical activity on sleep quality, well-being, and affect in academic stress periods. *Nature and Science of Sleep, 9*, 117.

Robin Sharma course

32. Mindvalley. (2019). *Becoming a 60-minute student: How to cultivate the habits of an eternal learner and unlock your greatest potential* [Video file]. Retrieved from https://blog.mindvalley.com/unlock-your-greatest-potential/

33. Mindvalley. (2019). Mindvalley quests. Retrieved from https://www.mindvalley.com/quests/

Richard Branson

34. Branson, R. (2014). Why I wake up early. Retrieved from https://www.virgin.com/richard-branson/why-i-wake-early

CHAPTER 25

Blue Zones

1. Robertson, R. (2017). Why people in "Blue Zones" live longer than the rest of the world. *Healthline*. Retrieved from https://www.healthline.com/nutrition/blue-zones
2. Buettner, D., & Skemp, S. (2016). Blue zones: Lessons from the world's longest lived. *American Journal of Lifestyle Medicine, 10*(5), 318-321.

The Human Longevity Project

3. Human Longevity Project. (2019). The secret to radiant health beyond 100... free of pain, disease, & prescription drugs. Retrieved from https://humanlongevityfilm.com/

The Secrets of a Long Life

4. Blue Zones, LLC. (2019). Dan Buettner. Retrieved from https://www.bluezones.com/dan-buettner/

Icaria longevity study

5. Panagiotakos, D. B., Chrysohoou, C., Siasos, G., Zisimos, K., Skoumas, J., Pitsavos, C., & Stefanadis, C. (2011). Sociodemographic and lifestyle statistics of oldest old people (> 80 years) living in Ikaria island: The Ikaria study. *Cardiology Research and Practice, 2011*.

Venn diagram

6. Blue zone. (2019). In *Wikipedia*. Retrieved July 16, 2019, from https://en.wikipedia.org/wiki/Blue_Zone

Cooked series

7. Del Deo, A., Gibney, A., Nishimura, L., Offman, S., Pollan, M., & Suh, C. (Producers). (2019). *Cooked* [Television series]. Retrieved from https://www.netflix.com/nl/title/80022456

Intermittent fasting Dr Valter

8. Longo, V. (2019). fasting-mimicking-diet-longevity. Retrieved from https://valterlongo.com/the-fasting-mimicking-diet-as-opposed-to-the-more-traditional-water-fasting-results-in-a-decrease-in-intestinal-diseases-in-mice-and-in-systemic-inflammation-in-humans/

9. Patterson, R. E., Laughlin, G. A., LaCroix, A. Z., Hartman, S. J., Natarajan, L., Senger, C. M., & Gallo, L. C. (2015). Intermittent fasting and human metabolic health. *Journal of the Academy of Nutrition and Dietetics, 115*(8), 1203-1212.

BDNF

10. Binder, D. K., & Scharfman, H. E. (2004). Brain-derived neurotrophic factor. *Growth Factors, 22*(3), 123.
11. Phillips, C. (2017). Brain-derived neurotrophic factor, depression, and physical activity: Making the neuroplastic connection. *Neural Plasticity, 2017*, 1-17.
12. Bathina, S., & Das, U. N. (2015). Brain-derived neurotrophic factor and its clinical implications. *Archives of Medical Science, 11*(6), 1164.
13. Brain-derived neurotrophic factor. (2019). In *Wikipedia*. Retrieved July 16, 2019, from https://en.wikipedia.org/wiki/Brain-derived_neurotrophic_factor

Mark Mattson study of intermittent fasting

14. Jarreau, P. (2019). 5 human fasting studies with Dr. Mark Mattson. Retrieved from https://lifeapps.io/fasting/5-human-fasting-studies-with-dr-mark-mattson/

Intermittent fasting

15. Tello, M. (2018). Intermittent fasting: Surprising update. *Harvard health publishing*. Retrieved from https://www.health.harvard.edu/blog/intermittent-fasting-surprising-update-2018062914156
16. Ganesan, K., Habboush, Y., & Sultan, S. (2018). Intermittent fasting: The choice for a healthier lifestyle. *Cureus, 10*(7).
17. Horne, B. D., Muhlestein, J. B., & Anderson, J. L. (2015). Health effects of intermittent fasting: Hormesis or harm? A systematic review. *The American Journal of Clinical Nutrition, 102*(2), 464-470.

Why does coffee make you feel tired?

18. Whitten, A. (2019). Science says: Coffee is secretly sabotaging your energy levels (why does coffee make me tired?) *The Energy Blueprint*. Retrieved from https://www.theenergyblueprint.com/why-does-coffee-make-me-tired/

Adenosine

19. Ribeiro, J. A., & Sebastiao, A. M. (2010). Caffeine and adenosine. *Journal of Alzheimer's Disease, 20*(s1), S3-S15.

Toxic phytochemicals

20. Karban, Richard; Anurag A. Agrawal; Marc Mangel (July 1997). "The benefits of induced defenses against herbivores". *Ecology*. 78 (5): 1351–1355.
21. Conrath, Uwe (2006). "Systemic Acquired Resistance". *Plant Signaling & Behavior*. 1(4): 179–184.
22. Choudhary, Devendra K.; Prakash, Anil; Johri, B. N. (December 2007). "Induced systemic resistance (ISR) in plants: mechanism of action". *Indian Journal of Microbiology*. 47 (4):

Benefits of fermented foods

23. Bilodeau, K. (2018). Fermented foods for better gut health. *Harvard health publishing*. Retrieved from https://www.health.harvard.edu/blog/fermented-foods-for-better-gut-health-2018051613841
24. Şanlier, N., Gökcen, B. B., & Sezgin, A. C. (2019). Health benefits of fermented foods. *Critical reviews in food science and nutrition*, 59(3), 506-527.
25. Rezac, S., Kok, C. R., Heermann, M., & Hutkins, R. (2018). Fermented foods as a dietary source of live organisms. *Frontiers in microbiology*, 9.

Gut bacteria need fiber

26. Aswell, S. (2018). For a longer life and happier gut, eat more fiber. *Healthline*. Retrieved from https://www.healthline.com/health/food-nutrition/fiber-diet-good-for-gut-and-health
27. Holscher, H. D. (2017). Dietary fiber and prebiotics and the gastrointestinal microbiota. *Gut microbes*, 8(2), 172-184.
28. Makki, K., Deehan, E. C., Walter, J., & Bäckhed, F. (2018). The impact of dietary fiber on gut microbiota in host health and disease. *Cell Host & Microbe*, 23(6), 705-715.

Polyphenols

29. Fraga, C. G., Galleano, M., Verstraeten, S. V., & Oteiza, P. I. (2010). Basic biochemical mechanisms behind the health benefits of polyphenols. *Molecular Aspects of Medicine*, 31(6), 435-445.
30. Williamson, G. (2017). The role of polyphenols in modern nutrition. *Nutrition bulletin*, 42(3), 226-235.
31. Cory, H., Passarelli, S., Szeto, J., Tamez, M., & Mattei, J. (2018). The role of polyphenols in human health and food systems: A mini-review. *Frontiers in nutrition*, 5.

Tryptophan

32. Friedman, M. (2018). Analysis, nutrition, and health benefits of tryptophan. *International Journal of Tryptophan Research, 11*, 117864691880228. doi: 10.1177/1178646918802282

Health benefits of green bananas

33. Birt, D. F., Boylston, T., Hendrich, S., Jane, J. L., Hollis, J., Li, L. & Schalinske, K. (2013). Resistant starch: Promise for improving human health. *Advances in Nutrition, 4*(6), 587-601.

Microbiome

34. Dave, M., Higgins, P. D., Middha, S., & Rioux, K. P. (2012). The human gut microbiome: Current knowledge, challenges, and future directions. *Translational Research, 160*(4), 246-257.
35. Reese, A. T., & Dunn, R. R. (2018). Drivers of microbiome biodiversity: A review of general rules, feces, and ignorance. *Mbio, 9*(4), e01294-18.

CHAPTER 26

Hormesis

1. Mattson, M. P. (2008). Hormesis defined. *Ageing research reviews, 7*(1), 1-7.
2. Hood, W. R., Zhang, Y., Mowry, A. V., Hyatt, H. W., & Kavazis, A. N. (2018). Life history trade-offs within the context of mitochondrial hormesis. *Integrative and Comparative Biology*, 58(3), 567-577.
3. Bárcena, C., Mayoral, P., & Quirós, P. M. (2018). Mitohormesis, an antiaging paradigm. In *International review of cell and molecular biology* (Vol. 340, pp. 35-77). Cambridge, MA: Academic Press.
4. Calabrese, E. J., & Mattson, M. P. (2017). How does hormesis impact biology, toxicology, and medicine? *NPJ aging and mechanisms of disease*, 3(1), 13.
5. Lee, D. H., & Jacobs, D. R. (2015). Hormesis and public health: Can glutathione depletion and mitochondrial dysfunction due to very low-dose chronic exposure to persistent organic pollutants be mitigated? *J Epidemiol Community Health*, 69(3), 294-300.
6. Radak, Z., Chung, H. Y., Koltai, E., Taylor, A. W., & Goto, S. (2008). Exercise, oxidative stress and hormesis. *Ageing research reviews*, 7(1), 34-42.
7. Ristow, M., & Zarse, K. (2010). How increased oxidative stress promotes longevity and metabolic health: The concept of

mitochondrial hormesis (mitohormesis). *Experimental gerontology*, 45(6), 410-418.

Mitochondria

8. Khan Academy. (2019). *Mitochondria* [Video file]. Retrieved from https://www.khanacademy.org/test-prep/mcat/cells/eukaryotic-cells/v/mitochondria
9. Friedman, J. R., & Nunnari, J. (2014). Mitochondrial form and function. *Nature*, 505(7483), 335.
10. Cooper, G.M. (2000). *The cell: A molecular approach* (2nd ed.). Sunderland, MA: Sinauer Associates. Retrieved from https://www.ncbi.nlm.nih.gov/books/NBK9896/Sage.

Essential phytochemicals

11. *Phytochemical*. (2019). In *Wikipedia*. Retrieved July 23, 2019, from https://en.wikipedia.org/wiki/Phytochemical
12. Leitzmann, C. (2016). Characteristics and health benefits of phytochemicals. *Complementary Medicine Research*, 23(2), 69-74.
13. Lee, M. T., Lin, W. C., Yu, B., & Lee, T. T. (2017). Antioxidant capacity of phytochemicals and their potential effects on oxidative status in animals - A review. *Asian-Australasian Journal of Animal Sciences*, 30(3), 299.
14. Granados-Chinchilla, F. (2017). A review on phytochemicals (including essential oils and extracts) inclusion in feed and their effects on food producing animals. *Journal of Dairy and Vetrinary Sciences*, 3(4), 555620.

The benefits of high-intensity interval training

15. Tinsley, G. (2017). 7 Benefits of high-intensity interval training (HIIT). *Healthline*. Retrieved from https://www.healthline.com/nutrition/benefits-of-hiit
16. Lucas, S. J., Cotter, J. D., Brassard, P., & Bailey, D. M. (2015). High-intensity interval exercise and cerebrovascular health: Curiosity, cause, and consequence. *Journal of Cerebral Blood Flow & Metabolism*, 35(6), 902-911.
17. Radak, Z., Ishihara, K., Tekus, E., Varga, C., Posa, A., Balogh, L. & Koltai, E. (2017). Exercise, oxidants, and antioxidants change the shape of the bell-shaped hormesis curve. *Redox Biology*, 12, 285-290.

Authopaghy

18. Thomas, R. L., & Gustafsson, Å. B. (2013). Mitochondrial autophagy. *Circulation Journal*, CJ-13.

19. Lee, J., Giordano, S., & Zhang, J. (2012). Autophagy, mitochondria and oxidative stress: Cross-talk and redox signalling. *Biochemical Journal, 441*(2), 523-540.

20. Okamoto, K., & Kondo-Okamoto, N. (2012). Mitochondria and autophagy: Critical interplay between the two homeostats. *Biochimica et Biophysica Acta (BBA) - General Subjects, 1820*(5), 595-600.

Xenohormesis

21. Hooper, P. L., Tytell, M., & Vígh, L. (2010). Xenohormesis: Health benefits from an eon of plant stress response evolution. *Cell Stress and Chaperones*, 15(6), 761-770.

22. Baur, J. A., & Sinclair, D. A. (2008). What is xenohormesis? *American journal of pharmacology and toxicology*, 3(1), 152.

23. Howitz, K. T., & Sinclair, D. A. (2008). Xenohormesis: Sensing the chemical cues of other species. *Cell, 133*(3), 387-391.

Hot and cold hormesis

24. Bujarrabal, A., & Schumacher, B. (2016). Hormesis running hot and cold. *Cell Cycle*, 15(24), 3335. *Cell Cycle*, 15(24), 3335.

25. Le Bourg, E. (2007). Hormetic effects of repeated exposures to cold at young age on longevity, aging and resistance to heat or cold shocks in Drosophila melanogaster. *Biogerontology*, 8(4), 431-444.

26. Dattilo, S., Mancuso, C., Koverech, G., Di Mauro, P., Ontario, M. L., Petralia, C. C., & Calabrese, V. (2015). Heat shock proteins and hormesis in the diagnosis and treatment of neurodegenerative diseases. *Immunity & Ageing*, 12(1), 20.

27. Marques, F. Z., Markus, M. A., & Morris, B. J. (2010). Hormesis as a pro-healthy aging intervention in human beings? *Dose-Response*, 8(1).

Hypoxia hormesis

28. Blagosklonny, M. V. (2011). Hormesis does not make sense except in the light of TOR-driven aging. *Aging*, 3(11), 1051.

29. Debevec, T., Millet, G. P., & Pialoux, V. (2017). Hypoxia-induced oxidative stress modulation with physical activity. *Frontiers in physiology*, 8, 84.

30. Oliveira, M. F., Geihs, M. A., FA França, T., Moreira, D. C., & Hermes-Lima, M. (2018). Is "preparation for oxidative stress" a case of physiological conditioning hormesis? *Frontiers in physiology*, 9, 945.

South Korean divers

31. United Nations Educational, Science And Cultural Organization. (2016). Culture of Jeju Haenyeo (women divers). Retrieved from https://ich.unesco.org/en/RL/culture-of-jeju-haenyeo-women-divers-01068

Intermittent hypoxia training (IHT)

32. Serebrovskaya, T. V., & Xi, L. (2016). Intermittent hypoxia training as non-pharmacologic therapy for cardiovascular diseases: Practical analysis on methods and equipment. *Experimental Biology and Medicine*, 241(15), 1708-1723.
33. Dale, E. A., Ben Mabrouk, F., & Mitchell, G. S. (2014). Unexpected benefits of intermittent hypoxia: Enhanced respiratory and nonrespiratory motor function. *Physiology*, 29(1), 39-48.

Resilience

34. Whitten, A., & Hofmekler, O. (2019). Hormesis - the hidden key to resiliency (plus, how to reduce stress and fix low energy levels). *The Energy Blueprint*. Podcast retrieved from https://www.theenergyblueprint.com/resiliency/

Children and fever early in life

35. Williams, L. K., Peterson, E. L., Ownby, D. R., & Johnson, C. C. (2004). The relationship between early fever and allergic sensitization at age 6 to 7 years. *Journal of Allergy and Clinical Immunology*, 113(2), 291-296.

Antifragile

36. Taleb, N. N. (2012). *Antifragile: Things that gain from disorder*. New York, NY: Random House.

CHAPTER 27

IMG models

1. IMG Worldwide Inc. (n.d.). IMG models. Retrieved from https://www.imgmodels.com/paris/home

Super recognizers

2. Super recognizer. (2019). In *Wikipedia*. Retrieved July 26, 2019, from https://en.wikipedia.org/wiki/Super_recogniser
3. Russell, R., Duchaine, B., & Nakayama, K. (2009). Super-recognizers: People with extraordinary face recognition ability. *Psychonomic bulletin & review*, 16(2), 252-257.

4. Lavoie, A. (2009). 'Super-recognizers' never forget a face. *The Harvard gazette.* Retrieved from https://news.harvard.edu/gazette/story/2009/05/super-recognizers-never-forget-a-face/

Retention of primitive reflexes

5. Marquis, P. J., Ruiz, N. A., Lundy, M. S., & Dillard, R. G. (1984). Retention of primitive reflexes and delayed motor development in very low birth weight infants. *Journal of Developmental and Behavioral Pediatrics*, 5(3), 124-126.
6. Gieysztor, E. Z., Choińska, A. M., & Paprocka-Borowicz, M. (2018). Persistence of primitive reflexes and associated motor problems in healthy preschool children. *Archives of Medical Science*, *14*(1), 167.
7. Damasceno, A., Delicio, A. M., Mazo, D. F., Zullo, J. F., Scherer, P., TY Ng, R., & Damasceno, B. P. (2005). Primitive reflexes and cognitive function. *Arquivos de Neuro-Psiquiatria*, 63(3A), 577-582.

Sucking reflex

8. Marcin, A. (2018). What is sucking reflex? *Healthline*. Retrieved from https://www.healthline.com/health/parenting/sucking-reflex
9. Lau, C. (2015). Development of suck and swallow mechanisms in infants. *Annals of Nutrition and Metabolism*, 66(Suppl. 5), 7-14.

Journal of Developmental and Behavioral Pediatrics.

Reflexes, Learning and Behavior

10. Goddard, S. B. (2002). Reflexes, learning and behavior: A window into the child's mind. Eugene, OR: Fern Ridge Press

Functional Neurology

11. Beck, R. W. (2011). *Functional neurology for practitioners of manual medicine*. Amsterdam, Netherlands: Elsevier.

Puebla

12. Puebla. (2019). In *Wikipedia*. Retrieved July 28, 2019, from https://en.wikipedia.org/wiki/Puebla_(city)

Pyramid of Cholula

13. Sic Mexico. (2019). Zona arqueológica de Cholula. Retrieved from https://sic.gob.mx/ficha.php?table=zona_arqueologica&table_id=80

CHAPTER 28

National Parc de Hoge Veluwe

1. De Hoge Veluwe National Park. (2019). Retrieved from https://www.hogeveluwe.nl/en

Brain map of the body

2. Cortical homunculus. (2019). In *Wikipedia*. Retrieved August 28, 2019, from https://en.wikipedia.org/wiki/Cortical_homunculus

Cartographers of the brain

3. World Science Festival. (2018). *Cartographers of the brain: Mapping the connectome* [Video file]. Retrieved from https://www.youtube.com/watch?v=OoU_GF4fc6w

Advantages of barefoot walking

4. Lindberg, S. (2018). Does walking barefoot have health benefits? *Healthline*. https://www.healthline.com/health/walking-barefoot#bottom-line
5. Hollander, K., Van der Zwaard, B. C., De Villiers, J. E., Braumann, K. M., Venter, R., & Zech, A. (2016). The effects of being habitually barefoot on foot mechanics and motor performance in children and adolescents aged 6–18 years: Study protocol for a multicenter cross-sectional study (Barefoot LIFE project). *Journal of Foot and Ankle Research*, 9(1), 36.
6. Hollander, K., Heidt, C., Van der Zwaard, B. C., Braumann, K. M., & Zech, A. (2017). Long-term effects of habitual barefoot running and walking: A systematic review. *Medicine & Science in Sports & Exercise*, 49(4), 752-762.
7. Hollander, K., De Villiers, J. E., Sehner, S., Wegscheider, K., Braumann, K. M., Venter, R., & Zech, A. (2017). Growing-up (habitually) barefoot influences the development of foot and arch morphology in children and adolescents. *Scientific Reports*, 7(1), 8079.

Brain.rehab

8. Brain.rehab Ltd. (2019). Stroke rehab 2.0: How you can go to the next level in your stroke recovery. Retrieved from https://www.brain.rehab/

CHAPTER 29

Marisa Peer

1. More Than Enough Limited. (2018). Audience with Marisa. Retrieved from https://marisapeer.com/
2. Mindvalley Talks. (2015). *Crash course for phenomenal success - Marisa Peer* [Video file]. Retrieved from https://www.youtube.com/watch?v=Iw3NyUMLh7Y

Hypnotherapy

3. Psychology Today. (2019). Hypnotherapy. Retrieved from https://www.psychologytoday.com/intl/therapy-types/hypnotherapy

Marisa Peer on Mindvalley

4. Mindvalley. (2019). How to capture the empowering beliefs, habits & thought patterns of the world's top super achievers - and instantly install them in your mind. Retrieved from https://www.mindvalley.com/uncompromised-life/

Man Up

5. Keuilian, B. (2018). *Man up: How to cut the bullshit and kick ass in business (and in life)*. Dallas, TX: BenBella Books.

CHAPTER 30

Wearing a cast changes your brain

1. Yong, T. (2009). How wearing a cast affects sense of touch and brain activity. *National Geographic*. Retrieved rom https://www.nationalgeographic.com/science/phenomena/2009/04/23/how-wearing-a-cast-affects-sense-of-touch-and-brain-activity/
2. Gauthier, L. V., Taub, E., Perkins, C., Ortmann, M., Mark, V. W., & Uswatte, G. (2008). Remodeling the brain plastic structural brain changes produced by different motor therapies after stroke. *Stroke: A journal of cerebral circulation*, 39(5), 1520.
3. American Academy of Neurology (2012). Broken arm? Brain shifts quickly when using a sling or cast. *Science daily*. Retrieved rom https://www.sciencedaily.com/releases/2012/01/120116200604.htm

Training plateau

4. Buttacio, J.L. (2017). The 8 reasons you hit a workout plateau (and how to beat it). *The healthy*. Retrieved from https://www.rd.com/health/fitness/workout-plateau/
5. Clark, J. E. (2016). The impact of duration on effectiveness of exercise, the implication for periodization of training and goal setting for individuals who are overfat, a meta-analysis. *Biology of Sport*, 33(4), 309.

Retrogression in the learning curve

6. Thomassen, A. (1998). Learning and forgetting curves: A practical study. *University of Waikato*. Retrieved from https://pdfs.semanticscholar.org/6c90/7ca3674dfc24f1f344b79d2b-693d98a0b92b.pdf

Nordic walking

7. Rutlin, T. (2019). Benefits of Nordic walking. Retrieved from https://sportmedbc.com/article/benefits-nordic-walking
8. Tschentscher, M., Niederseer, D., & Niebauer, J. (2013). Health benefits of Nordic walking: A systematic review. *American Journal of Preventive Medicine*, *44*(1), 76-84.
9. Takeshima, N., Islam, M. M., Rogers, M. E., Rogers, N. L., Sengoku, N., Koizumi, D. & Naruse, A. (2013). Effects of nordic walking compared to conventional walking and band-based resistance exercise on fitness in older adults. *Journal of sports science & medicine*, 12(3), 422.
10. Cugusi, L., Solla, P., Serpe, R., Carzedda, T., Piras, L., Oggianu, M., & Marrosu, F. (2015). Effects of a nordic walking program on motor and non-motor symptoms, functional performance and body composition in patients with Parkinson's disease. *NeuroRehabilitation*, 37(2), 245-254.

Cross-crawl exercises

11. Kang, J. I., Park, J. S., Jeong, D. K., Choi, H. H., & Moon, Y. J. (2018). Effects on muscle activities according to the type of bodyblade exercise in quadruped position. *Journal of Physical Therapy Science*, 30(6), 862-865.
12. Imai, A., Kaneoka, K., Okubo, Y., & Shiraki, H. (2014). Effects of two types of trunk exercises on balance and athletic performance in youth soccer players. *International journal of sports physical therapy*, 9(1), 47.
13. Kalish, L. (2016). 10 benefits of cross crawl - brain hemisphere synching exercise. *Move with me*. Retrieved from https://move-with-me.com/self-regulation/10-benefits-of-cross-crawl-brain-hemisphere-synching-exercise/

Embrace the suck

14. Goalcast. (2017). *How to conquer your mind and embrace the suck - David Goggins - Goalcast* [Video file]. Retrieved from https://www.youtube.com/watch?v=_J_bOqPhuZA
15. Brendon.com (2017). *Embrace the suck!* [Video file]. Retrieved from https://www.youtube.com/watch?v=AGH8P70Tn-s
16. Bay, A. (2007). 'Embrace the suck' and more military speak. *NPR*. Retrieved from https://www.npr.org/2007/03/08/7458809/embrace-the-suck-and-more-military-speak?t=1560833851254

Arambhashura

17. Wisdom Library. (2019). Arambhashura, aka: ārambhaśūra; 2 definition(s). Retrieved from https://www.wisdomlib.org/definition/arambhashura

CHAPTER 31

Eulogy

1. Eulogy. (2019). In *Cambridge dictionary*. Retrieved from https://dictionary.cambridge.org/dictionary/english/eulogy

Philip Stutz

2. The Tools. (2017). About Phil. Retrieved from https://www.thetoolsbook.com/about

The Tools

3. The Tools. (2017). Turn challenges into opportunities. Retrieved from https://www.thetoolsbook.com/

Aphasia

4. Aphasia. (2019). In *Wikipedia*. Retrieved from August 2, 2019, from https://en.wikipedia.org/wiki/Aphasia

Dysarthria

5. Dysarthria. (2019). In *Wikipedia*. Retrieved August 2, 2019, from https://en.wikipedia.org/wiki/Dysarthria

TED

6. TED. (2019). Our organization. Retrieved from https://www.ted.com/about/our-organization

Gargling for vagus nerve stimulation

7. Kharrazian, D. (2013). The gut-brain axis. In *Why isn't my brain working? A revolutionary understanding of brain decline and effective strategies to recover your brain's health*. San Diego, CA: Elephant Press.

Peripheral nerve stimulator

8. International Neuromodulation Society. (2019). Peripheral nerve stimulation. Retrieved from https://www.neuromodulation.com/PNS
9. Wilson, R. D., Knutson, J. S., Bennett, M. E., & Chae, J. (2017). The effect of peripheral nerve stimulation on shoulder biomechanics: A randomized controlled trial in comparison to physical therapy. *American journal of Physical Medicine & Rehabilitation, 96*(3), 191.

10. Trent, A. R., & Jain, A. (2019). Peripheral nerve stimulator. *StatPearls*. Retrieved from https://www.ncbi.nlm.nih.gov/books/NBK539703/

Whistling

11. Meyer J. Whistle production and physics of the signal. (2015) Whistled Languages. Berlin, Germany: Springer, 74–77.

Vestibular dysfunction after stroke

12. Marsden, J. F., Playford, D. E., & Day, B. L. (2005). The vestibular control of balance after stroke. *Journal of Neurology, Neurosurgery & Psychiatry*, 76(5), 670-679.

The effect of crossed exercises

13. Demirakca, T., Cardinale, V., Dehn, S., Ruf, M., & Ende, G. (2016). The exercising brain: Changes in functional connectivity induced by an integrated multimodal cognitive and whole-body coordination training. *Neural Plasticity*, 2016.

N-Back app

14. Mindware. Dual N-Back Pro. Retrieved from https://dual-n-back-pro.com/

15. Jaeggi, S. M., Buschkuehl, M., Jonides, J., & Perrig, W. J. (2008). Improving fluid intelligence with training on working memory. *Proceedings of the National Academy of Sciences*, 105(19), 6829-6833.

16. Au, J., Sheehan, E., Tsai, N., Duncan, G. J., Buschkuehl, M., & Jaeggi, S. M. (2015). Improving fluid intelligence with training on working memory: A meta-analysis. *Psychonomic bulletin & review*, 22(2), 366-377.

Optimize app

17. Apple. (2019). Optimize with Brian Johnson. Retrieved from https://apps.apple.com/us/app/optimize-with-brian-johnson/id1135159918

Claire Wineland's speech

18. Klick. (2016). *Claire Wineland gives inspirational talk at Klick MUSE New York* [Video file]. Retrieved from https://www.youtube.com/watch?v=kP41Zv3CaSo

Claire Wineland

19. Claire Wineland. (2019). In *Wikipedia*. Retrieved August 15, 2019, from https://en.wikipedia.org/wiki/Claire_Wineland

Cystic fibrosis

20. Mayo Clinic Staff. (2019). Cystic fibrosis. Retrieved from https://www.mayoclinic.org/diseases-conditions/cystic-fibrosis/symptoms-causes/syc-20353700
21. Naehrlich, L., Chao, C. & Naehring, S. (2017). Cystic fibrosis diagnosis and treatment. *Continuing Medical Education, 114*(33-34): 564–574.

Linda's first speech and the same speech in English, half a year later

22. Kuipers, J.A. & Rådestad, L.J.P. [Arjan Kuipers]. (2018). *Hoe herstel je verder na een herseninfarct/bloeding? Deel I* [Video file]. Retrieved from https://www.youtube.com/watch?v=5weLxVDaK04&feature=youtu.be
23. Rådestad, L.J.P. & Kuipers, J.A. [brain.rehab channel]. (2019). *How you can continue to improve after your stroke* [Video file]. Retrieved from https://www.youtube.com/watch?v=7IdCqnz16gQ&feature=youtu.be

Claire's Place Foundation

24. Claire's Place Foundation (2019). Claire's Place Foundation, Inc. Retrieved from https://clairesplacefoundation.org

CHAPTER 32

Stress weakens the brain

1. Arnsten, A. F. (2015). Stress weakens prefrontal networks: Molecular insults to higher cognition. *Nature neuroscience, 18*(10), 1376.
2. Lupien, S. J., Juster, R. P., Raymond, C., & Marin, M. F. (2018). The effects of chronic stress on the human brain: From neurotoxicity, to vulnerability, to opportunity. *Frontiers in neuroendocrinology*, 49, 91-105. 9, 91-105.Stress can shrink the brain
3. Bremner, J. D. (2006). Stress and brain atrophy. *CNS & Neurological Disorders - Drug Targets*, 5(5), 503-512.
4. Arnsten, A. F. (2009). Stress signalling pathways that impair prefrontal cortex structure and function. *Nature Reviews Neuroscience, 10*(6), 410.

Stress contributing to brain inflammation

5. Liu, Y. Z., Wang, Y. X., & Jiang, C. L. (2017). Inflammation: The common pathway of stress-related diseases. *Frontiers in human neuroscience, 11*, 316.

6. Douglas Bremner, J. (2006). Stress and brain atrophy. *CNS & Neurological Disorders - Drug Targets*, 5(5), 503-512.
7. McEwen, B. S. (2017). Neurobiological and systemic effects of chronic stress. *Chronic stress, 1*, 2470547017692328.

Stress contributing to Alzheimer's or degenerative brain diseases

8. Esch, T., Stefano, G. B., Fricchione, G. L., & Benson, H. (2002). The role of stress in neurodegenerative diseases and mental disorders. *Neuroendocrinology Letters*, 23(3), 199-208.
9. Justice, N. J. (2018). The relationship between stress and Alzheimer's disease. *Neurobiology of stress, 8*, 127-133.

Stress and its effect on memory

10. McEwen, B. S., Nasca, C., & Gray, J. D. (2016). Stress effects on neuronal structure: Hippocampus, amygdala, and prefrontal cortex. *Neuropsychopharmacology, 41*(1), 3.
11. Valero, J., Bernardino, L., Cardoso, F. L., Silva, A. P., Fontes-Ribeiro, C., Ambrósio, A. F., & Malva, J. O. (2017). Impact of neuroinflammation on hippocampal neurogenesis: Relevance to aging and Alzheimer's disease. *Journal of Alzheimer's Disease*, 60(s1), S161-S168.
12. Luethi, M., Meier, B., & Sandi, C. (2009). Stress effects on working memory, explicit memory, and implicit memory for neutral and emotional stimuli in healthy men. *Frontiers in behavioral neuroscience*, 2, 5.

CDC statement on coping with stress

13. Centers for Disease Control and Prevention (n.d.). Coping with stress. Retrieved from https://www.cdc.gov/features/copingwith-stress/index.html

Chemical stress

14. Jager, T. (2013). Making sense of chemical stress. *VU University.*
15. Amiard-Triquet, C., Amiard, J. C., & Mouneyrac, C. (2015). Predictive ecotoxicology and environmental assessment. In *Aquatic ecotoxicology* (pp. 463-496). Cambridge, MA: Academic Press.
16. Świergosz-Kowalewska, R., Molenda, P., & Halota, A. (2014). Effects of chemical and thermal stress on acetylcholinesterase activity in the brain of the bank vole, Myodes glareolus. *Ecotoxicology and Environmental Safety, 106*, 204-212.

Physical stress

17. Kavushansky, A., Ben-Shachar, D., Richter-Levin, G., & Klein, E. (2009). Physical stress differs from psychosocial stress in the

pattern and time-course of behavioral responses, serum corticosterone and expression of plasticity-related genes in the rat. *Stress, 12*(5), 412-425.

18. Yaribeygi, H., Panahi, Y., Sahraei, H., Johnston, T. P., & Sahebkar, A. (2017). The impact of stress on body function: A review. *EXCLI journal, 16*, 1057.

Psychological stress

19. Monroe, S. M., & Cummins, L. F. (2015). Stress: Psychological perspectives. *Science direct*. Retrieved from https://www.sciencedirect.com/topics/social-sciences/psychological-stress
20. Schneiderman, N., Ironson, G., & Siegel, S. D. (2005). Stress and health: Psychological, behavioral, and biological determinants. *Annual Review on Clinical Psychology, 1*, 607-628.
21. McEwen, B. S. (2017). Neurobiological and systemic effects of chronic stress. *Chronic stress, 1*, 2470547017692328.

Amygdala

22. Kavushansky, A., Ben-Shachar, D., Richter-Levin, G., & Klein, E. (2009). Physical stress differs from psychosocial stress in the pattern and time-course of behavioral responses, serum corticosterone and expression of plasticity-related genes in the rat. *Stress, 12*(5), 412-425.

Sympathetic nervous system

23. Science Daily. (2019). Sympathetic nervous system. *Science daily.* Retrieved from https://www.sciencedaily.com/terms/sympathetic_nervous_system.htm
24. Khan Academy. (2019). *Autonomic nervous system (ANS) and physiologic markers of emotion* [Video file]. Retrieved from https://www.khanacademy.org/science/health-and-medicine/executive-systems-of-the-brain/emotion-lesson/v/autonomic-nervous-system-ans-and-physiologic-markers-of-emotion

Function of cortisol

25. Thau, L., & Sharma, S. (2019). Physiology, cortisol. *StatPearls*. Retrieved from https://www.ncbi.nlm.nih.gov/books/NBK538239/

Aspartame

26. Aspartame. (2019). In *Wikipedia*. Retrieved August 24, 2019, from https://en.wikipedia.org/wiki/Aspartame
27. Choudhary, A. K., & Pretorius, E. (2017). Revisiting the safety of aspartame. *Nutrition reviews, 75*(9), 718-730.

Aspartame and stress response

28. Choudhary, A. K., & Lee, Y. Y. (2018). Neurophysiological symptoms and aspartame: What is the connection? *Nutritional neuroscience, 21*(5), 306-316.

Sleep deprivation causing stress response

29. Joo, E. Y., Yoon, C. W., Koo, D. L., Kim, D., & Hong, S. B. (2012). Adverse effects of 24 hours of sleep deprivation on cognition and stress hormones. *Journal of Clinical Neurology*, 8(2), 146-150.
30. Han, K. S., Kim, L., & Shim, I. (2012). Stress and sleep disorder. *Experimental neurobiology, 21*(4), 141-150.

Sleep and stroke risk

31. Phua, C. S., Jayaram, L., & Wijeratne, T. (2017). Relationship between sleep duration and risk factors for stroke. *Frontiers in neurology, 8*, 392.
32. Koo, D. L., Nam, H., Thomas, R. J., & Yun, C. H. (2018). Sleep disturbances as a risk factor for stroke. *Journal of Stroke*, 20(1), 12.

CHAPTER 33

The Shortness of Life

1. Daily Stoic. (2019). On the shortness of life: Book summary, key lessons, and best quotes. Retrieved from https://dailystoic.com/on-the-shortness-of-life-seneca/

Meditation benefits

2. Hölzel, B. K., Carmody, J., Vangel, M., Congleton, C., Yerramsetti, S. M., Gard, T., & Lazar, S. W. (2011). Mindfulness practice leads to increases in regional brain gray matter density. *Psychiatry Research: Neuroimaging, 191*(1), 36-43.
3. Laneri, D., Schuster, V., Dietsche, B., Jansen, A., Ott, U., & Sommer, J. (2016). Effects of long-term mindfulness meditation on brain's white matter microstructure and its aging. *Frontiers in aging neuroscience, 7*, 254.
4. Fox, K. C., Nijeboer, S., Dixon, M. L., Floman, J. L., Ellamil, M., Rumak, S. P. & Christoff, K. (2014). Is meditation associated with altered brain structure? A systematic review and meta-analysis of morphometric neuroimaging in meditation practitioners. *Neuroscience & Biobehavioral Reviews, 43*, 48-73.
5. Fox, K. C., Dixon, M. L., Nijeboer, S., Girn, M., Floman, J. L., Lifshitz, M. & Christoff, K. (2016). Functional neuroanatomy of meditation: A review and meta-analysis of 78 functional

neuroimaging investigations. *Neuroscience & Biobehavioral Reviews*, 65, 208-228.

6. Canter, P. H. (2003). The therapeutic effects of meditation. Retrieved from https://www.bmj.com/content/326/7398/1049.short

Meditation is an aerobic training for the brain

7. Bergland, C. (2016). Combining aerobic exercise and meditation reduces depression. *Psychology today*. Retrieved from https://www.psychologytoday.com/intl/blog/the-athletes-way/201602/combining-aerobic-exercise-and-meditation-reduces-depression

Headspace app

8. Headspace. (2019). Your guide to health and happiness. Retrieved from https://www.headspace.com/

The importance of forgiveness

9. Mindvalley. (2018). *Why you should forgive people who hurt you - Vishen Lakhiani* [Video file]. Retrieved from https://www.youtube.com/watch?v=a7flaCA3Qr4

40 Years of Zen

10. 40 Years of Zen. (2019). 40 years of Zen. Retrieved from https://www.40yearsofzen.com/

Emily Fletcher

11. Ziva. (2019). Meditation for high performance. Retrieved from https://zivameditation.com/

Michael Beckwith

12. Mindvalley. (2019). How to manifest your soul's purpose. Retrieved from https://www.mindvalley.com/power-of-visioning/masterclass/invite

13. Mindvalley. (2016). *Discovering your greatest gifts from the universe - Michael Beckwith* [Video file]. Retrieved from https://www.youtube.com/watch?v=SDfgPoYm03k

Grey matter in the prefrontral cortex and forgiveness

14. Leaf, C. (2018). Why you should embrace the forgiveness mindset. If you don't, you're only hurting yourself. *Thrive global*. Retrieved from https://thriveglobal.com/stories/why-you-should-embrace-the-forgiveness-mindset/

Emotional regulation in the orbitofrontal cortex and hippocampus

15. Jin, J., & Maren, S. (2015). Prefrontal-hippocampal interactions in memory and emotion. *Frontiers in systems neuroscience*, 9, 170.
16. Gagnepain, P., Hulbert, J., & Anderson, M. (2017). Parallel regulation of memory and emotion supports the suppression of intrusive memories. *The Journal of Neuroscience*, 37(27), 6423-6441.

More grey matter in the brain, high correlation with ability to cultivate positive emotions, emotional stability, and engage in mindful behavior

17. Grecucci, A., Pappaianni, E., Siugzdaite, R., Theuninck, A., & Job, R. (2015). Mindful emotion regulation: Exploring the neurocognitive mechanisms behind mindfulness. *BioMed research international*, 2015.
18. Guendelman, S., Medeiros, S., & Rampes, H. (2017). Mindfulness and emotion regulation: Insights from neurobiological, psychological, and clinical studies. *Frontiers in psychology*, 8, 220.

George Eliot

19. George Eliot. (2019). In *Wikipedia*. Retrieved August 30, 2019, from https://en.wikipedia.org/wiki/George_Eliot

Crying to help combat stress

20. Dodgson, L. (2018). Crying once a week can reduce stress, according to a Japanese professor who calls himself a 'tears teacher'. *Insider*. Retrieved from https://www.insider.com/how-crying-helps-reduce-stress-2018-10

Amygdala

21. Amygdala. (2019). In *Wikipedia*. Retrieved August 30, 2019, from https://en.wikipedia.org/wiki/Amygdala
22. Rasia-Filho, A. A., Londero, R. G., & Achaval, M. (2000). Functional activities of the amygdala: An overview. *Journal of Psychiatry and Neuroscience*, 25(1), 14.

Hypothalamus

23. Lechan, R. M., & Toni, R. (2016). Functional anatomy of the hypothalamus and pituitary. In *Endotext*. South Dartmouth, MA: MDText.com, Inc.

Tears contain leucine enkephalin

24. Baeyens, V., & Gurny, R. (1997). Chemical and physical parameters of tears relevant for the design of ocular drug delivery formulations. *Pharmaceutica Acta Helvetiae, 72*(4), 191-202.
25. Mukamal, R. (2019). All about emotional tears. Retrieved from https://www.aao.org/eye-health/tips-prevention/all-about-emotional-tears
26. Whitney, D. (2018). The science of tears. Retrieved from https://psychcentral.com/blog/the-science-of-tears/

Rui-katsu (tear-seeking)

27. Shimbun, C. (2013). Participants ease stress levels at crying events. *The Japan times.* Retrieved from https://www.japantimes.co.jp/news/2013/06/22/national/participants-ease-stress-levels-at-crying-events/#.XQ8lvegzY2w

Risk of taking prescription drugs

28. Light, D. W. (2010). *The risks of prescription drugs.* New York, NY: Columbia University Press. Retrieved from https://cup.columbia.edu/book/the-risks-of-prescription-drugs/9780231146937
29. Blenkinsopp, A., Bond, C., & Raynor, D. K. (2012). Medication reviews. *British Journal of Clinical Pharmacology, 74*(4), 573-580.

Natural antibiotics

30. Park M., Bae J., Lee D.S. (2008). Antibacterial activity of [10]-gingerol and [12]-gingerol isolated from ginger rhizome against periodontal bacteria. *Phytother. Res.* 22, 1446–1449.
31. Singh G., Marimuthu P., Murali H.S., Bawa A.S.(2005) Antioxidative and antibacterial potentials of essential oils and extracts isolated from various spice materials—Part 48. *J. Food Saf.* 25, 130–145.
32. Baris D., Kizil M., Aytekin C., Kizil G., Yavuz M., Ceken B., Ertekin A.S. In vitro antimicrobial and antioxidant activity of ethanol extract of three *Hypericum* and three *Achillea* species from Turkey. (2011) *Int. J. Food Prop.*14, 339–355.

Foods that are good for your microbiome

33. Petre, A. (2019). The microbiome diet: Can it restore your gut health? *Healthline.* Retrieved from https://www.healthline.com/nutrition/microbiome-diet
34. Singh, R. K., Chang, H. W., Yan, D., Lee, K. M., Ucmak, D., Wong, K. & Bhutani, T. (2017). Influence of diet on the gut microbiome

and implications for human health. *Journal of Translational Medicine*, 15(1), 73.

35. Ercolini, D., & Fogliano, V. (2018). Food design to feed the human gut microbiota. *Journal of Agricultural and Food Chemistry*, 66(15), 3754-3758.
36. Sentenac, H. (2019). Why healing your gut (and keeping your gut happy) is essential for good health. Retrieved from https://foodrevolution.org/blog/best-foods-for-gut-health/

Natural probiotics

37. Kechagia, M., Basoulis, D., Konstantopoulou, S., Dimitriadi, D., Gyftopoulou, K., Skarmoutsou, N., & Fakiri, E. M. (2013). Health benefits of probiotics: A review. *ISRN Nutrition, 2013.*
38. Moloney, M. G. (2016). Natural products as a source for novel antibiotics. *Trends in pharmacological sciences*, *37*(8), 689-701.
39. Dresden, D. (2018). Top seven safe, effective natural antibiotics. *Medical news today*. Retrieved from https://www.medicalnewstoday.com/articles/321108.php

Hormesis

40. Mattson, M. P. (2008). Hormesis defined. *Ageing research reviews*, *7*(1), 1-7.

Overachievement

41. Eliot, J. (2015). *Overachievement: The science of working less to accomplish more*. New York, NY: Diversion Books.

Ikigai by Hector Garcia and Frances Mirales

42. García, H., & Miralles, F. (2017). *Ikigai: The Japanese secret to a long and happy life*. London, England: Penguin.
43. Ikigai. (2019). In *Wikipedia*. Retrieved August 31, 2019, from https://en.wikipedia.org/wiki/Ikigai

Clarity reduces stress

44. Frögéli, E., Rudman, A., Ljótsson, B., & Gustavsson, P. (2018). Preventing stress-related ill health among newly registered nurses by supporting engagement in proactive behaviors: Development and feasibility testing of a behavior change intervention. *Pilot and Feasibility Studies*, *4*(1), 28.

Memento mori

45. Daily Stoic. (2019)."Memento mori": The reminder we all desperately need. Retrieved from https://dailystoic.com/memento-mori/

Kensho moments

46. Lakhiani, V. (2016). *The code of the extraordinary mind: 10 unconventional laws to redefine your life and succeed on your own terms.* Emmaus, PA: Rodale.

Kensho

47. Quora (n.d.). What is kensho. Retrieved from https://www.quora.com/What-is-kensho

CHAPTER 34

Behavior and identity

1. Clear, J. (2019). How to change your beliefs and stick to your goals for good. Retrieved from https://jamesclear.com/identity-votes

Identity

2. Social science. (2019). In *Wikipedia*. Retrieved September 2, 2019, from https://en.wikipedia.org/wiki/Identity_(social_science)
3. Identity. (2019). In *Online etymology dictionary*. Retrieved from https://www.etymonline.com/word/identity

Homunculus of man

4. Cortical homunculus. (2019). In *Wikipedia*. Retrieved September 2, 2019, from https://en.wikipedia.org/wiki/Cortical_homunculus
5. Disability Science Review. (2017). Your brain is made of maps. *Medium*. Retrieved from https://medium.com/@mosaicofminds/maps-in-the-brain-f236998d544f

Body map study with string musicians

6. Elbert, T., Pantev, C., Wienbruch, C., Rockstroh, B., & Taub, E. (1995). Increased cortical representation of the fingers of the left hand in string players. Science, *270*(5234), 305-307.
7. Catani, M. (2017). A little man of some importance. *Brain, 140*(11), 3055-3061.

Dormant neurons and neurogenesis after stroke

8. Small, S. L., Buccino, G., & Solodkin, A. (2013). Brain repair after stroke - a novel neurological model. *Nature Reviews Neurology, 9*(12), 698.
9. Marlier, Q., Verteneuil, S., Vandenbosch, R., & Malgrange, B. (2015). Mechanisms and functional significance of stroke-induced neurogenesis. *Frontiers in neuroscience, 9*, 458.

Atomic Habits

10. Clear, J. (2019). *Atomic habits*. New York, NY: Penguin Random House.

Game Changers

11. Asprey, D. (2018). *Game changers: What leaders, innovators, and mavericks do to win at life*. New York, NY: HarperCollins.

Mini Habits

12. Guise, S. (2013). *Mini habits: Smaller habits, bigger results*. Seattle, WA: Selective Entertainment LLC.

How does bamboo grow?

13. Lewis Bamboo. (2019). How does bamboo grow? Retrieved from https://lewisbamboo.com/how-bamboo-grows/

Khan Academy

14. Khan Academy. (2019). For every student, every classroom. Real results. Retrieved from https://www.khanacademy.org/

N-Back app

15. Brain Scale. (2019). Dual N-Back. Retrieved from http://brainscale.net/dual-n-back

Working memory is critical to fluid intelligence

16. Hershey, D. A., Austin, J. T., & Gutierrez, H. C. (2015). Financial decision making across the adult life span: Dynamic cognitive capacities and real-world competence. In *Aging and decision making* (pp. 329-349). Cambridge, MA: Academic Press.
17. Unsworth, N., Fukuda, K., Awh, E., & Vogel, E. K. (2014). Working memory and fluid intelligence: Capacity, attention control, and secondary memory retrieval. *Cognitive Psychology, 71*, 1-26.
18. Salthouse, T. A., & Pink, J. E. (2008). Why is working memory related to fluid intelligence? *Psychonomic bulletin & review, 15*(2), 364-371.
19. Au, J., Sheehan, E., Tsai, N., Duncan, G. J., Buschkuehl, M., & Jaeggi, S. M. (2015). Improving fluid intelligence with training on working memory: A meta-analysis. *Psychonomic bulletin & review*, 22(2), 366-377.

Susanne Jaeggi and Martin Buschkuehl

20. Jaeggi, S. M., Buschkuehl, M., Jonides, J., & Perrig, W. J. (2008). Improving fluid intelligence with training on working memory. *Proceedings of the National Academy of Sciences, 105*(19), 6829-6833.

Limited beliefs

21. Cooper, R. K. (2002). *The other 90%: How to unlock your vast untapped potential for leadership and life.* New York, NY: Crown Business.

Aging and the brain

22. Peters, R. (2006). Ageing and the brain. *Postgraduate Medical Journal*, 82(964), 84-88.

Warren Buffet on compound interest

23. Miller, J.C. (2016). Opinion: This Warren Buffett rule can work wonders on your portfolio. *Market watch*. Retrieved from https://www.marketwatch.com/story/this-warren-buffett-rule-can-work-wonders-on-your-portfolio-2016-04-26

Aristotle, probably misquoted

24. Herron, F. (2012). It's a much more effective quotation to attribute it to Aristotle, rather than to Will Durant. The Art of "Quotemanship" and "Misquotemanship." Retrieved from http://blogs.umb.edu/quoteunquote/2012/05/08/its-a-much-more-effective-quotation-to-attribute-it-to-aristotle-rather-than-to-will-durant/

CHAPTER 35

Erik Kandel

1. Kandel, E., Greengard, P. & Calrsson, A. (2019). Eric Kandel biographical. Retrieved from https://www.nobelprize.org/prizes/medicine/2000/kandel/biographical/

The Disordered Mind

2. Kandel, E. R. (2018). *The disordered mind: What unusual brains tell us about ourselves*. London, England: Hachette UK.

Can't Hurt Me

3. Goggins, D. (2018). *Can't hurt me: Master your mind and defy the odds*. Austin, TX: Lioncrest.

Neuroplasticity

4. Fuchs, E., & Flügge, G. (2014). Adult neuroplasticity: More than 40 years of research. *Neural Plasticity, 2014.*

5. Shaffer, J. (2016). Neuroplasticity and clinical practice: Building brain power for health. *Frontiers in psychology, 7, 1118.*

6. Voss, P., Thomas, M. E., Cisneros-Franco, J. M., & de Villers-Sidani, É. (2017). Dynamic brains and the changing rules of neuroplasticity:

Implications for learning and recovery. *Frontiers in psychology, 8*, 1657.

7. Sharma, N., Classen, J., & Cohen, L. G. (2013). Neural plasticity and its contribution to functional recovery. In *Handbook of clinical neurology* (Vol. 110, pp. 3-12). Amsterdam. Netherlands: Elsevier.

Ramón y Cajal

8. Santiago Ramón y Cajal. (2019). In *Wikipedia*. Retrieved September 6, 2019, from https://en.wikipedia.org/wiki/Santiago_Ram%C3%B3n_y_Cajal

Norman Doidge books with references to Merzenich, Bach Y Rita, Taub, and phases of neuroplasticity

9. Doidge, N. (2007). *The brain that changes itself: Stories of personal triumph from the frontiers of brain science*. London, England: Penguin.
10. Doidge, N. (2016). *The brain's way of healing: Remarkable discoveries and recoveries from the frontiers of neuroplasticity*. London, England: Penguin.

Broken Movement

11. Krakauer, J. W., & Carmichael, S. T. (2017). *Broken movement: The neurobiology of motor recovery after stroke*. Cambridge, MA: The MIT Press.

Healing process after a stroke

12. Lee, K. B., Lim, S. H., Kim, K. H., Kim, K. J., Kim, Y. R., Chang, W. N., & Hwang, B. Y. (2015). Six-month functional recovery of stroke patients: A multi-time-point study. *International Journal of Rehabilitation Research, 38*(2), 173.
13. Hillis, A. E., & Tippett, D. C. (2014). Stroke recovery: Surprising influences and residual consequences. *Advances in Medicine, 2014*.

Microglial cells, the brains defense system

14. Faustino, J. V., Wang, X., Johnson, C. E., Klibanov, A., Derugin, N., Wendland, M. F., & Vexler, Z. S. (2011). Microglial cells contribute to endogenous brain defenses after acute neonatal focal stroke. *Journal of Neuroscience, 31*(36), 12992-13001.
15. Kraft, A. D., & Harry, G. J. (2011). Features of microglia and neuroinflammation relevant to environmental exposure and neurotoxicity. *International Journal of Environmental Research and Public Health, 8*(7), 2980-3018.

Effects on remote areas after a stroke

16. Baron, J. C., Yamauchi, H., Fujioka, M., & Endres, M. (2014). Selective neuronal loss in ischemic stroke and cerebrovascular disease. *Journal of Cerebral Blood Flow & Metabolism*, 34(1), 2-18.

17. Mendelow, A. D., Lo, E. H., Sacco, R. L., Faan, M. M. F., & Wong, L. K. (2015). *Stroke: Pathophysiology, diagnosis, and management*. Amsterdam, Netherlands: Elsevier.

Wallerian degeneration

18. Carroll, S.L. (2009). Wallerian degeneration. *Science direct*. Retrieved from https://www.sciencedirect.com/topics/neuroscience/wallerian-degeneration

19. Conforti, L., Gilley, J., & Coleman, M. P. (2014). Wallerian degeneration: An emerging axon death pathway linking injury and disease. *Nature Reviews Neuroscience*, 15(6), 394.

20. Gaudet, A. D., Popovich, P. G., & Ramer, M. S. (2011). Wallerian degeneration: Gaining perspective on inflammatory events after peripheral nerve injury. *Journal of Neuroinflammation*, 8(1), 110.

Diaschisis

21. Seitz, R. J., Azari, N. P., Knorr, U., Binkofski, F., Herzog, H., & Freund, H. J. (1999). The role of diaschisis in stroke recovery. *Stroke*, 30(9), 1844-1850.

22. Strother, M. K., Buckingham, C., Faraco, C. C., Arteaga, D. F., Lu, P., Xu, Y., & Donahue, M. J. (2016). Crossed cerebellar diaschisis after stroke identified noninvasively with cerebral blood flow-weighted arterial spin labeling MRI. *European journal of radiology*, 85(1), 136-142.

23. Carrera, E., & Tononi, G. (2014). Diaschisis: Past, present, future. *Brain*, 137(9), 2408-2422.

24. Beldarrain, G., García-Moncó, C., Quintana, M., Llorens, V., & Rodeño, E. (1997). Diaschisis and neuropsychological performance after cerebellar stroke. *European neurology*, 37(2), 82-89.

Increased function in opposite hemisphere after stroke

25. Buetefisch, C. M. (2015). Role of the contralesional hemisphere in post-stroke recovery of upper extremity motor function. *Frontiers in neurology*, 6, 214.

26. Mani, S., Mutha, P. K., Przybyla, A., Haaland, K. Y., Good, D. C., & Sainburg, R. L. (2013). Contralesional motor deficits after unilateral stroke reflect hemisphere-specific control mechanisms. *Brain*, 136(4), 1288-1303.

Health before stroke determines outcome

27. Mani, S., Mutha, P. K., Przybyla, A., Haaland, K. Y., Good, D. C., & Sainburg, R. L. (2013). Contralesional motor deficits after unilateral stroke reflect hemisphere-specific control mechanisms. *Brain, 136*(4), 1288-1303.
28. Wolfe, C. D., Crichton, S. L., Heuschmann, P. U., McKevitt, C. J., Toschke, A. M., Grieve, A. P., & Rudd, A. G. (2011). Estimates of outcomes up to ten years after stroke: Analysis from the prospective South London Stroke Register. *PLOS Medicine*, 8(5), e1001033.
29. Rist, P. M., Buring, J. E., Kase, C. S., & Kurth, T. (2016). Healthy lifestyle and functional outcomes from stroke in women. *The American Journal of Medicine, 129*(7), 715-724.

Ventricular system

30. Ventricular system. (2019). In *Wikipedia*. Retrieved September 8, 2019, from https://en.wikipedia.org/wiki/Ventricular_system
31. Shenoy, S. S., & Lui, F. (2018). Neuroanatomy, ventricular system. *StatPearls*. Retrieved from https://www.ncbi.nlm.nih.gov/books/NBK532932/
32. Purves, D., Augustine, G.J. & Fitzpatrick, D. (2001). The ventricular system. In *Neuroscience* (nd2nd ed.). Sunderland, MA: Sinauer Associates.

Stem cells near ventricular system

33. Lu, J., Manaenko, A., & Hu, Q. (2017). Targeting adult neurogenesis for poststroke therapy. *Stem cells international, 2017*.
34. Gonzalez-Perez, O. (2012). Neural stem cells in the adult human brain. *Biological and Biomedical Reports*, 2(1), 59.
35. Duan, X., Kang, E., Liu, C. Y., Ming, G. L., & Song, H. (2008). Development of neural stem cell in the adult brain. *Current opinion in neurobiology*, 18(1), 108-115.
36. Johansson, C. B., Svensson, M., Wallstedt, L., Janson, A. M., & Frisén, J. (1999). Neural stem cells in the adult human brain. *Experimental cell research*, 253(2), 733-736.

Glial cells can turn into neurons

37. Penn State. (2019). New gene therapy reprograms brain glial cells into neurons. *Science daily*. Retrieved from https://www.sciencedaily.com/releases/2018/11/181105122433.htm
38. Lu, Jianfeng, Robert A. Bradley, and Su-Chun Zhang. Turning reactive glia into functional neurons in the brain. *Cell Stem Cell* 14.2 (2014): 133-134.

39. Li, H., & Chen, G. (2016). In vivo reprogramming for CNS repair: Regenerating neurons from endogenous glial cells. *Neuron, 91*(4), 728-738.

40. Jäkel, S., & Dimou, L. (2017). Glial cells and their function in the adult brain: A journey through the history of their ablation. *Frontiers in cellular neuroscience, 11*, 24.

Microglial cells

41. Kraft, A. D., & Harry, G. J. (2011). Features of microglia and neuroinflammation relevant to environmental exposure and neurotoxicity. *International Journal of Environmental Research and Public Health, 8*(7), 2980-3018.

Astrocytes

42. Sofroniew, M. V., & Vinters, H. V. (2010). Astrocytes: Biology and pathology. *Acta neuropathologica, 119*(1), 7-35.

Oligodendrocytes

43. Bradl, M., & Lassmann, H. (2010). Oligodendrocytes: Biology and pathology. *Acta neuropathologica, 119*(1), 37-53.

Neuronal sprouting

44. Sobkowicz, H. M., & Slapnick, S. M. (1992). Neuronal sprouting and synapse formation in response to injury in the mouse organ of Corti in culture. *International journal of developmental neuroscience, 10*(6), 545-566.

Networks of the brain

45. Sporns, O. (2013). Structure and function of complex brain networks. *Dialogues in Clinical Neuroscience, 15*(3), 247.

46. Yao, Z., Hu, B., Xie, Y., Moore, P., & Zheng, J. (2015). A review of structural and functional brain networks: Small world and atlas. *Brain informatics*, 2(1), 45-52.

Chaos in the brain after a stroke

47. Carmichael, S. T. (2016). The 3 Rs of stroke biology: Radial, relayed, and regenerative. *Neurotherapeutics, 13*(2), 348-359.

48. Falcon, M. I., Riley, J. D., Jirsa, V., McIntosh, A. R., Chen, E. E., & Solodkin, A. (2016). Functional mechanisms of recovery after chronic stroke: Modeling with the Virtual Brain. *Eneuro, 3*(2).

Cell danger response

49. Naviaux, R. K. (2014). Metabolic features of the cell danger response. *Mitochondrion, 16*, 7-17.

50. The Human Longevity Project. (n.d.). Episode 1 - the truth about aging: Can it be slowed or even reversed? Retrieved from https://humanlongevityfilm.com/downloads/transcripts/thlp_ep_1_transcript.pdf

Reticular system of the brain

51. Reticular formation. (2019). In *Wikipedia*. Retrieved September 9, 2019, from https://en.wikipedia.org/wiki/Reticular_formation
52. Yeo, S. S., Chang, P. H., & Jang, S. H. (2013). The ascending reticular activating system from pontine reticular formation to the thalamus in the human brain. *Frontiers in human neuroscience, 7*, 416.

Neuronal plasticity is often a random event

53. Dennis, M., Spiegler, B. J., Juranek, J. J., Bigler, E. D., Snead, O. C., & Fletcher, J. M. (2013). Age, plasticity, and homeostasis in childhood brain disorders. *Neuroscience & Biobehavioral Reviews, 37*(10), 2760-2773.
54. Cramer, S. C., Sur, M., Dobkin, B. H., O'Brien, C., Sanger, T. D., Trojanowski, J. Q. & Chen, W. G. (2011). Harnessing neuroplasticity for clinical applications. *Brain, 134*(6), 1591-1609.

Reactivation of dormant neurons after a stroke

55. Lindvall, O., & Kokaia, Z. (2015). Neurogenesis following stroke affecting the adult brain. *Cold Spring Harbor perspectives in biology, 7*(11), a019034.
56. Guruswamy, R., & ElAli, A. (2017). Complex roles of microglial cells in ischemic stroke pathobiology: New insights and future directions. *International journal of molecular sciences, 18*(3), 496.

CHAPTER 36

Curt Richter

1. Curt Richter. (2019). In *Wikipedia*. Retrieved September 12, 2019, from https://en.wikipedia.org/wiki/Curt_Richter
2. Schulkin, J. (2005). *Curt Richter: A life in the laboratory*. Baltimore, MD: Johns Hopkins University Press.

The brain uses much of available energy

3. Raichle, M. E., & Gusnard, D. A. (2002). Appraising the brain's energy budget. *Proceedings of the National Academy of Sciences*, 99(16), 10237-10239.
4. Falkowska, A., Gutowska, I., Goschorska, M., Nowacki, P., Chlubek, D., & Baranowska-Bosiacka, I. (2015). Energy metabolism of the brain, including the cooperation between astrocytes and neurons,

especially in the context of glycogen metabolism. *International journal of molecular sciences, 16*(11), 25959-25981.

5. Berg, J. M., Tymoczko, J. L., & Stryer, L. (2002). Section 30.2, each organ has a unique metabolic profile. In *Biochemistry* (5th ed.). New York, NY: W.H. Freeman and Company.

Mitochondria are either in energy production or cell defence mode

6. Tatsuta, T., & Langer, T. (2008). Quality control of mitochondria: Protection against neurodegeneration and ageing. *The EMBO Journal, 27*(2), 306-314.
7. Seppet, E., Gruno, M., Peetsalu, A., Gizatullina, Z., Nguyen, H. P., Vielhaber, S., & Sonnabend, M. (2009). Mitochondria and energetic depression in cell pathophysiology. *International journal of molecular sciences, 10*(5), 2252-2303.
8. Madreiter-Sokolowski, C., Sokolowski, A., Waldeck-Weiermair, M., Malli, R., & Graier, W. (2018). Targeting mitochondria to counteract age-related cellular dysfunction. *Genes, 9*(3), 165.

Reasons why mitochondria go into cell defence mode

9. Meyer, J. N., Leung, M. C., Rooney, J. P., Sendoel, A., Hengartner, M. O., Kisby, G. E., & Bess, A. S. (2013). Mitochondria as a target of environmental toxicants. *Toxicological Sciences, 134*(1), 1-17.
10. Ledderose, C., Bao, Y., Ledderose, S., Woehrle, T., Heinisch, M., Yip, L. & Junger, W. G. (2015). Mitochondrial dysfunction, depleted purinergic signaling, and defective T cell vigilance and immune defense. *The Journal of Infectious Diseases, 213*(3), 456-464.
11. Kubli, D. A., & Gustafsson, Å. B. (2012). Mitochondria and mitophagy: The yin and yang of cell death control. *Circulation Research, 111*(9), 1208-1221.

The effects of blue light

12. Bradford, A. (2016). How blue LEDs affect sleep. *Live science*. Retrieved from https://www.livescience.com/53874-blue-light-sleep.html
13. Tosini, G., Ferguson, I., & Tsubota, K. (2016). Effects of blue light on the circadian system and eye physiology. *Molecular Vision*, 22, 61.*Molecular vision*, 22, 61.
14. Harvard Medical School. (2018). Blue light has a dark side. *Harvard health publishing*. Retrieved from https://www.health.harvard.edu/staying-healthy/blue-light-has-a-dark-side

Melatonin is a powerful antioxidant

15. Chrono Biology. (2019). New insights into the use of melatonin as an antioxidant. Retrieved from https://www.chronobiology.com/new-insights-use-melatonin-antioxidant/
16. Reiter, R. J., Mayo, J. C., Tan, D. X., Sainz, R. M., Alatorre-Jimenez, M., & Qin, L. (2016). Melatonin as an antioxidant: Under promises but over delivers. *Journal of Pineal Research, 61*(3), 253-278.

Vegetable fats cause inflammation

17. Fritsche, K. L. (2015). The science of fatty acids and inflammation. *Advances in Nutrition*, 6(3), 293S-301S.
18. Galland, L. (2010). Diet and inflammation. *Nutrition in Clinical Practice*, 25(6), 634-640.
19. Dobarganes, C., & Márquez-Ruiz, G. (2015). Possible adverse effects of frying with vegetable oils. *British Journal of Nutrition, 113*(S2), S49-S57.
20. Kummerow, F. A. (2009). The negative effects of hydrogenated trans fats and what to do about them. *Atherosclerosis*, 205(2), 458-465.
21. Ng, C. Y., Leong, X. F., Masbah, N., Adam, S. K., Kamisah, Y., & Jaarin, K. (2014). Heated vegetable oils and cardiovascular disease risk factors. *Vascular Pharmacology, 61*(1), 1-9.

Food intolerances causing cell danger response

22. Mansueto, P., Montalto, G., Pacor, M. L., Esposito-Pellitteri, M., Ditta, V., Bianco, C. L. & Di Lorenzo, G. (2006). Food allergy in gastroenterologic diseases: Review of literature. *World Journal of Gastroenterology, 12*(48), 7744.
23. Trinchese, G., Paparo, L., Aitoro, R., Fierro, C., Varchetta, M., Nocerino, R., & Berni Canani, R. (2018). Hepatic mitochondrial dysfunction and immune response in a murine model of peanut allergy. *Nutrients, 10*(6), 744.

Sugar causes mitochondrial damage

24. Mansueto, P., Montalto, G., Pacor, M. L., Esposito-Pellitteri, M., Ditta, V., Bianco, C. L. & Di Lorenzo, G. (2006). Food allergy in gastroenterologic diseases: Review of literature. *World Journal of Gastroenterology, 12*(48), 7744.
25. Cioffi, F., Senese, R., Lasala, P., Ziello, A., Mazzoli, A., Crescenzo, R., & Iossa, S. (2017). Fructose-rich diet affects mitochondrial DNA damage and repair in rats. *Nutrients*, 9(4), 323.

Advanced glycation end products causing mitochondrial damage

26. Fournet, M., Bonte, F., & Desmouliere, A. (2018). Glycation damage: A possible hub for major pathophysiological disorders and aging. *Aging and disease*, 9(5), 880.

Medication and mitochondrial malfunction

27. Neustadt, J., & Pieczenik, S. R. (2008). Medication-induced mitochondrial damage and disease. *Molecular Nutrition & Food Research*, 52(7), 780-788.
28. Will, Y., Shields, J. E., & Wallace, K. B. (2019). Drug-induced mitochondrial toxicity in the geriatric population: Challenges and future directions. *Biology*, 8(2), 32.
29. Varga, Z. V., Ferdinandy, P., Liaudet, L., & Pacher, P. (2015). Drug-induced mitochondrial dysfunction and cardiotoxicity. *American Journal of Physiology - Heart and Circulatory Physiology*, 309(9), H1453-H1467.

Overexercising causing mitochondrial shutdown

30. Menshikova, E. V., Ritov, V. B., Fairfull, L., Ferrell, R. E., Kelley, D. E., & Goodpaster, B. H. (2006). Effects of exercise on mitochondrial content and function in aging human skeletal muscle. *The Journals of Gerontology Series A: Biological Sciences and Medical Sciences*, 61(6), 534-540.
31. Ostojic, S. M. (2016). Exercise-induced mitochondrial dysfunction: A myth or reality? *Clinical Science*, 130(16), 1407-1416.
32. Stawski, R., Walczak, K., Kosielski, P., Meissner, P., Budlewski, T., Padula, G., & Nowak, D. (2017). Repeated bouts of exhaustive exercise increase circulating cell free nuclear and mitochondrial DNA without development of tolerance in healthy men. *PLOS One*, 12(5), e0178216.

Psychological stress and mitochondrial malfunction

33. Picard, M., & McEwen, B. S. (2018). Psychological stress and mitochondria: A systematic review. *Psychosomatic Medicine*, 80(2), 141.
34. Picard, M., & McEwen, B. S. (2018). Psychological stress and mitochondria: A conceptual framework. *Psychosomatic Medicine*, 80(2), 126.
35. Allen, J., Romay-Tallon, R., Brymer, K. J., Caruncho, H. J., & Kalynchuk, L. E. (2018). Mitochondria and mood: Mitochondrial dysfunction as a key player in the manifestation of depression. *Frontiers in neuroscience*, 12, 386.

Bacterial and viral infections causing mitochondrial malfunction

36. Herst, P. M., Rowe, M. R., Carson, G. M., & Berridge, M. V. (2017). Functional mitochondria in health and disease. *Frontiers in endocrinology*, *8*, 296.
37. Luethy, L. N., & Pfeiffer, J. K. (2012). Viral infection brings mitochondrial traffic to a standstill. *Cell host & microbe*, *11*(5), 420-421.
38. Reshi, L., Wang, H. V., & Hong, J. R. (2018). Modulation of mitochondria during viral infections. *Mitochondrial Diseases*, 443.

Insulin resistance and mitochondrial damage

39. Montgomery, M. K., & Turner, N. (2015). Mitochondrial dysfunction and insulin resistance: An update. *Endocrine connections*, *4*(1), R1-R15.
40. Sivitz, W. I., & Yorek, M. A. (2010). Mitochondrial dysfunction in diabetes: From molecular mechanisms to functional significance and therapeutic opportunities. *Antioxidants & Redox Signaling*, *12*(4), 537-577.

Environmental toxins and their effect on mitochondria

41. Meyer, J. N., Leung, M. C., Rooney, J. P., Sendoel, A., Hengartner, M. O., Kisby, G. E., & Bess, A. S. (2013). Mitochondria as a target of environmental toxicants. *Toxicological Sciences*, *134*(1), 1-17.
42. Zolkipli-Cunningham, Z., & Falk, M. J. (2017). Clinical effects of chemical exposures on mitochondrial function. *Toxicology*, *391*, 90-99.

The effect of fluoride on mitochondrial function

43. Fina, B. L., Lombarte, M., Rigalli, J. P., & Rigalli, A. (2014). Fluoride increases superoxide production and impairs the respiratory chain in ROS 17/2.8 osteoblastic cells. *PLOS One*, *9*(6), e100768.

Processed foods contain bisphenols, phthalates, and artificial colorings

44. Trasande, L., Shaffer, R. M., & Sathyanarayana, S. (2018). Food additives and child health. *Pediatrics*, *142*(2), e20181410.

Organic food contains less herbicides and pesticides

45. Robinson, L., Segal, J., & Segal, R. (2019). Organic foods: What you need to know. *HelpGuide*. Retrieved from https://www.helpguide.org/articles/healthy-eating/organic-foods.htm
46. Smith-Spangler, C., Brandeau, M. L., Hunter, G. E., Bavinger, J. C., Pearson, M., Eschbach, P. J., & Olkin, I. (2012). Are organic foods

safer or healthier than conventional alternatives?: A systematic review. *Annals of internal medicine*, 157(5), 348-366.

47. Barański, M., Rempelos, L., Iversen, P. O., & Leifert, C. (2017). Effects of organic food consumption on human health; the jury is still out! *Food & nutrition research*, 61(1), 1287333.
48. Crinnion, W. J. (2010). Organic foods contain higher levels of certain nutrients, lower levels of pesticides, and may provide health benefits for the consumer. *Alternative medicine review*, 15(1).

Alcohol is a mitochondrial toxin

49. Hoek, J. B., Cahill, A., & Pastorino, J. G. (2002). Alcohol and mitochondria: A dysfunctional relationship. *Gastroenterology*, 122(7), 2049-2063.

Toxins in our drinking water

50. Pascus, B. (2019). New study claims 43 states expose millions to dangerous chemical in drinking water. *CBC news*. https://www.cbsnews.com/news/drinking-water-may-contain-pfas-chemicals-in-43-states-according-to-new-study-by-environmental-working-group/
51. National Research Council, & Safe Drinking Water Committee. (1983). Toxicity of selected contaminants in drinking water. In *Drinking water and health* (Vol. 5). Washington, DC: National Academies Press.
52. Popkin, B. M., D'Anci, K. E., & Rosenberg, I. H. (2010). Water, hydration, and health. *Nutrition reviews*, 68(8), 439-458.in Drinking Water. In *Drinking Water and Health:* Volume 5. National Academies Press (US).

Air purification to decrease toxic load

53. Vijayan, V. K., Paramesh, H., Salvi, S. S., & Dalal, A. A. K. (2015). Enhancing indoor air quality - the air filter advantage. *Lung India: Official Organ of Indian Chest Society*, 32(5), 473.
54. Morishita, M., Adar, S. D., D'Souza, J., Ziemba, R. A., Bard, R. L., Spino, C., & Brook, R. D. (2018). Effect of portable air filtration systems on personal exposure to fine particulate matter and blood pressure among residents in a low-income senior facility: A randomized clinical trial. *JAMA Internal Medicine*, 178(10), 1350-1357.

Get rid of kitchen utensils containing toxins

55. Maceachern, D. (2016). The 9 most toxic items in your kitchen. *Country living*. Retrieved from https://www.countryliving.com/home-maintenance/cleaning/g3210/toxic-pantry-items/

56. Sajid, M., & Ilyas, M. (2017). PTFE-coated non-stick cookware and toxicity concerns: A perspective. *Environmental Science and Pollution Research, 24*(30), 23436-23440.

57. Inan-Eroglu, E., & Ayaz, A. (2018). Is aluminum exposure a risk factor for neurological disorders? *Journal of Research in Medical Sciences: The Official Journal of Isfahan University of Medical Sciences, 23.*

Hormone disrupting chemicals in cosmetics

58. Nicolopoulou-Stamati, P., Hens, L., & Sasco, A. J. (2015). Cosmetics as endocrine disruptors: Are they a health risk? *Reviews in Endocrine and Metabolic Disorders, 16*(4), 373-383.

59. Engeli, R., Rohrer, S., Vuorinen, A., Herdlinger, S., Kaserer, T., Leugger, S., & Odermatt, A. (2017). Interference of paraben compounds with estrogen metabolism by inhibition of 17β-hydroxysteroid dehydrogenases. *International Journal of Molecular Sciences, 18*(9), 2007.

60. Nowak, K., Ratajczak-Wrona, W., Górska, M., & Jabłońska, E. (2018). Parabens and their effects on the endocrine system. *Molecular and Cellular Endocrinology, 474*, 238-251.

61. Street, M., Angelini, S., Bernasconi, S., Burgio, E., Cassio, A., Catellani, C., & Gargano, G. (2018). Current knowledge on endocrine disrupting chemicals (EDCs) from animal biology to humans, from pregnancy to adulthood: Highlights from a national Italian meeting. *International journal of molecular sciences, 19*(6), 1647.

Chemicals in cleaning products can disrupt mitochondria

62. De Coster, S., & Van Larebeke, N. (2012). Endocrine-disrupting chemicals: Associated disorders and mechanisms of action. *Journal of Environmental and Public Health, 2012.*

Cell defence mode and important nutrients

63. Hughes, A. L., Hughes, C. E., Henderson, K. A., Yazvenko, N., & Gottschling, D. E. (2016). Selective sorting and destruction of mitochondrial membrane proteins in aged yeast. *Elife, 5*, e13943.

Mitochondrial damage responsible for ageing

64. Hughes, A. L., Hughes, C. E., Henderson, K. A., Yazvenko, N., & Gottschling, D. E. (2016). Selective sorting and destruction of mitochondrial membrane proteins in aged yeast. *Elife, 5*, e13943.

65. Srivastava, S. (2017). The mitochondrial basis of aging and age-related disorders. *Genes, 8*(12), 398.

66. Bratic, A., & Larsson, N. G. (2013). The role of mitochondria in aging. *The Journal of Clinical Investigation*, *123*(3), 951-957.

67. Payne, B. A., & Chinnery, P. F. (2015). Mitochondrial dysfunction in aging: Much progress but many unresolved questions. *Biochimica et Biophysica Acta (BBA)-Bioenergetics*, *1847*(11), 1347-1353.

Foods that boost mitochondrial function

68. Jørgensen, W., Rud, K. A., Mortensen, O. H., Frandsen, L., Grunnet, N., & Quistorff, B. (2017). Your mitochondria are what you eat: A high-fat or a high-sucrose diet eliminates metabolic flexibility in isolated mitochondria from rat skeletal muscle. *Physiological Reports*, 5(6), e13207.

69. Du, J., Zhu, M., Bao, H., Li, B., Dong, Y., Xiao, C. & Vitiello, B. (2016). The role of nutrients in protecting mitochondrial function and neurotransmitter signaling: Implications for the treatment of depression, PTSD, and suicidal behaviors. *Critical reviews in food science and nutrition*, 56(15), 2560-2578.

70. Metabolic Meals. (2019). How to improve mitochondrial function for better energy. Retrived from Metabolic Meals. (2019). How to Improve Mitochondrial Function for Better Energy.Retrived from https://www.mymetabolicmeals.com/how-to-improve-mitochondrial-function-for-better-energy/

Phospholipids can reduce fatigue significantly

71. Nicolson, G. L., & Ash, M. E. (2014). Lipid replacement therapy: A natural medicine approach to replacing damaged lipids in cellular membranes and organelles and restoring function. *Biochimica et Biophysica Acta (BBA) - Biomembranes*, *1838*(6), 1657-1679.

72. Imai, A., Oda, Y., Ito, N., Seki, S., Nakagawa, K., Miyazawa, T., & Ueda, F. (2018). Effects of dietary supplementation of astaxanthin and sesamin on daily fatigue: A randomized, double-blind, placebo-controlled, two-way crossover study. *Nutrients*, *10*(3), 281.

73. Nicolson, G. L. (2014). Mitochondrial dysfunction and chronic disease: Treatment with natural supplements. *Integrative Medicine: A Clinician's Journal*, *13*(4), 35.

What foods contain phospholipids?

74. Küllenberg, D., Taylor, L. A., Schneider, M., & Massing, U. (2012). Health effects of dietary phospholipids. *Lipids in Health and Disease*, *11*(1), 3.

Asthaxanthin powerfully protects the mitochondrial membrane

75. Davinelli, S., Nielsen, M., & Scapagnini, G. (2018). Astaxanthin in skin health, repair, and disease: A comprehensive review. *Nutrients, 10*(4), 522.*Nutrients, 10*(4), 522.

The danger of toxins in our environment

76. Gross, L., & Birnbaum, L. S. (2017). Regulating toxic chemicals for public and environmental health. *PLOS Biology*. Retrieved from https://journals.PLOS.org/PLOSbiology/article?id=10.1371/journal.pbio.2004814
77. Crinnion, W. J. (2000). Environmental medicine, part one: The human burden of environmental toxins and their common health effects. *Alternative medicine review: A journal of clinical therapeutic*, 5(1), 52-63.

Negative influence of toxins on energy production and your health

78. Johnson, A. R., Justin Milner, J., & Makowski, L. (2012). The inflammation highway: Metabolism accelerates inflammatory traffic in obesity. *Immunological reviews*, 249(1), 218-238.
79. Carpenter, D. O., Arcaro, K., & Spink, D. C. (2002). Understanding the human health effects of chemical mixtures. *Environmental health perspectives*, 110(suppl 1), 25-42.

How many toxins do we have in our body

80. Murdock, B. S. (2005). Tracking toxins. *EMBO reports*, 6(8), 701-705.
81. Silins, I., & Högberg, J. (2011). Combined toxic exposures and human health: Biomarkers of exposure and effect. *International Journal of Environmental Research and Public Health*, 8(3), 629-647.

Toxins in car exhaust

82. Goldsmith, J. R., & Rogers, L. H. (1959). Health hazards of automobile exhaust. *Public Health Reports, 74*(6), 551.
83. Sekine, K., Shima, M., Nitta, Y., & Adachi, M. (2004). Long term effects of exposure to automobile exhaust on the pulmonary function of female adults in Tokyo, Japan. *Occupational and Environmental Medicine*, 61(4), 350-357.
84. Hutchinson, E. J., & Pearson, P. J. (2004). An evaluation of the environmental and health effects of vehicle exhaust catalysts in the UK. *Environmental health perspectives*, 112(2), 132-141.

The most common toxins in our environment

85. Chin, N. P. (2010). Environmental toxins: Physical, social, and emotional. *Breastfeeding Medicine*, 5(5), 223-224.

86. Sexton, K., & Hattis, D. (2007). Assessing cumulative health risks from exposure to environmental mixtures - three fundamental questions. *Environmental health perspectives*, *115*(5), 825-832.

87. Duncan, D.E. (2019). Chemicals within us. *National Geographic*. Retrieved From https://www.nationalgeographic.com/science/health-and-human-body/human-body/chemicals-within-us/

Mercury and aluminium are common toxins in our environment

88. Jaishankar, M., Tseten, T., Anbalagan, N., Mathew, B. B., & Beeregowda, K. N. (2014). Toxicity, mechanism and health effects of some heavy metals. *Interdisciplinary toxicology*, *7*(2), 60-72.

Toxins from molds

89. Brewer, J., Thrasher, J., & Hooper, D. (2014). Chronic illness associated with mold and mycotoxins: Is naso-sinus fungal biofilm the culprit? *Toxins*, 6(1), 66-80.

Skin and liver as detoxifying organs

90. Artemis. (n.d.). Your detoxification pathway explained. Retrieved from https://international.artemis.co.nz/your-detox-pathway-explained

91. Hodges, R. E., & Minich, D. M. (2015). Modulation of metabolic detoxification pathways using foods and food-derived components: A scientific review with clinical application. *Journal of Nutrition and Metabolism*, *2015*.

92. Zhou, S. S., Li, D., Zhou, Y. M., & Cao, J. M. (2012). The skin function: A factor of anti-metabolic syndrome. *Diabetology & metabolic syndrome*, *4*(1), 15.

Storage of toxins in our body

93. La Merrill, M., Emond, C., Kim, M. J., Antignac, J. P., Le Bizec, B., Clément, K., & Barouki, R. (2012). Toxicological function of adipose tissue: Focus on persistent organic pollutants. *Environmental health perspectives*, *121*(2), 162-169.

Vegetable fiber binds toxins

94. Lattimer, J. M., & Haub, M. D. (2010). Effects of dietary fiber and its components on metabolic health. *Nutrients*, 2(12), 1266-1289.

Green leafy vegetables

95. Guan, Y. S., & He, Q. (2015). Plants consumption and liver health. *Evidence-based complementary and alternative medicine, 2015.*

Foods that help the detoxification process

96. Van de Walle, G. (2019). Full body detox: 9 ways to rejuvenate your body. *Healthline.* Retrieved from https://www.healthline.com/nutrition/how-to-detox-your-body
97. Hodges, R. E., & Minich, D. M. (2015). Modulation of metabolic detoxification pathways using foods and food-derived components: A scientific review with clinical application. *Journal of Nutrition and Metabolism, 2015.*

Vitamin C-rich foods help production of gluthation

98. Ribas, V., García-Ruiz, C., & Fernández-Checa, J. C. (2014). Glutathione and mitochondria. *Frontiers in pharmacology*, 5, 151.

Detoxification through herbs such as dandelion, milk thistle, turmeric

99. Balaban, Y. H., Aka, C., & Koca-Caliskan, U. (2017). Liver immunology and herbal treatment. *World Journal of Hepatology*, 9(17), 757.
100. Guan, Y. S., & He, Q. (2015). Plants consumption and liver health. *Evidence-based complementary and alternative medicine, 2015.*
101. Hanje, A. J., Fortune, B., Song, M., Hill, D., & McClain, C. (2006). The use of selected nutrition supplements and complementary and alternative medicine in liver disease. *Nutrition in clinical practice, 21*(3), 255-272.
102. Hodges, R. E., & Minich, D. M. (2015). Modulation of metabolic detoxification pathways using foods and food-derived components: A scientific review with clinical application. *Journal of Nutrition and Metabolism, 2015.*

CHAPTER 37

Robert Melillo

1. Dr. Robert Melillo. (2019). Dr. Robert Melillo. Retrieved from https://www.drrobertmelillo.com/about/

Brain balance achievement centers

2. Brain Balance Achievement Centers. (2019). Brain Balance has a plan for kids who struggle. Retrieved from https://www.brainbalancecenters.com/

Autism and imbalances between the hemispheres

3. Melillo, R., & Leisman, G. (2009). Autistic spectrum disorders as functional disconnection syndrome. *Reviews in the neurosciences, 20*(2), 111-132.
4. O'Reilly, C., Lewis, J. D., & Elsabbagh, M. (2017). Is functional brain connectivity atypical in autism? A systematic review of EEG and MEG studies. *PLOS One, 12*(5), e0175870.

Neuroinflammation and autism spectrum disorder

5. Matta, S. M., Hill-Yardin, E. L., & Crack, P. J. (2019). The influence of neuroinflammation in autism spectrum disorder. *Brain, Behavior, and Immunity, 79*, 75-90.

Primitive reflexes

6. Gieysztor, E. Z., Choińska, A. M., & Paprocka-Borowicz, M. (2018). Persistence of primitive reflexes and associated motor problems in healthy preschool children. *Archives of Medical Science, 14*(1), 167.
7. Bain Balance Achievement Centers. (2019). Retained primitive reflexes as a sign of brain imbalance. Retrieved from https://blog.brainbalancecenters.com/2014/09/retained-primitive-reflexes-sign-brain-imbalance
8. Mehta, U. M., Sanjay, T. N., Venkatasubramanian, G., & Muralidharan, K. (2019). Cortical inhibition and primitive reflexes in remitted first-episode mania. *Brain Stimulation: Basic, Translational, and Clinical Research in Neuromodulation, 12*(4), 1093–1094.
9. Futagi, Y., Toribe, Y., & Suzuki, Y. (2012). The grasp reflex and moro reflex in infants: Hierarchy of primitive reflex responses. *International Journal of pPediatrics, 2012.*
10. Panteliadis, C. P., Hagel, C., Karch, D., & Heinemann, K. (2015). Cerebral palsy: A lifelong challenge asks for early intervention. *The Open Neurology Journal, 9*, 45.
11. Niklasson, M., Rasmussen, P., Niklasson, I., & Norlander, T. (2015). Adults with sensorimotor disorders: Enhanced physiological and psychological development following specific sensorimotor training. *Frontiers in psychology, 6*, 480.
12. Schott, J. M., & Rossor, M. N. (2003). The grasp and other primitive reflexes. *Journal of Neurology, Neurosurgery & Psychiatry, 74*(5), 558-560.

Babinsky reflex

13. U.S. National Library of Medicine. (2019). Babinski reflex. Retrieved from https://medlineplus.gov/ency/article/003294.htm

14. Van Gijn, J. (1995). The Babinski reflex. *Postgraduate Medical Journal, 71*(841), 645-648.
15. Acharya, A. B., Jamil, R. T., & Dewey, J. J. (2019). Babinski reflex. *StatPearls*. Retrieved from https://www.ncbi.nlm.nih.gov/books/NBK519009/

Primitive reflexes in stroke patients

16. Botvin, J. G., Keith, R. A., & Johnston, M. V. (1978). Relationship between primitive reflexes in stroke patients and rehabilitation outcome. *Stroke*, 9(3), 256-258.
17. Arima, M., Ogata, A., Kawahira, K., & Shimodozono, M. (2017). Improvement and neuroplasticity after combined rehabilitation to forced grasping. *Case reports in neurological medicine, 2017*.

Harvard study

18. Teicher, T. (n.d.). *White paper: Profound effects of brain balance exercises and interactive metronome and on a subset of children with attention deficit hyperactivity disorder*. Retrieved from https://cdn2.hubspot.net/hubfs/3798961/Harvard%20White%20Paper%20BB%20August%202019.pdf

Low-level light laser has a positive effect on traumatic brain injury

19. Thunshelle, C., & Hamblin, M. R. (2016). Transcranial low-level laser (light) therapy for brain injury. *Photomedicine and laser surgery*, 34(12), 587-598.
20. A.G.N. (1940). Food for health in peace and war. *Canadian Medical Association Journal*, 42(6): 578–579.

Synkinesis

21. U.S. National Library of Medicine. (2019). Babinski reflex. Retrieved from https://medlineplus.gov/ency/article/003294.htm
22. Husseman, J., & Mehta, R. P. (2008). Management of synkinesis. *Facial plastic surgery*, 24(02), 242-249.
23. Hwang, I. S., Tung, L. C., Yang, J. F., Chen, Y. C., Yeh, C. Y., & Wang, C. H. (2005). Electromyographic analyses of global synkinesis in the paretic upper limb after stroke. *Physical Therapy*, 85(8), 755-765.
24. Kang, J. A., Chun, M. H., Choi, S. J., Chang, M. C., & Yi, Y. G. (2017). Effects of mirror therapy using a tablet PC on central facial paresis in stroke patients. *Annals of Rehabilitation Medicine*, 41(3), 347.

CHAPTER 38

Constraint-induced movement therapy (CIMT)

1. Corbetta, D., Sirtori, V., Castellini, G., Moja, L., & Gatti, R. (2015). Constraint-induced movement therapy for upper extremities in people with stroke. *Cochrane Database of Systematic Reviews*, (10).
2. Kwakkel, G., Veerbeek, J. M., van Wegen, E. E., & Wolf, S. L. (2015). Constraint-induced movement therapy after stroke. *The Lancet Neurology*, *14*(2), 224-234.
3. Thrane, G., Friborg, O., Anke, A., & Indredavik, B. (2014). A meta-analysis of constraint-induced movement therapy after stroke. *Journal of rehabilitation medicine*, 6(9), 833-42

Mental visualisation in stroke recovery

4. Ietswaart, M., Johnston, M., Dijkerman, H. C., Joice, S., Scott, C. L., MacWalter, R. S., & Hamilton, S. J. (2011). Mental practice with motor imagery in stroke recovery: Randomized controlled trial of efficacy. *Brain*, *134*(5), 1373-1386.
5. Zimmermann-Schlatter, A., Schuster, C., Puhan, M. A., Siekierka, E., & Steurer, J. (2008). Efficacy of motor imagery in post-stroke rehabilitation: A systematic review. *Journal of Neuroengineering and rehabilitation*, 5(1), 8.
6. Ploderer, B., Fong, J., Klaic, M.,Nair, S., Vetere, F., Lizama, L. E. C., & Galea, M. P. (2016). How therapists use visualizations of upper limb movement information from stroke patients: A qualitative study with simulated information. *JMIR rehabilitation and assistive technologies*, 3(2), e9.Ploderer, B., Fong, J., Klaic, M., Nair, S., Vetere, F., Lizama, L. E. C., & Galea, M. P. (2016). How therapists use visualizations of upper limb movement information from stroke patients: a qualitative study with simulated information. *JMIR rehabilitation and assistive technologies*, 3(2), e9.
7. Loudon, D., Macdonald, A. S., Carse, B., Thikey, H., Jones, L., Rowe, P. J., & Baillie, L. (2012). Developing visualisation software for rehabilitation: Investigating the requirements of patients, therapists and the rehabilitation process. *Health Informatics Journal*, *18*(3), 171-180.

Raising temperature to increase nerve conduction speed in rehabilitation

8. Carr, R. W., Pianova, S., Fernandez, J., Fallon, J. B., Belmonte, C., & Brock, J. A. (2003). Effects of heating and cooling on nerve terminal impulses recorded from cold-sensitive receptors in the guinea-pig cornea. *The Journal of General Physiology*, *121*(5), 427-439.

9. Kiernan, M. C., Cikurel, K., & Bostock, H. (2001). Effects of temperature on the excitability properties of human motor axons. *Brain, 124*(4), 816-825.

Hypnotherapy in stroke recovery

10. Holroyd, J., & Hill, A. (1989). Pushing the limits of recovery: Hypnotherapy with a stroke patient. *International Journal of Clinical and Experimental Hypnosis*, 37(2), 120-128.

Edward Taub

11. UAB Medicine. (2019). Constraint-induced therapy (CI therapy) - Taub Therapy Clinic. Retrieved from https://www.uabmedicine.org/patient-care/treatments/ci-therapy

Corpus Callosum

12. Bloom, J. S., & Hynd, G. W. (2005). The role of the corpus callosum in interhemispheric transfer of information: Excitation or inhibition? *Neuropsychology Review*, 15(2), 59-71.

Interhemispheric inhibition with motor activity

13. Ward, N. S., & Cohen, L. G. (2004). Mechanisms underlying recovery of motor function after stroke. *Archives of Neurology*, *61*(12), 1844-1848.

14. Fling, B. W., & Seidler, R. D. (2012). Task-dependent effects of interhemispheric inhibition on motor control. *Behavioural Brain Research*, 226(1), 211-217.

15. Hübers, A., Orekhov, Y., & Ziemann, U. (2008). Interhemispheric motor inhibition: Its role in controlling electromyographic mirror activity. *European Journal of Neuroscience*, 28(2), 364-371.

Redundancy in the networks of the brain

16. Fallani, F. D. V., Rodrigues, F. A., da Fontoura Costa, L., Astolfi, L., Cincotti, F., Mattia, D. & Babiloni, F. (2011). Multiple pathways analysis of brain functional networks from EEG signals: An application to real data. *Brain topography*, 23(4), 344-354..

Sarah Towers monkey experiments

17. Tower, S. S. (1940). Pyramidal lesion in the monkey. *Brain*, 63(1), 36-90.

The importance of motivation in stroke recovery

18. Maclean, N., Pound, P., Wolfe, C., & Rudd, A. (2000). Qualitative analysis of stroke patients' motivation for rehabilitation. *Bmj*, 321(7268), 1051-1054.

19. Kristensen, H. K., Tistad, M., Von Koch, L., & Ytterberg, C. (2016). The importance of patient involvement in stroke rehabilitation. *PLOS One*, *11*(6), e0157149.

20. Maclean, N., Pound, P., Wolfe, C., & Rudd, A. (2002). The concept of patient motivation: A qualitative analysis of stroke professionals' attitudes. *Stroke*, 33(2), 444-448.

Chapter 39

Bruce Lipton

1. Mountain of Love Productions. (2019). What would your life be like if you learned that you are more powerful than you have ever been taught? Retrieved from https://www.brucelipton.com/

The Biology of Belief

2. Lipton, B. H. (2010). *The biology of belief: Unleashing the power of consciousness, matter, and miracles*. Carlsbad, CA: Hay House.

Epigenetics

3. Weinhold, B. (2006). Epigenetics: The science of change. *Environmental health perspectives*. Retrieved from https://ehp.niehs.nih.gov/doi/abs/10.1289/ehp.114-a160

4. Deans, C., & Maggert, K. A. (2015). What do you mean,"epigenetic"? *Genetics*, *199*(4), 887-896.

5. Moosavi, A., & Ardekani, A. M. (2016). Role of epigenetics in biology and human diseases. *Iranian biomedical journal*, 20(5), 246.

6. What is Epigenetics? (2018). A super brief and basic explanation of epigenetics for total beginner. Retrieved from https://www.whatisepigenetics.com/what-is-epigenetics/

Nobel prize winner Elisabeth Blackburn

7. Nobel Media AB. (2019). Elizabeth H. Blackburn facts. Retrieved from https://www.nobelprize.org/prizes/medicine/2009/blackburn/facts/

Genes and the environment

8. Bray, G. A. (2004). The epidemic of obesity and changes in food intake: The fluoride hypothesis. *Physiology & Behavior*, *82*(1), 115-121.

9. Olden, K., & White, S. L. (2005). Health-related disparities: Influence of environmental factors. *Medical Clinics*, 89(4), 721-738.

10. Ramos, R., & Olden, K. (2008). Gene-environment interactions in the development of complex disease phenotypes. *International Journal of Environmental Research and Public Health*, 5(1), 4-11.

Jim Kwik

11. Jim Kwik. (2019). If knowledge is power, learning is a superpower. Retrieved from https://jimkwik.com/

Kwik Learning

12. Kwik Learning. (2019). Read faster. Work smarter. Think better. Retrieved from https://kwiklearning.com/

The Big Leap by Gay Hendricks

13. Hendricks, G. (2010). *The big leap: Conquer your hidden fear and take life to the next level.* San Fransisco, CA: HarperOne.

Printed in Great Britain
by Amazon

44488878R00241